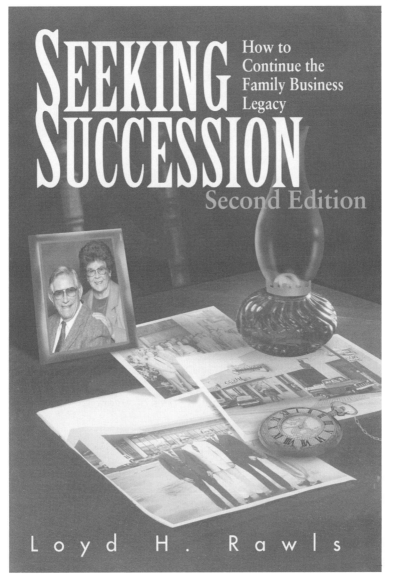

SEEKING SUCCESSION

How to
Continue the
Family Business
Legacy

SUCCESSION

Second Edition

Loyd H. Rawls

J

Published and distributed exclusively by
The Family Business Resource Center
2420 Martin Road, Suite 300
Fairfield, CA 94533
707.428.6300
www.seekingsuccession.com

First Edition Editor, Layout and Artistic Design: Ricci Mann Victorio
Second Edition Editor: Michael Ludden

Printed in the United States of America

A b o u t   t h e   A u t h o r

Loyd H. Rawls has a passion for keeping the family business in the family and helping business owners achieve their succession goals. He has conveyed his theories and passion to an impressive group of business consultants and professional educators, and together they have developed the Rawls Succession Planning Group, with two dynamic divisions: The Rawls Company addresses the financial planning issues of business succession. The Family Business Resource Center is dedicated to promoting the success and succession of family owned businesses through training family principals, successors, key personnel and family members in the three most significant factors effecting business succession: leadership development, management team enhancement, and communication.

Advisors often ask what the secret is to Loyd Rawls' success as a succession planner. The answer is that Loyd provides significant services that support his clients in maximizing their business productivity and for the ultimate succession of the family business legacy. Loyd's unique concepts of "Succession Success^{sm}" and "Succession Certification^{sm}" add recognizable value to these businesses. Loyd and his associates are known for their core operating goal: to exceed the expectations of their clients by addressing any and all critical issues that impact the achievement of family business succession.

"The Rawls Company has given us advice and guidance concerning day-to-day operations and especially in establishing the road map for family succession of our four corporations."
B.W. Simpkins, Chairman, S&S Enterprises, Inc.

"What appeared to be a straightforward estate planning issue in my eyes grew into a successful effort to tie all these larger issues together. While it seemed overwhelming at first, I am excited that we stayed with it, and did some much needed strategic planning and addressed head-on many related areas as well. It was worth every penny we spent."
Jim Graham, President, Santa Margarita Ford

Dedication

Two equally diverse groups that have abounding passions are the recipients of this dedication. Business owners (and their supporting family members) lead this recognition. The economies of the world owe you a debt of gratitude for your brave initiative to pursue your dreams. Beyond the family legacy, you have endured the financial risks and emotional stress to provide the foundation for every vibrant economy. You have been a strong advocate of less regulatory impediments to success and succession. Implicit with the concept of family business, acknowledgment is also extended to the parents, spouses, children and in-laws who provide the vital family support, and persevere through those challenges and frustrations unique to those who do not participate in the family business.

This book is also dedicated to a unique set of advisors who provide critically needed support and services to the family business. These financial planners, attorneys, accountants, estate planners, trust officers, bankers, psychologists, insurance executives and other advisors who have stepped beyond the normal confines of their profession and taken a proprietary interest in the success of one or more family businesses. Driven by an understanding of the importance of the family business and a compassion for the circumstances, they have paid a high price of service beyond expectation.

In recognition of these heroes of private enterprise and family values, I dedicate Seeking Succession. It is my hope and prayer that the hard earned wisdom and experiences offered herein will provide you encouragement and guidance in your pursuit of family business succession.

Acknowledgments

I give my deepest expression of appreciation to the following who have supported me in the creation, development and refinement of this outpouring of my heart. Without their help, this work could have never been completed.

Pat Rawls, my beloved wife, thank you for your never ending love, encouragement and sacrifice beyond what anyone could imagine.

Amy, Kendall and Champ, my wonderful children, thank you for your unconditional love and confidence in me.

Loyd and Flora Rawls, my dear parents, thank you for your blessing and your confidence.

Dora and Richard Majer, my dear sister and brother in-law, thank you for confidence and encouragement.

Ricci M. Victorio, my business associate and editor, thank you for your unrelenting effort and talent in producing this book. Without you, my dream would still be a dream.

Dan Thill, Peggy Hite and John J. Higgins, my business associates, thank you for sharing the dream and supporting the effort.

Richard Young, Jimmy Page, Paul Kuck, Greg Amundson, Wayne Burroughs, Joanne Helphenstine and Ken Rosenfield, thank you for your review of this work and encouragement to carry it through.

Ernie and Susan Kelly, thank you for your journalistic guidance.

Jim Hinckley, Esq., my supporting technical advisor, thank you for your methodical review and technical guidance. You are indeed an outstanding attorney with a magnificent heart for your clients and estate planning.

Lou Bachrodt, Jr. and Lou Bachrodt, III, thank you for your inspiration regarding the real importance of succession and enabling me to understand the value of what I offer.

Eric DeArrigottia, Duane Kuck, Jim Ford, Paul Fannin, Tom Connell, Nurmal Sirvotham, Blake Lorenz, Pete Radcliff and Hugh Roberts for unconditional friendship and unrelenting prayer.

Delta Airlines and US Airlines for fine service and the compatible conditions in which I have been able to write most of this book.

Lord God Almighty, for Your Mercy and Grace through Your Son, Jesus Christ, the Alpha and the Omega.

From the Editor

It is with profound humility that we are publishing the second edition of *Seeking Succession*. Since it's initial publication, we have received an overwhelming outpouring of gratitude and praise from business owners, attorneys, financial planning experts, professional associations, educational institutions, libraries and other business related publications. *Seeking Succession* is an exceptional awareness and training tool and has established a leadership position in promoting a greater understanding of all of the critical interdependent elements that affect succession planning for a family owned business. The acceptance and acknowledgment of this succession aid is more than we could have ever imagined.

Seeking Succession was written specifically for the purpose of education and not as a substitute for the advice of your lawyer, accountant, financial planner, insurance professional or any of your personal or professional advisors. We have divided this diverse and complicated subject into 6 categorical sections. Some chapters are directed specifically to the business owner, key manager or family successor, who will rely upon their financial advisors to handle the actual details of their succession planning. Other chapters address more technical issues that will interest the technically adept business owner, attorneys, accountants and financial planners who are actually in the succession planning process.

Within each chapter, the author has illustrated the concepts with case histories and examples. I suggest you begin by reading the first section, and then select the chapters that are most appropriate and interesting for your needs and questions. Regardless of where you start, or how much you absorb, you should achieve a greater understanding for what initially must feel is an overwhelming endeavor. Remember, a journey will only be successfully completed if you take one step at a time, stay on the path and follow the advice of one who has traveled the road before you!

Ricci M. Victorio
Senior Editor & Vice President
The Family Business Resource Center

Table of Contents

Introduction

*T*he beginning is the most important part of the work.

~ Plato ~

The Family Business Legacy

Surprisingly alert after a late-evening meal, he came forward in his arm chair, leaned against the table and responded to my question, "How important is the succession of my business? Loyd, I am almost embarrassed to tell you how important succession of this business is to me."

Lou Bachrodt, Jr. was a grand gentleman in his late 60s who was from the old era of hard work and sacrifice. He had been an automobile dealer for 49 years. He was a man possessing great pride in his family and business.

We were in the initial discussions about my firm helping him establish a business succession plan that would perpetuate his three automobile dealerships and his accumulated wealth for his three sons and daughter.

"This business is like one of my children," he continued. "It's part of my soul. Bachrodt Chevrolet is a member of our family, even though it doesn't have skin and bones like the rest of us. I've devoted my adult life to its development, just as I have done for each of my children. For this business to fail and not succeed to the next generation would be a tragedy and a disappointment that I just don't have words to describe."

I could see the emotion well up in his eyes, just as I had seen it when he described the death of his youngest daughter in a car accident. "It is probably not healthy to feel this way, but honestly that is where I am. Regarding your question about peace of mind and my objectives, I feel that peace of mind for me is to know that I have done everything within my ability to provide for the succession of these businesses."

Over the last 30 years, those same feelings have been expressed to me repeatedly in different words and surroundings by countless men and women who own family businesses and intend to pass those businesses to their children or prized employees.

It is not at all uncommon for owners to develop feelings for their businesses that are comparable with those they have for their children. The closely held family business is an amazing entity that can generate phe-

3

nomenal emotions of love, happiness, gratification, anxiety, disappointment, frustration and sadness.

And that is nothing new. Since the industrial revolution, America has enjoyed a unique environment of free enterprise. Our open society has encouraged hard work and has provided opportunities to choose any vocation.

Over the generations, all one really needed was a dedicated family to cover the bases and watch the cash, as it did not require much capital to start a business. Large, closely-knit families were commonplace. Children were an asset to help carry the workload. There was little or no regulation or taxation.

For 200 years America has grown and prospered through the creation of family businesses. In some cases, they were passed on to the children. Yet, most of these businesses failed to go beyond the founder's generation.

Children were drawn away to pursue "better opportunities." Major wars consumed successors.

However, more businesses were started to fill the void and to take advantage of the growing opportunities of an expanding economy. Some of the family businesses that achieved succession and ultimately became institutions were Ford, DuPont, and Anheuser-Busch.

A profound aspect of the emerging American culture was that the "little guys" were challenged by these success stories. In addition, the little guys were not restricted by tax regulations and were actually encouraged by government to break out on their own. Many Americans made their mark in business, saying: "If Henry Ford can do it, so can I."

Today, the environment for starting and building a business is different. Cash is king and debt is difficult to manage. Substantial capital is required to do everything, from opening the doors to financing accounts receivable. Capital is more difficult to accumulate because of taxation and a more competitive global economy. Where capital is inadequate, debt equity is required.

Operating credit lines are more difficult to establish and maintain as a result of the defensive posture at lending institutions after the real estate problems of the 1980's. The ambient risks of business created by open market competition are further complicated by overzealous government agencies that regulate everything from the environment to hiring practices.

Now it is difficult to find motivated employees, including family members, who are really willing to work. Unions, entitlement programs, workmen's compensation regulations and a "do your own thing" mentality have hindered the development of a stable, dedicated work force.

With regard to succession, educational opportunities allow prospective successors to pursue their own unique interests outside of the family business. Today there are fascinating job opportunities across towns, the country and the globe that were not available before. Thus, the percentage of family businesses achieving succession today is significantly less than it was 50 years ago. The continuation of a family business from one generation to the next has become progressively more difficult.

> *The family business is a vital part of our economy and culture. It holds a unique position in our society - the most <u>sought-after business entity in America.</u>*

The desire for independence and growth still exists and the emotions associated with children, family and making a mark are alive and well. Most importantly, the motivating forces of power, prosperity, freedom and creativity, although frustrated, are as strong as ever.

The family is a natural structure for business. God, through His divine wisdom, established the family as the basic structure of man. He recognized the need for a fundamental organization that nurtures, protects and instructs mankind in the critical aspects of life. Long before there were governments, prisons or social security, man was thriving through the family structure.

God established basic procedures to assure the effective operation of the family. These procedures are written into the hearts of mothers, fathers and children and automatically go into operation at birth. Parents love, children cling; parents provide, children honor; parents lead, children follow. Everyone is programmed with the basic knowledge needed for the family to function effectively.

Thousands of years of experience, from Cain and Abel to the Ford Motor Company, illustrate the family structure. The success of the family as a business unit, using these God-given instincts of unity and synergy, has been illustrated repeatedly over the ages.

Unfortunately, the vulnerability of family operated businesses has also been illustrated. Once we recognize the potential effectiveness of unified families, the efficiency and productivity of highly structured groups are not a mystery. As an example, the Japanese culture has demanded compliance with the basic family principles of respect and unity to enhance survival for thousands of years. Japanese society continues to capitalize upon the belief in the family principle of respect at the highest corporate level.

Large Japanese corporations make sure employees receive the family feelings of being valued and needed. Regardless of the size of the business, each employee is made to feel important, a vital part of the business, which makes a significant impact upon their success. As a result, the everyday Japanese employee of a large industrial company performs beyond the norm, striving to work harder and more efficiently. Through the amazing strength of its cultural tradition, the average Japanese employer thinks in terms of the group's (the business') welfare before his own needs or those of his family.

According to statistics provided by the U.S. Commerce Department, the family business accounts for 60% of our country's gross national product and employs approximately 60% of the work force. The family business is, pound-for-pound, the strongest, most responsive and productive of all business units. Efficiency is reached through inbred unity and synergy with strong motivation for proficiency and productivity. Members of a family business have a clear understanding that waste comes right out of the family's pocket. Phenomenal production levels are realized through a willingness to go the extra mile and a desire to bring honor and prosperity to the family name.

Although coveted by the masses, its make-up and operation are understood by only a small minority. The uneducated ranks include the federal government, the general public, and even the owners of family businesses themselves.

Unfortunately, the federal government does not understand that the family business is a vital, fundamental production unit, not an immediate, unending source for tax revenue. The family business is not bulletproof and is easily choked by unreasonable taxation and smothered by regulation and reporting. On one hand, the federal government professes how important small businesses are to America, and on the other hand, it continues to break the back of the family business with never-ending reports, regulations, taxes and fees. As a motivational mystery, government actually discourages people from continuing the production and tax paying abilities of the family business by imposing confiscatory estate taxes. It is confusing how our government claims to promote private business while simultaneously killing the goose that lays the golden eggs of jobs and income taxes with regulations and estate taxes.

The general public certainly is unaware of the challenges and hardships of the family business. The typical man or woman on the street feels that the family business owner is just the lucky beneficiary of the "sperm lottery." They feel that owning a successful family business is due to the luck of inheritance or having a great break. They see a private business as an easy street where one can live out of the business' checkbook, have a new car every year, work half days and play golf every Wednesday afternoon. When Dad gets tired, he just cashes a business check and turns the company over to Junior, who, without ever doing a solid day's work, becomes blessed with a life of conspicuous consumption.

The family business is also the least understood member of the American business community.

The general public does not understand that private business, not the government, is the base of the economic chain that creates jobs, products and prosperity. John Q. Public does not understand that private business is his friend and the champion of individual rights. The average man on the street does not recognize that, through lobbying, financial contributions and trade associations, family businesses battle big government and fight for not only themselves, but all private citizens. The family business struggles against Big Brother and the quagmire of regulations and programs that can destroy an individual's motivation and dignity.

Finally, what the general public does not realize is that whatever is good for the family business is good for America. Family businesses employ most of the private citizens in America and do not lay off masses of employees just to maintain profits and justify big bonuses to management. On the contrary, the average confused citizen feels that what is good for the family business only makes the fat cats get fatter. They do not understand that many of the business assets, such as buildings, plants, and equipment do not represent wealth, but liabilities to the bank, tax collectors and the EPA. These are obviously the attitudes that come into play when private citizens become legislators and impose upon the family business more regulation and taxes.

Additionally, there is the individual family business owner who commonly does not understand how fortunate he is to independently own a business. The typical family business owner does not realize that success and succession are not synonymous, and that succession is not an inherent right of his children. He may not understand the hard, cold odds his children are facing.

Many are ill informed regarding the everyday problems of cash flow, regulation, competition, and employee motivation. These are monumental problems of succession. These same parents usually overlook the growing probability that their children will avoid these problems and skip the family business to pursue other careers. They do not recognize the natural hesitancy of a child to stay under the controlling wing of a parent who is slow to recognize their maturity and capability. Parents tend to think their children will naturally want to be in the family business when, in reality, most of the time the sharp kids have to be sold on the idea.

Finally, there is the business owner who is out of touch with the value of his company and does not fathom the cost of selling the business or passing it on to the children. He has not recognized that, if he sells the business, the net after-tax returns on the proceeds will probably not equal the salary and benefits the family realizes from the business.

Or he has not accepted the fact that, from an estate tax perspective, he may be worth more dead than alive. There are some people who just cannot accept the harsh and often gruesome reality of estate taxes. As a result, the process of developing ways to finance the projected estate tax to enable the business to be passed to the next generation without the burden of debt is beyond the understanding of some business owners. Far too many businesses are in harm's way of impending estate taxes that will ultimately cause the sale or liquidation of a business that could otherwise be passed on to heirs.

When questioned about the areas of successor management development or family harmony, most family business owners respond that they'll work it out. In saying this, they fail to reflect on past experiences with their friends and even their own family, where loving brothers and sisters not only failed to work it out, but threatened the unity of the family with petty jealousy and greed.

Nevertheless, the resiliency of the family business is an utterly amazing phenomenon. In the midst of all this misunderstanding by the federal government, the general public and the business owner, it is remarkable that the family business endures so much abuse and continues to be the bedrock in the contemporary American economy. However, these misunderstandings have begun to erode this foundation. There is a crisis looming on the horizon of this great country if this trend is not reversed. Many highly productive family businesses originated in the 1950's and 1960's are now at the threshold of succession. As the pressure against the succession of family businesses continues, this pivotal sector of our economy gets weaker and weaker.

Yet this trend can be reversed and America can continue to be a world leader in innovation, creativity, productivity, and most importantly, freedom.

Without a doubt, what is good for the family business is good for America Increased education and understanding are the greatest hopes for reversing this trend of the declining family business. The stakes are high. It is important to everyone in America that we improve the perceptiveness of government and the general public toward the succession of the family business. And it is critical that those of you who own family businesses develop an understanding of your greatest resource and what it will take to pass it to the next generation.

The Succession Process

Case History: The Timber Family

Quite a few years ago I was making an initial presentation to a prospect in the lumber business whose family had an interesting perspective on the succession process. We began by discussing what had already been done to provide for the succession of their business. The father, son and daughter were involved in our discussion. The mother was not involved in the business. All three were full time employees. The son and daughter, who both appeared to be about 30, apparently were beginning to take over management control from their father, who appeared to be about 65.

Their softwood timber products business was very successful as a result of a housing boom. The client who had referred me said the family was worth about $30 million, primarily because they owned more than 20,000 acres of pine forest. The father, Mr. Timber, had inherited a few thousand acres of forest from his father and had scrimped and sacrificed through his working career to buy additional acreage to build a saw mill.

Mr. Timber carried himself like the classic conservative farmer who had been successful through hard work and good fortune. In our initial discussion he was careful not to make presumptuous statements about his personal success or the success of the business. However, he did give the message that he had labored through many thin years to build his business.

In contrast, the son and daughter, Jack and Jennifer, came across as arrogant. This was an apparent result of entering the business directly from their high-bred college years. Neither had married yet. Their father had given each of them 24% of the business.

I asked questions to learn more about their goals and their existing succession planning so I could identify any shortcomings to highlight the value of my firm's service. Mr. Timber was attentive but unresponsive. Jack and Jennifer, however, interrupted before I was finished, contending that their succession planning was complete. Jack was the more outspoken of the two. With a smile on his face, he said that he and his sister each owned 24% of the stock, as well as an insurance policy to purchase the balance of stock from their father's estate. He confidently stated that the cash would then be used to pay estate taxes after supporting his mother for the balance of her lifetime.

My referral had said the family really needed my help and he was depending upon me to assist his close friends with their problems. I had originally thought their problem was a lack of knowledge; however, as Jack convinced me that he was an "expert" on the subject, I began to realize I was dealing with another type of problem. I was desperate to achieve credibility because Jack, with all his bragging, was doing all the talking.

As Jack took a breath, I grabbed the lead. "I commend you for the succession work you have done. You are light years ahead of most of your colleagues. To your credit, you have made a very good start; however, I don't believe that you fully understand the definition of succession."

I was hoping that I could grab their attention on an academic point that was beyond Jack's experience and save myself from being pushed out the door, although I wasn't sure I even wanted to work with this family, especially the close-minded children. I did at least want to share some of the unique benefits of my experience so they would say nice things about me to the gentleman who had referred me.

"Succession is the process of preserving the real assets, spirit, ideology and mission of a family business through the next generation without extreme financial, emotional or management hardship.

And keep in mind the operative word in this definition is extreme. Succession predictably involves financial, emotional and management challenges.

The goal of succession planning is to keep the challenges from creating extreme hardships that can imperil or prevent the continuity of the business."

The two kids sitting on the sofa on the other side of their father's big desk did not appear at all impressed, but did seem willing, for the moment, to let me talk.

"There are two major activities involved in the process of family business succession. The first is the actual transfer of ownership and management of a family business to the next generation through sales, gifts and estate. You seem to be well on your way with this first activity with the initial gifting of business equity and the insurance policy.

The second activity is the operational survival and continuity of the business. The point is, just because the next generation owns the business, that does not mean that succession will take place."

The son and daughter did not seem moved. I could feel the pressure mounting. They shifted their eyes toward each other with smiles as if to say, "Get a life." Their father, on the other hand, was leaning back in his swivel chair and now listening to me intently. He glanced over to catch his children's expression and leaned forward on his desk with an affirming nod, encouraging me to continue. Taking his cue, I figured it was time to go for the throat because I probably would not get another chance.

"You may think that you have achieved succession by owning 48% of the stock and an insurance policy to buy the balance. But the reality is you are just getting started, and you have a long way to go. If you don't get your attitudes straight, you can still blow it."

The two young adults sat with crossed arms and legs. They showed no reaction and did not seem interested in more advice. The dynamics between father and children were not clear, so I did not know if Dad was in control or if he was under his children's leadership.

However, based upon the stiffening silence in the room, it looked like they had good ol' dad right where they wanted him and I was soon to be history.

I let it roll, "In just the few minutes I have been here, you two kids have acted like you have the succession tiger by the tail with your stock and insurance policy. However, I question if the two of you have really grasped the spirit, ideology and mission of this business. If not, you are in for a bitter disappointment. This business appears to have achieved success based upon your father's conservatism and his sacrificial willingness to grow this business over a long period of time. The two of you have only been around during the good times. Your most significant contribution has been in determining how to spend money, not make it. You really don't know what this business is all about yet."

Jack flashed an expression of indignation as he slipped to the edge of his seat, obviously preparing to get up and leave the room or show me the door. I quickly intercepted his attempt to interrupt. "Please let me finish, and I'll be on my way so you can get back to your busy schedule. I know each of you brings valuable education and talents to this business, but I am not at all sure that the two of you share your father's philosophy about business. This is important, because it was your father's feelings about expenses, retained earnings and growth that has brought this business to where it is today."

"Actually, my guess is that there is an internal struggle going on right now between the two of you and your father about what the mission of this business is, how you are going to make your money, and what you are going to do with the profits. The three of you probably could not currently agree on where to go for lunch, much less what this business should be doing next year. I am certain you are not prepared for the future challenges you are sure to incur."

Both Jack and Jennifer showed a shocked expression as they looked to each other and then to their dad. It appeared that I had finally struck a nerve. Jack was still sitting on the edge of the sofa, staring off in space, apparently searching for the appropriate words to tell me to get lost without provoking his dad. Preempting Jack, I stood up, walked to the window and gazed out in my best controlling demeanor and continued. "The hardships of succession are inevitable. Times change, markets change, profits change and parents retire. Taxes are inevitable and there is always debt tempting you to buy more equipment or timberland."

Then I turned around and addressed the two children directly. "You can be sure that these delightful business conditions you are experiencing are going to change. The question is, how prepared will you be to make the difficult decisions that owner/managers have to make to survive in down markets? Also, the two of you probably have not discussed your foremost succession challenge -- how you will work together to manage this company! My guess is that you have not discussed who will lead and who will follow or how future in-laws and children will be involved in the business. Both of you are currently unmarried with no family diversions competing for your time and emotional energy. When you do marry, decisions regarding time commitments, compensation, and involvement of other family members will become more complicated. I do not think that you have taken a realistic look into the future. You are currently very confident, but I assure you that future challenges are going to be humbling. I do not think you understand what succession really is, and I believe you are far from having, in your words, taken care of succession."

I walked back across the room to my chair and picked up my briefcase, assuming it was time for me to leave. As I turned to Mr. Timber to express my appreciation for the meeting, I saw he was leaning forward, elbows on his desk with his palms holding his forehead. He obviously was thinking as he rubbed his hands through his thinning, grayish-brown hair.

Jack leaned back on the sofa and said, "That was most eloquent, Mr. Rawls, but I really don't think we are going to have those kinds of problems. I regret that you are offended by our confident attitude, but we sincerely feel we are effectively addressing our needs. And if we find that we do need help, our attorney will be here to advise us as he has in the past."

His sister Jennifer had been amazingly quiet. To my surprise, she was not showing agreement with what her brother said. She grinned slightly, as if embarrassed by him, and looked to the floor, squirming in her seat a bit. Still looking at the floor, she said, "I am not sure that our attorney can help us with these issues. I have been asking him for two years to draw up an agreement on the insurance policy we own and it has not been done yet. Besides, what does he know about running a business, taxes and estate planning? What he really knows is how to sue people to collect our money."

"AHEM!" Mr. Timber blurted out with conviction in his voice, which apparently was tempered by past frustrations on the points that I had made. "Jack, you have missed the point. Keep your mouth shut for awhile and maybe you will learn something." I now knew who was in control! "Mr. Rawls, thank you for being candid under these awkward circumstances. You are right on point with this family. I gave them stock in this company on impulse, against the advice of our attorney. As it has turned out, the gifts were probably a good idea; however, the move could have just as easily been a bad idea if one of my children turned the wrong way. "

"I was sold the insurance policy by my agent, more because he needed a commission than because we needed funding for my wife's security and estate taxes. Until you mentioned estate taxes a few minutes ago, I assumed the only purpose of the policy was to give my wife cash security if these kids run the business down the tubes after my death. These kids know I struggled to get this business started, but they don't seem to appreciate that they will have to struggle to keep it going. They are constantly on me to borrow money for plant expansion and product diversification. I control the finances now, but, at 68 years old, I am tired of arguing. We are mere babes in the realm of succession planning. I want to know that we have a plan and that our plan can work."

This was the beginning of a client relationship that continues to this day. Needless to say, I had struck a hot point. The father had been concerned about the struggles within the business; however, he did not really enjoy talking about his retirement, his death or his children's ability to run the business. Arguments always seemed to develop and he hated family arguments. With the business doing so well, he had managed to put off the dialogue required to develop family mission statements or how decisions were going to be made after his departure. Both he and his children were blind to the need for business agreements and estate planning that addressed succession and taxes.

As a result of our involvement with this family, we were able to consider the total succession process. A few things did change, including the heirs' perspective on the idea of succession. We created a structure for effectively and efficiently transferring the business to Jack and Jennifer and we addressed the critical intra-family business management process that would determine the future success of the business. The cockiness of the son and daughter subsided as they considered the realities of managing the business in their father's absence. They agreed that the family attorney was a good litigator, but did not know much about estate taxation, probate, stock redemptions and buy/sell agreements. Our meeting was a pivotal point to bring back the reality of business cycles and the spirit of conservatism needed to carry the business forward. Our efforts on this point were very timely. Two years later, their business followed the housing industry downturn. Fortunately, they were prepared and not only survived, but have continued to grow.

The point of this story is that succession extends beyond the classic activities of making gifts and buying an insurance policy to cover estate taxes. Succession planning also involves other critical subjects, such as the development of successor managers and the interactive relationships of family members working in the business. It was enormously important that Mr. Timber and his children understood that -- no matter how harmonious the family -- succession of their family business was not something to be taken for granted. They couldn't achieve succession without a pragmatic, disciplined roadmap.

Succession Action Program

The succession process involves more than passing total ownership of a business from one generation to the next. Actually, transferring the business is the easiest aspect of succession. If you have the money and time, you can buy the talent, documents and insurance policies that will get the job done. What you cannot buy is success beyond the transfer.

In the relay of business succession, once the baton is passed, the next generation must run its own race and win or lose based upon the quality of its training and its dedication to business continuity.

Business disposition planning is a long-range activity influenced by many factors, such as taxes, family, feelings and health. A Succession Planning Action Program provides focus and structure to deal with the inevitable distractions and challenges to the succession process.

If your planning is going to survive the inevitable excitement, you had better have a "no brainer" action program to keep you on track. The typical succession planning process involves elements of family and business that easily can become combustible when mixed. These well-chronicled volatile combinations include business control, money, taxes, family relationships and personal health. Unfortunately, in the touchy, emotional family environment, there is no way of predicting which issues will cause an explosion.

Let's outline the steps you'll need to take:

1. Getting started

2. Establishing succession objectives

3. Assembling a capable planning team

4. Reviewing alternative action steps

5. Reconfirming objectives

6. Developing an action plan

7. Identifying a planning leader

8. Following through with the action plan

9. Passing the baton of management control

10. Achieving succession success

Now let's look at each step.

1. Getting started is no easy task. Although the Timber family was not as far along as they had thought, to their credit, they had begun. That's more than can be said for many family businesses caught up in procrastination or denial. Planning the succession of a business is easy to postpone. Understandably, it is often uncomfortable for parents to initiate discussions about turning over to their children a business that took a lifetime to develop.

Talking about death and how wealthy the kids are going to be as a result of it is no fun either.

Still, you have to get the succession process started. In more than 25 years of succession planning, I have witnessed far more creativity from parents finding excuses to postpone their planning than I have seen used in transferring the business.

2. Establishing succession objectives provides a foundation for the planning process. Stating specific goals may seem elementary, yet most family business principals overlook this important step with the thought that they clearly understand what they want to accomplish. Everyone has ideas and dreams. However, ideas and dreams are just thoughts. They can easily be modified or dropped with changes in mood or circumstances. The process of transferring those ideas and dreams into black and white provokes analysis and refinement. And that process results in a greater commitment within a more realistic plan.

Equally important, stated objectives provide a foundation or starting point to measure your progress and ultimate success. Stating objectives can be simple or challenging, depending upon the degree of forethought.

3. Assembling a capable planning team is essential. Your advisors will help you address a variety of factors that impact your decision, such as cash flow needs, time commitment, the capabilities of children, availability of support staff, estate taxes and the marketplace. The quality of your succession planning will be directly dependent upon the technical ability and experience of your advisor team.

4. Reviewing alternative action steps will give you peace of mind that you are pursuing the right course of action. There are a variety of succession-planning avenues. The diversity of alternative estate structures, stock transfer methods and business structures can and often does create confusion.

Each alternative has an impact on the family and business; however, there is a plan that will satisfy the unique circumstances of your finances, family and business environment. If you will just spend the necessary time and energy to consider the various disposition alternatives, you can determine your most appropriate course of action.

Make sure you consider alternative succession plans. Otherwise, you will never have confidence that you are doing the right thing. Confidence gives momentum to propel the planning through difficult issues. Rest assured, there is a way to achieve any objective.

5. Reconfirming objectives is a necessary step in building confidence in your succession plan. Be prepared to return to step one and change your objectives. As an example, you may want to be financially independent and retire from your business by age 60; however, when you understand the financial commitment required to achieve this goal and the current lifestyle sacrifices required, you may decide to plan to retire at 65.

6. Developing an action plan establishes the essential structure and organization. An action plan contains specific instructions for each member of the planning team, such as attorneys and accountants, which will enable them to clearly understand their responsibilities within a defined schedule. A regularly updated and circulated action plan will do much to coordinate the team's efforts while maintaining a focused vision of goals. Your plan should be an effective roadmap of the action you will be taking with as much detail as possible. You will rely upon this action plan for guidance for weeks, months and even years.

7. Identify a planning leader to bring order to what can otherwise be a confusing and frustrating process. There is great value in a leader who will take charge and do whatever is necessary to keep the ball rolling. This may involve keeping notes, following up with family members and supporting advisors who have volunteered to do certain tasks or have been assigned tasks important to the succession process. All too often, after expensive frustrating delays, one or more members of the planning team gives that familiar shrug of the shoulders and says, "I thought you were going to do that," or "Nobody told me I was supposed to do that."

Each time coordination and follow-up delays occur, the planning process loses valuable momentum. A committed leader can prevent these mishaps. It is critical to have a planning leader or quarterback who will take responsibility for preparing the action plan and monitoring progress of the various projects.

8. Following through with the action plan is essential. An action plan by itself will not get the job done. It must be propelled by a sense of urgency as you methodically address the business at hand. Achieving succession is dependent upon relentless commitment. Reluctance to take action creates delays, and delays increase the hazards to the succession process.

Emotions can go ballistic, creating rifts and cracks in the <u>*supporting family infrastructure.*</u>

A change in health during delays can wreak havoc. The hazards of losing planning momentum are endless. The cost of losing momentum can be devastating.

Following through with the action plan is the simple formula for success and cannot be overemphasized. The greatest of intentions for business succession are commonly never fulfilled because shortcuts appear attractive and one of the basic steps is omitted.

Fear and disagreement are the two most common reasons for not following through.

Business owners can get cold feet when they consider the implications of turning over management or ownership of their business to their children or in-laws. This fear of stepping down usually creates varying degrees of second-guessing, with such questions as; "Am I ready?" "What will I do with myself if I am not running the business?" "Am I going to have enough money to retire?"

If there is waning confidence and no support, uncertainty can grow. As a result of this natural fear, owners frequently demand more time to think things over and put off advisors who are endeavoring to continue the planning process. In some unfortunate circumstances, advisors become frustrated and stop calling to reschedule meetings. If owners are not reassured and given peace of mind that they are pursuing the right course of action, succession can come to a regrettable halt.

Parents, don't be embarrassed or discouraged by your fear that you are about to destroy the business or become dependent upon your children. Your concern is natural and more than likely justified. When I see fear paralyze parents, my conclusion is that we have gone too far, too fast.

And so, while I advise a powerful commitment to the process, there may be times when you must back up to a place where you are more comfortable, especially if you are really concerned about what is being recommended or even about what you have already done. Do not be embarrassed to say you are uncomfortable with any decision or action. Eventually your concern or hesitancy will surface anyway. If you need more time, take it. Just don't carry all of the pressure by keeping your feelings to yourself. Let others know your concerns so they can work on alternatives If you don't say anything, you become the problem.

Continue the dialogue. Continue the succession process. Back up. Call for a "think about it" period. Stay in the process. A good way to evaluate the success of a meeting is if the next meeting is scheduled. If you keep scheduling your next meeting, you will eventually work out your concerns. If you share your feelings, you will identify the problem and ultimately solve it.

The other momentum killer is disagreement. Parents and/or their children rarely agree on all facets of succession. Usually, mutual respect will support reasonable productive compromise. However, if the disagreeing parties stand firm, they can sidetrack the process.

With no encouraging signs of compromise or reconciliation, the succession effort is often abandoned.

In those unfortunate circumstances we typically hear, "I wish we had never started this, we were better off doing nothing rather than tearing our family apart."

The reality is that succession planning does not tear families apart. Self-centered, unreasonable family members do. The succession planning process can bring personality or relationship problems that already exist to the surface.

Disagreements are inevitable, so the question is how they will be addressed. An experienced planning leader can serve as a facilitator, but the responsibility ultimately falls upon family members to subordinate individual feelings and agendas for the betterment of the family. If this cannot be accomplished, succession may not be a viable option.

If you'll follow these eight steps, you can establish an environment where confidence in decisions can be sustained and family bonds can be strengthened through continual review and confirmation of decisions. Your evaluation should carry an attitude of trust that past decisions may be good, but can always be refined. As the various players begin to feel better about what has been done and what will take place, the process becomes substantially easier. Succession planning is a masterpiece under development, which needs time, patience and diligence to reach perfection.

9. Passing the baton is the defining step of family business succession. Two events must take place in the transfer: parents must let go, and heirs must take control. Parents cannot do it all and, regardless of how badly they want to retire, they cannot just turn the business over to their children and expect it to survive. Neither can the heirs do it all. Regardless of how strongly they want to assume control, they cannot make their parents abandon control. Passing the baton appropriately is a coordinated effort. After ample preparation and planning, the handoff takes place with a simultaneous release by the parents and grasping by the heirs.

Unfortunately, most succession environments are not ideal.

Either the owner/parent wants to hang on too long, or the successor/child attempts to seize control too early.

Regardless of which end of the "stick" you are on, the key is to have empathy and compassion for the feelings and actions of those on the other end. Parents, choose not to be offended with children who are overzealous or under motivated. Children, do not be offended with parents who lack the confidence to let go. Stand strong in your beliefs, but do not let unbridled emotion ruin the process in the final stage. Your empathy, coupled with strong convictions, can carry the succession process to completion.

Ideally, parents should have gradually allowed their children to assume more responsibility. Turning over total control is a function of the heirs' age, maturity and business acumen. However, extended joint management by parents and their heirs is the most effective environment for teaching the critical management techniques.

Attitude is the most important ingredient for a harmonious and effective working relationship between parents and their heirs. Heirs should have the confidence that they can be successful and have a willingness to assume responsibility; however, they must also realize that they have a lot to learn and that many challenges lie ahead. The peculiar combination of confidence and humility ideally positions an heir to handle the demands of the high learning curve of succession and maintain the respect of both parents and employees. Heirs should realize that, although parents may have slowed down physically and even mentally, they still merit respect as founders and/or owners of the business. Parents who have successfully operated a business are a resource of time-tested experience, which is invaluable to someone learning a business.

Parents should have patience with their children's aggressiveness or lack thereof, keeping in mind that, if their children were not aggressive, they would not be good succession candidates. An effective, but difficult, way of teaching children is to allow them to make mistakes, then coach them on how to avoid those mistakes the next time.

It takes courage to overlook children's shortcomings, give them the opportunity to lead and allow them to make mistakes. However, there are incentives for taking chances with children. The sooner they learn the ropes, the sooner parents can step off the firing line and draw on their experience to lead the business to higher levels of achievement. The sooner children step into management responsibility, the sooner parents can worry less about operations and spend more time on creative business ideas or recreational activities.

Parents, however, should not plan to give the kids the keys and hit the road. Parents provide guidance and, sometimes, checks and balances for children who have already assumed management control. It is ever so comforting to call upon a parent for advice on a challenging situation that they have dealt with many times during their years at the helm. The availability and use of parental advice is one of the common characteristics of family businesses that have smooth succession experiences.

Achieving succession success is the final aspect of the process. This may seem to be stating the obvious, but far too often families overlook continuity of success. Parents feel that they have accomplished their goal by simply transferring the business from one generation to the next. In reality, when the next generation gets the stock or property, the most challenging aspect of the succession process has just begun. It is now time for the successors to apply what they have learned for the succession and continued growth of the business. No matter how easy it was with Mom or Dad, when there is no one else to rely upon, succession takes on a whole new aura.

There are many factors that impact succession success in the next generation. These are the critical factors:

- Succession Success

- Manager Development

- Teamwork

- Communication

- Estate Planning

- Strategic Financial Planning

It is imperative to realize that, regardless of how well we have addressed the first nine steps, succession success will ultimately rest in the hands of the successors. Right now this thought may be frightening, but do not panic. If you follow the steps and address the critical factors, you can be confident you have done all you can do. You must then rely upon your preparation and your faith.

Financial Issues

*I*f you have built castles in the air, your work need not be lost; that is where they should be. Now put foundations under them.

~ Henry David Thoreau ~

Strategic Financial Planning

The purpose of succession is to continue a business into the next generation. Family members and managers provide the medium. Financial planning protects the business unit during the succession process and makes best use of financial resources toward the achievement of succession goals.

Strategic financial planning does not involve day-to-day personal financial management or business activities.

The three disciplines of family business succession are personal financial planning, business planning and estate planning. These elements overlap and work interdependently to significantly impact the succession process. For example, personal financial security has a profound impact on the succession process. However, personal financial security of parent principals is dependent upon an efficient flow of business profitability through corporations, real estate and partnerships during working years and after retirement. Personal guarantees of business debt are typical in a family business.

Yet, contingent liabilities can have a significant impact upon personal financial planning, business planning and certainly estate planning.

Estate planning directs the flow of personal assets and business assets to the heirs and beneficiaries of parent principals. The flow of personal and business assets through an estate is dictated by the titling and the structure of these assets. Estate tax has a major impact on estate taxation; and one of the major determinants of estate taxation is business structuring.

There are two major goals in financial planning relating to the succession of a family business. Establishing a state-of-the-art, technically correct financial plan is first. The familiar technical objectives are:

- Achieving the highest possible return on investments

- Minimizing income tax

- Minimizing personal business liability

- Avoiding estate tax

- Reducing probate

- Providing for asset management

Although initially less obvious, the second and equally important goal is personal compatibility. There is limited long-term fruit to a financial plan that produces fear, frustration and confusion as a by-product. It is also profoundly true that being technically correct and being comfortable can be contradictory goals. The goal is to be as technically correct (advanced) while being as personally comfortable as possible.

Succession planning is a long-term endeavor. There is no long-term viability to a succession plan built on financial structures that rub against fundamental feelings. As you embark upon financial planning filled with new concepts and structures, follow the proven conservative wisdom and do not enter into an investment or business structure that will give you a rash down the road. Getting a bit outside of your comfort zone is okay, but do not deny your fundamental beliefs about risk, control or liquidity.

If your attorney, accountant or financial planner is offering updated recommendations that you do not accept, tell them you want a plan you can live with and to keep bringing their ideas to you. If it is a good idea, over time you will become comfortable with the concept and adopt it into your plans.

Case History: To Gift or Not To Gift?

As an illustration, consider the case of the grand widow who was matriarch of a very successful family-owned beer wholesaler. I had been working with her family for several years to analyze and update their business succession and estate continuity planning. In this follow-up service meeting, I was discussing ways to reduce her estate taxes.

"I am not going to do it," she said emphatically. "You might as well forget the subject. And don't ask me again. I will never put myself in a position where there is any chance that I will be dependent upon my children.

I would rather die than ask them for money. What if I get sick? Or need to go to a nursing home? Who would pay for that?"

I had obviously struck a sensitive subject with my suggestion that she make a gift to her son. She stood up, and with both hands on the table, leaned over and looked directly at me with squinting, intense eyes, to finish speaking her mind.

"Loyd, you have no idea what it is like to have no one to depend upon. As a widow, I have no one. You may think I have it all together, but I am scared and I am not going to let you push me into something that I may regret."

This 73 year-old matriarch, whose deceased husband was the founder of a very profitable Anheuser-Busch beer wholesaler was, to put it mildly, excited. Typically a very sweet and passive grandmother who baked a killer pound cake for me to take home after each visit, she was amazingly trans-formed and she shocked me back into my seat with my mouth open for mentioning gifting. I was aware that the idea of gifting could bring panic to the psyche of the uninformed, the confused or the insecure; but never had I thought that this lady was scared about her financial security. Based upon the color in her face and the fire in her eyes, she qualified on all three counts. She was fuming. Knowing her normal sweet nature, I sensed that these feelings had been building as I mentioned gifting over a period of time. I had been totally insensitive to her insecurity. Having given up on the prospect of getting my normal pound cake, I was concerned about what else I might lose from this experience.

You may think her response to my logical recommendation was humorous. Her reaction was more extraordinary as you understand her cir-cumstances. Her son owed her about $60,000 for the purchase of stock in the family business when his father died 10 years earlier. I was recom-mending that this lady consider forgiving (gifting) the note in an effort to manage the growth of her estate and reduce future estate taxes. The last thing she needed was another $60,000. You see, she had a multi-million dollar net worth. Her cash and cash equivalents were in excess of $3 million, and her personal income from the family business was more than $450,000 per year. Furthermore, as you might have expected, her living expenses were less than $60,000 per year and she was a compulsive saver. In overview, with a net worth approaching $10 million earned, income in excess of $450,000 per year and living expenses of less than $60,000 per year, she was about to pound my head for suggesting that she make a $10,000 debt forgiveness gift to her son.

So, why did this normally quiet, gentle lady almost stick my hand in the garbage disposal when I mentioned gifting? It was because she did not care about being technically correct. Her sole interest was in being com-fortable with her circumstances. In contrast to what was clearly technically correct, forgiveness of a relatively insignificant debt to reduce her estate

taxes and her son's income taxes was not compatible. Not being the passive
type, she let me know the moment I stepped over the line.

Having provided appropriate emphasis on the importance of compatibility in financial planning, our continuing discussion of financial planning
will not dwell on specific investments, business structures or estate documents common to traditional financial planning. Those topics are secondary
to compatibility, as well as too broad and heavy for this discussion. Our
approach to financial planning will focus on the strategic philosophies and
structures that are critical to succession planning to enhance your ability to
work with your investment advisors, attorney and accountant to achieve
your financial planning objectives and succession goals.

Personal Financial Planning

Personal financial planning addresses four points: establishing goals,
organizing assets, addressing personal financial security and asset management. Personal financial planning is the compass for the succession
planning process. It carries the responsibility for determining the direction
and specific course of the succession planning program.

Establishing Goals

The goals established in personal financial planning should address all
aspects of personal business and estate planning that sustain the dream of
transferring the business to the next generation.

Goal setting and refinement sets the tone of conviction and dedication to the formidable challenge of succession. The quality of the succession
planning process is dependent upon the amount of time, effort and thought
put into the establishment and refinement of your goals.

It might be said that establishing goals is juvenile because everyone
has goals, especially ambitious business owners. Wrong! Sure, they have
goals regarding the operation of the business, but they rarely have well-
defined personal financial goals relating to business succession. To merely
state, "I want my kids to continue my business," is not adequate goal
setting. While a business owner will commonly spend extended time with
his managers in business analysis and strategic planning, he will rarely
follow the same process in establishing succession related goals until retirement or death is imminent. Even when asked to define and evaluate
financial security as mentioned earlier, business owners tend to be satisfied

with general parameters versus specific goals. Maybe this is caused by a fear of mortality or aversion to discussions about giving up control and retiring. Regardless of the reason, goal setting is one of the most challenging areas of succession planning.

Most business owners think they have established succession goals when all they have done is expressed intentions. If personal and private intentions are not subjected to the analysis of being written down and communicated to others, they are just ideas that change with the wind. To say that you have your long term goals in your mind is a fantasy. Intentions are held in the brain and not exposed to the refinement of paper allowing an individual to avoid accountability. Inherent in the term "goal" is a commitment to achieve. When intentions are written and communicated, the idea becomes a goal, making it real and therein the intention becomes a commitment.

When intentions are expressed, they become goals and are enhanced by the critique of others.

The process of writing, sharing and refining goals is critical to succession planning.

Any long range undertaking, such as succession planning, requires a willingness to express goals along with commitment and direction that the goal making process establishes.

Organizing and Evaluating Personal Assets

In order to effectively react to your current financial position, you must organize and analyze assets from a succession planning perspective. Organization of financial data describes a process of developing a realistic description of an individual's financial affairs. This financial description could be as simple as pulling out the latest comprehensive financial statement; however, experience has shown that the owners of closely-held family businesses rarely keep financial statements that are effective for succession planning purposes.

When typical business owners provide financial statements to the banks, they usually underestimate the value of the business and overestimate the value of personal assets. They commonly play "paper" games with their banks and bonding companies to project a financial picture according to the specific need at hand. Business owners rarely have a comprehensive, realistic succession-oriented financial statement.

Financial statements often omit important assets and contingent liabilities. Classically, a client will react to questions regarding personal financial organization with, "Oh, I just remembered another asset that I forgot to mention." The impact of income tax, inflation, depreciation and liquidation cost on retirement plans and personal assets is frequently not considered. The organization of personal financial planning should address the impact of an individual's assets upon their income and security.

The personal financial planning process must determine the real value of assets as it relates to personal financial security. Business owners typically must readjust their financial perspective of assets for the personal financial planning aspect of succession planning. The adjustments involve considering the utility of an asset for income and security purposes. To determine the utility of your assets, you must develop an understanding of the assets. This means that you should be asking questions such as:

- Will you depend directly upon the business for income after retirement?

- What income can be expected from specific assets?

- Will projected income be sufficient to satisfy specific goals?

- How can additional assets be obtained?

- Will there be continuing post-retirement liability for business debt?

- Can the children run the business in your absence?

- Will they need assistance and if so, what will be the cost?

- What assets are family heirlooms that are not available for liquidation to satisfy cash needs?

- What will be the time and cost involved in liquidating specific assets?

Typically, the questions about assets are easier than the answers; however, the more questions that are generated, the higher the probability that the personal financial needs of both parents and children will be addressed effectively in the succession plan.

After assets are organized from a utility perspective, personal, business and estate goals can be confirmed as unreasonable or realistic. If the analysis points out that the goals are unrealistic, the goals should be adjusted to prevent unnecessary pressure and frustration.

> *Confronting the bad news that a goal is unrealistic under current circumstances is better than failing to reach an important goal after years of expectations.*

The path to the achievement of goals is through evaluation and diligent pragmatic follow up action. If you can develop a plan of action for attaining a goal, you are halfway home. An Action Agenda is a product for analyzing assets in relationship to goals. The Action Agenda specifies and prioritizes the specific action required to accomplish the goals by specific parties of the planning team.

Continuing Case History:

Referring again to the widowed beer wholesaler, we remember that she was personally insecure and, without hesitation, put me on notice to back off. Needless to say, I got her message. However, her technical financial circumstances were contradictory to her personal concerns. I concluded that her reaction was not because of greed or resentment toward her son, as she was not that kind of person. Her reaction stemmed from her circumstances and a lack of understanding regarding her resources.

Although being widowed was beyond my control, the area I could affect was her understanding of her resources; so I dropped the subject of gifting and began a very fundamental program of organization and education to help her better understand her situation. I made every effort to explain the capability of her assets and the resulting impact the excess income was having on her estate and estate taxes. We very deliberately projected her liberal income needs and identified the sources of her secure income. We also projected the cost of full-time private duty nursing, beginning immediately and lasting for five years beyond her projected life expectancy. Assuming a conservative passbook rate on investments and a 50% income tax bracket, we helped this lady organize and evaluate her assets to give her peace of mind that her definition of financial security was in the bag.

About eighteen months later, during a regularly scheduled review, she put me back on my heels with an unsolicited and totally unexpected comment. "I suppose, Loyd, I could afford to do a little gifting." She not only forgave the relatively tiny note to her son, she also utilized all of her

$600,000 unified tax credit gifting capability. She later became a gifting machine, even executing taxable gifts. We continue to discuss how she can go on making gifts to both children and grandchildren and how she can leverage these gifts through various asset transfer techniques.

Personal Financial Security

Addressing financial security is an analytical process that depends directly upon the organization of assets described above. Unrealistic or incorrect conclusions about underlying assets will bring improper conclusions about financial security, which can bring a tragic halt or frustrating anguish to the succession planning process.

I am frequently asked, "What does personal financial planning have to do with passing a business to heirs?" The answer is, a great deal. The senior generation controlling a family business is not going to get serious about turning over ownership and management of their business to their successors until they know that their personal financial security is not in doubt.

Although some parents are crazy for their kids, the vast majority consciously or subconsciously believe in the succession planning axiom: do not put yourself in a position where you depend upon your children for financial security.

The experience shared earlier with my client who owned the beer distributorship illustrated that succession planning maneuvers, such as gifting or transition of management or the sale of portions of the business to children, will not be addressed openly and freely until personal financial security has been addressed.

Looking back, I can identify many instances in which my planning was side-tracked or just appeared to run out of gas. As I think about each situation, I believe the cause of most of these problems was the financial insecurity of the planning principals. Either by natural instinct or pro-active choice, the parents lost enthusiasm for the direction of the planning because they perceived that the planning would put their financial security at risk; and unfortunately, I did not have the savvy to identify the real problem and address the security concerns of the principals. Although some parents are crazy for their kids, the vast majority consciously or subconsciously believe in the succession planning axiom: Do not put yourself in a position where you depend upon your children for financial security.

Financial security is defined through a personal decision about financial expectations based upon a personal point of view. Each individual's definition of financial security comes from the amalgamation of their experiences, values and family culture. With encouragement and assistance, you can develop a definition based upon your unique education, experience and values. This definition will provide a benchmark to determine your current position.

As a business owner, do not complicate this issue. Develop a detailed personal definition of what financial security would be for you. Share your definition with respected friends and advisors. With an understanding of where you are relative to your goals, you can evaluate the virtue of future activity that would impact your definition of financial security.

As an example, in the process of addressing your financial security, you may determine that you have insufficient assets and/or income streams to retire and turn the business over to the kids with peace of mind. Coming to grips with this reality, you can discard the thoughts of giving away income producing assets and draft a supporting remedial action plan to develop the needed assets to satisfy your definition of financial security. Under different circumstances, you may determine that you have sufficient assets independent from the business to satisfy all of your financial needs. In this case, you may be inclined to begin an aggressive gifting program. Addressing financial security is the passkey for other activities that are very important to succession planning.

Asset Management

In the words of a successful business owner, "It is more difficult to manage money than it is to earn money." During his business career, he and his partner developed and operated a multifaceted business covering a wide geographical area. Approaching retirement, this business owner liquidated a major portion of his business and began devoting the bulk of his time and effort to managing a portfolio and not running a business. With this management transition came recognition of the profound difference between operating a business and managing a portfolio.

The talents and skills required to develop and operate a business are not necessarily the same as those required to successfully manage the fruits of the business.

Although family business owners have their share of problems, lack of intelligence is not usually one. Without bright minds and sound judgment, they never would have been able to originate and develop a valuable business. A bright mind and sound judgment are also required to manage assets; however, the talents and skills required to develop and operate a business are not necessarily the same as those required to successfully manage the fruits of the business.

Managing assets also requires an in-depth understanding of the stocks, bonds, real estate and business in which you are investing, plus the environment of that asset. In other words, if you are going to buy a stock, you need to know about the specific stock being purchased and the stock market that dictates pricing, liquidation procedures, dividends, options, acquisition costs and carrying costs. The same simple concept would apply to bonds, real estate, commodities and investments into other businesses.

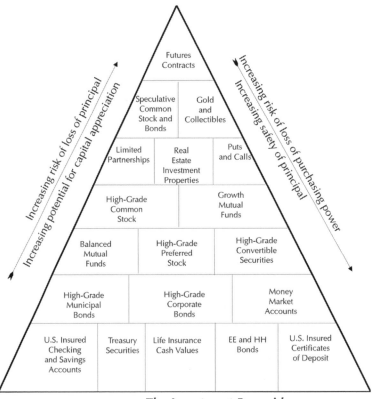

The Investment Pyramid

It is very easy to make a good investment and, over the long term, lose your profit if you do not understand the market environment. It is also easy and very common to understand a market environment but not carry out the proper due diligence research, which could result in a bad investment. Although this is a simple concept and an imminently logical investment philosophy, investment failures outpace successes because of ignorance or apathy regarding either the investment asset or the asset environment.

> ***Do not invest your hard earned money unless you thoroughly <u>understand both the asset and the asset environment.</u>***

Otherwise, the assets of your success may become liabilities to the succession process.

The highest priority during working years for a business owner is learning and operating the business in a fast-moving, competitive environment. Learning the ropes of asset management is a totally separate business that requires study, concentration and practice. Because of the high concentration required to operate a business, it is rare for a business owner who is also a successful asset manager to know anything more than the "Penelope Program" for investment.

Case History: The Penelope Program

The Penelope Program was named after a most unique and delightful client who owned and operated a successful equipment rental business. Among her other admirable characteristics, she was decisive. The fruits of her labor were impressive. She was realistic in her evaluation of her ability to manage assets and her unwillingness to invest in assets she could not understand or control, such as the stock market. She invested her funds only in certificates of deposit of $100,000 or less with FDIC insured institutions across the fruited plain. She realized the investment return shortcomings of her program; however, based upon her definition of financial security, her program worked wonderfully.

I had many debates with her as to how she could reduce her taxation and/or increase her investment return. As I mentioned, she was decisive; so I never moved her one inch. Penelope was also an advocate of another financial management axiom: know what you do and do what you know. She would not give any serious consideration to an investment in any variable annuity, mutual fund, stock or bond. Her explanation of her exclusive focus on the equipment rental business was that 50 years of twelve hour days had brought her to the point of understanding the equipment rental business; and at her age, she obviously did not have time to undertake the expensive learning curve with any other business.

Penelope was realistic regarding the availability of her time for learning about other investment opportunities. She was willing to accept a very conservative return by just pursuing certificates of deposit; however, this philosophy may not suit you and I do not recommend this approach to investing. The business owners I have worked with who are also good asset managers either know and respect their limitations or approach asset management (investing) as a labor of love. When they recognize their limitations, they get professional help. When investing is a labor of love, they spend the time to understand the market and effectively research specific investments. For vacation, they go to investment seminars, and in their spare time, they work the Internet seeking investment ideas.

> ### The business owners who are good asset managers either know their limitations or approach asset management as a labor of love.

I recommend that you seek the highest return on your assets within your personal risk tolerance environment. Become as informed as possible about investment opportunities within your time, interest and physical limitations. Do not invest a penny until you have total peace of mind about either the portfolio manager's philosophy and techniques, or specific investment you have selected and the corresponding asset environment. Address your highest priority, the family business, first. You should be realistic about your genuine interest in asset management and the time you are willing to apply to exploit your interest. If you are still an active manager, make a realistic appraisal of your ability to climb the investment learning curve. In the absence of adequate time, if your desired return exceeds your capability, seek professional assistance.

Some people are just turned on by investments. If you need professional assistance, and the vast majority of us do, draw upon your bright mind and sound judgment to build a successful investment management program. The world is full of asset managers, portfolio managers and investment managers. Some are good, some are bad and some are wolves looking for their next lamb. Just apply your common sense and experience to separate the good from the bad. As you think about how you would select an asset manager, investment advisor or portfolio manager, consider asking these questions:

- How long have they been in the investment management business?

- What is their training, professional designation, and background?

- What are their general investment preferences: bonds, stocks, real estate, etc?

- What has been their investment history experience? (Please provide a sample of work.)

- Do they have errors and omissions insurance?

- What are their commissions and fees?

- Who are three references that have at least three years experience with their service?

- What service reports will be received, and when should they be received?

- Are they receiving any expense reimbursements or back-end fees from the investment companies?

- Have they ever had any complaints filed (with the SEC or NASD) regarding their service?

- Who is their supervisor, and when can we meet to discuss the above?

The investment management industry is very mobile and supervisory. Beware of individuals who move around and do not have supervisors. When you ask to meet a supervisor, everyone will be on notice that you will not be a passive, vulnerable investor. Your good business sense and discernment can enable you to pick a thoroughbred professional to manage your hard earned money. Be as demanding of an asset manager/investment advisor as you would of an employee. Do not accept mediocrity. Performance is the test.

Financial Planning for Successor Heirs

Our emphasis has been on the parent principals and rightly so, because the succession process will never get started until their needs are properly addressed. However, the needs of children who will be taking over the business should also be addressed.

The prospective successors who are anticipating continuing a family business do so with expectations. Generally, children expect that when mom and/or dad retire, they will step into their parents' lifestyles. Upon retirement, parents are usually enjoying the most attractive earnings/workload/lifestyle of their careers. Successors should be given the news early on in their careers that this will probably not be the lifestyle they will assume when their parents retire. If there are two or more successor heirs, when they divide cash flow freed by their parents' retirement, their portion of the cash flow will be less than their parents.

Furthermore, when mom and dad retire, they will probably continue to draw some form of salary and benefits. There may also be a stock redemption that will consume the cash flow. Invariably, there is some form of payout of salary, benefits or debt that consumes cash flow that the successors might otherwise get. In the vast majority of businesses, if the successors get a pay or benefit raise shortly after their parents retire, it is because they have expanded the business or dropped expenses other than those associated with their parents. If the successors want to live the good life and take bundles of money out, they had better be prepared to put bundles of effort in. Parents who are taking more out of the business than they appear to be contributing are merely drawing upon a buildup of income earning ability that occurred when they were barely taking anything out of the business. In other words, it is payback time.

> *n the vast majority of businesses, if the successors get a pay or benefit raise immediately after their parents retire, it is because they have expanded the business or dropped expenses.*

To help support this reality, parents are urged to pay children what they are really worth, not what they need to live a lifestyle that they should have. Do not pay them less than they are worth, or you will create resentment that can never be erased. Also, do not pay them more. "Enabling" will promote incorrect conclusions about the input versus takeout concept of the family business.

In concert with the education about what children should expect to take out of the family business, it should also be explained that they are paid according to a compensation policy that is critical to the overall harmony of employees and productivity of the business. Further, there are two elements of earning from a family business. The first is compensation for services. The second aspect of compensation is return on equity ownership. When the children own stock via gifts or purchases, they can enjoy the second aspect of compensation from the family business.

Most family business owners are required to personally guarantee business debt.

At the risk of expressing the obvious, parents should not transfer operational control to their children without being relieved of liability.

History has proven that facts are stranger than fiction. There is no way to determine today what bizarre circumstances may occur in the future that converts a simple loan guarantee into a personal disaster. It is okay for children to think they are in control, but parents should maintain sufficient voting stock or contractual power to regain control if the need arises.

How do you determine what children are worth? This is difficult because of the subjective nature of the situation. You may feel they should have a nicer home or their children should go to private schools. Commonly, the income of successors is inflated to artificially support their standard of living. The best approach is to simply pay children what you would pay a non-family member. Any other compensation criteria can create problems, either with a child's entitlement attitude or with the frustration of managers who are working hard for every dollar they earn. Do not be naive and believe that you can keep a child's compensation secret. If you feel that you need to supplement a child's cash flow, do not distort their reasonable income from the business. You can make annual spendable cash gifts or make creative equity gifts that will either enhance income or provide a specific benefit, such as a home.

In review, personal financial planning is critical to effective succession planning. Parents with rational minds must have confidence in their personal financial security before they will release their most productive asset: the family business. Transferring portions of the business during a parent's lifetime is important to minimizing estate tax. Transferring management control during this lifetime is important to the development of effective business management skills and practices. The disciplined accumulation and management of assets is critical to achieving financial security and peace of mind. The senior generation's peace of mind about personal financial security is in the best interest of all benefactors (children, employees, vendors) of the business succession process.

Business Financial Planning

What does business financial planning have to do with turning the business over to the successors? This second aspect of financial planning positions the business, and to some degree family members, for the smoothest, most efficient transition possible. Just as parents must be prepared for succession, the business must be equally well-prepared to serve the parents' needs, respond to the successors' direction and avoid as much tax and estate administration as possible.

In this chapter we will review aspects of business structuring that facilitate the unique needs of succession. Consistent with our approach to personal financial planning, we are not going to delve into the detailed structuring of corporations, partnerships, limited liability corporations, joint ventures, and other structures. But we will provide enough detail to give you a sense of the complexities involved and the breadth of options available.

Business financial planning must be implemented by competent attorneys and accountants. What we will do here is discuss the important business-planning principles that should be addressed during the planning process.

The business planning effort confirms that your goals can be satisfied by the existing business structure or it identifies structuring problems so that they can be appropriately addressed. As an example, you may want to periodically redeem a few shares of stock in your business to fund retirement income or specific needs. However, there may be punitive personal income tax on partial stock redemptions in a regular C-corporation. You may need to develop alternate methods of generating cash to achieve your goal. And this review may identify other goals that are unrealistic within the current business structure. Sometimes it is not feasible to conform business structures to goals. Some changes in the business structure might bring unrealistic costs or take too much time. In this event, the planning effort should conform succession goals to business structures. This is usually a slower moving, even emotional process, because we may be talking about modifying a lifelong dream.

As an example, during a planning feasibility review, we frequently identify business succession goals that are in conflict with estate distribution goals. The cause of the contradiction is insufficient non-business assets in the family's estate to accomplish the fundamental goal of equal estate-asset distribution to children both in and out of the business.

After directing adequate assets to children operating the business, there are essentially no assets remaining to direct to the children outside the business.

Under such circumstances, goals actually have to be conformed to the situation.

Business financial planning should be approached under the assumption that, for every family business environment, there is an optimum method of structuring corporations, partnerships, and agreements to achieve the family's succession goals. Just as people and businesses vary, so does the "optimum structure." There is no cookie cutter program that effectively structures all family businesses for succession. Some families are more concerned about security; others about control, and others about taxation. The unique concerns of each family determine the optimum structure.

Let's review the definition of a business and what is involved in business succession planning. A business is the administrative structure that manages and directs a specific commercial activity. Documentation of ownership, records of activity, records of policies and collection of accepted procedures provide the embodiment of the business. There are a variety of methods through which a business can be administered: proprietorships, partnerships, corporations, limited liability corporations and joint ventures. There are also many variations of partnerships and corporations. Business financial planning addresses how the business should be structured to achieve a variety of succession objectives pertaining to ownership, income, control and taxation. The nexus of business planning is to further the achievement of expressed succession goals through business vehicles and business agreements.

There are two approaches to business planning: organization and reorganization. The family members who have birthed and nurtured a business into success already have business entities in place when succession planning becomes a priority. The reality of the situation is that the vast majority of families organize their businesses without any thought to succession. Who can blame them? In the beginning, when one does not even know if the business will survive, why spend valuable time and money considering how the next generation will take over?

Initial business structuring decisions are most often based upon concerns of liability or income tax, not succession. Business planning identifies and addresses the incompatible structures and systems and reorganizes them to conform to succession goals and new financial planning priorities.

Unfortunately, there are some restrictions and limitations to business reorganization because of income tax and gift tax regulations.

As an example, to facilitate business credit, you may have put your real estate in your C-corporation when you started. Many years later, when credit worthiness is not an issue, you may want to own the real estate separately from the business to facilitate retirement income or equitable asset distribution. Removal of the real estate from the corporation may create a personal income tax that can be a major deterrent. Fortunately, even with the restrictions, there is substantial latitude for reorganization that can enhance your succession plans. You must rely on your attorney and accountant to keep you informed of the do's and don'ts of business reorganization.

Additionally, if that C-corporation had been organized from a succession perspective, it could be an S-corporation to facilitate the pass-through of rents and capital gains, or the real estate could be owned personally and pledged as security for loan guarantees. When succession-planning goals are in place, advisors can adapt business structures to meet them.

Admittedly, working with corporations, partnerships, and legal documents can get complicated. In the absence of solid goals as reference points, you could find yourself in a black hole of confusion and frustration. Regardless of whether business planning is reorganizing old enterprises or organizing new endeavors, the first step is to review expressed goals to ensure that you are moving in the right direction.

Business planning begins the never-ending process of reevaluation and refinement of goals. This does not have to be a major undertaking; however, a deliberate effort should be made to evaluate how well business structures match goals. That means a review of the technical aspects of business ownership, taxation, liability and control, along with personal feelings.

Predictably, inconsistencies are found. This process can be very simple or quite involved, depending upon the aggressiveness of goals and the level of prior business planning.

Each family business environment has its own unique goals and needs. From a succession perspective, there are time-tested business structuring principles.Rely upon your advisors to help you build the most compatible, technically advanced business structure available.

> *Keep in mind, though, that it is very easy to become so technically correct that you have no earthly idea what has been done, or why.*

Keep the business as simple as possible. Remember, there are two competing issues in almost every aspect of financial planning for succession: being technically correct and being personally compatible.

Business Structures

I am not going to attempt to define what business structure is best. The appropriate answer depends totally upon your circumstances. However, we will address important business succession structuring principles.

When appropriate, utilize "pass through conduit" business vehicles. Unless there is an ulterior motive, avoid business vehicles such as regular C-corporations and complex trusts that pay income tax at the business level. However, if your advisor can provide adequate explanation as to why a taxed entity such as a regular C-corporation is more appropriate, by all means, take his advice. Otherwise, utilize vehicles such as subchapter S-corporations and partnerships to pass through to the business owners the taxable income, which is only taxed once. These vehicles also generally enable retained earnings to be withdrawn without double taxation. Of great importance, pass through business structures enable retired parents and passive siblings to obtain a return on their equity without incurring punitive double income tax.

When appropriate, own business real estate separately from the operating business. That will facilitate other aspects of succession planning, such as creating an additional source of retirement income. Also, separate real estate will facilitate estate planning by providing a passive asset that can be directed to inactive children to achieve equitable asset distribution.

Assuming that you understand these principles and are relying upon qualified advisors, the actual brick and mortar structure of your business will meet your succession needs. Let's now focus on business ownership policies and agreements that are fundamentally important.

Additionally look for opportunities to establish both an active and a passive form of business ownership. For both regular C and Subchapter-S corporations, this means two series of common stock, voting and non-voting. For partnerships, this means the designation of both general (controlling) partners and limited (passive) partners. For other hybrid business structures, such as Limited Liability Corporations and Limited Liability Partnerships, this means designating a controlling member or partner.

Having an active and a passive form of ownership provides several succession planning advantages.

Owners can gift or sell non-controlling equity ownership to successors to supplement their income without relinquishing control of the business. When equitable estate distribution dictates that non-actively employed children receive equity ownership, control of the business can be transferred to actively employed children. Finally, as will be discussed in a later chapter, utilization of a controlling and non-controlling form of business equity can substantially reduce the gift tax or estate tax cost of business equity transfers.

Whenever possible, restrict business ownership to actively employed family members who seek a full time career. Rarely have I seen ongoing harmony between active and inactive family stockholders in a business. The adversarial opportunities between active and inactive business partners are endless. The combination of money, control and sweat generate phenomenal selfish emotions between family members, which frequently results in relationship stress.

Case History: The Inactive Stockholder
A classic example of the hazards of an inactive stockholder is illustrated in a fast food restaurant franchise we have worked with for several years. Dad had two children, a son and a daughter, and owned a very profitable store in a rural community of approximately 400,000 people. Son was a businessman like his dad, and pretty good at it. He loved the fast food business and considered no other career options. Dad was semi-retired, so

Son was running the business as the general manager. Dad was proud of his son for following in his footsteps and intended to give the business to him.

Dad, however was also proud of his daughter. She was well-trained and was pursuing her dad's passion, horses. Daughter had an eye for quality and, in the horse world, that is spelled M-O-N-E-Y. The fast food business was profitable and the horses were expensive. The horse farm was a monetary black hole, promising "one day to start making money."

Dad was just as determined to help Daughter with her career as he was to help Son with his. Dad's solution to the cash flow imbalance between Son's fast food chain and Daughter's horses was to give Daughter stock in the business. Daughter did nothing but work horses, making zero contribution to the supporting business. She was paid a salary from the business, given 24% of the stock, and received 24% of the profits through subchapter-S dividends.

Son was not particularly pleased with the situation; however, he was no fool. Dad, having given him 25% of the stock, was also paying him a great salary. In addition, Dad had estate documents that would pass an additional 26% of his stock to his son, giving him control after Dad's death. Son recognized that he was getting the best of a bad deal. Moreover, he was concerned that he did not want to appear greedy or unappreciative to parents who had their idealistic hearts set on their children harmoniously continuing to share business profits after they retired.

I offered an observation to Dad that his good intentions were actually creating a problem, which could become nasty in the event of his death or if circumstances changed. We pointed out that, in the absence of parents, the true feelings of children would prevail; and Son did not think Daughter should be paid from the business if she did not contribute to its success.

His reaction: "Okay then, give me a better idea of how I can support my daughter's horse business without personally having to pay income tax on the cash flow."

My response was that income tax was important, but not more important than family harmony. I suggested that Dad pay Daughter a return on her equity ownership of the restaurant through Sub-S dividends. The balance of the cash needed would come from gifts to their daughter or their investment in the farm. I also suggested that he not plan for her to be a continuing passive stockholder after his death.

Unfortunately, Dad was not convinced. He continued with his program of supporting Daughter's horse-breeding career from the family business through salary and dividends. To make things even more exciting, he purchased a ranch for Daughter two years later and leased it to the business to make the mortgage payments tax deductible.

The next year, the fast food business began a declining cycle and historically very high profits went into the tank. Son was working a 70-hour week to keep the business in the black and did not receive any bonus, *partly because of the expense of Daughter's salary and the farm payment. The tension between Son, Father and Sister grew to an explosive level. The son's anguish was not an issue of greed. He had to earn enough to support his family, and he saw those horses reducing the lifestyle of his wife and children. Heated arguments ensued.*

The following year, the fast food business continued to weaken. Son was upset with Dad as the business lost money and he received no bonuses. As mortgage and tuition mounted, the son felt compelled to get a higher paying job in an adjoining community; so Son left and Dad came back to work full time.

Meanwhile, in the midst of a banking crunch, the bank refused to renew the note on the ranch, so Dad was forced to sell it. As a result, Daughter also became upset with Dad. Without a ranch to breed horses, she decided to move to Miami to collaborate with friends who were training horses at the Hialeah breeding grounds.

At 68, Dad had lost his ability and desire to operate the business, which was further declining because of his poor management and insufficient working capital. He asked his son to rejoin him with a promise that he would rectify the stock situation. The son said no. He had taken a job in an urban community and his wife did not want to move back to the country. Dad was forced to sell the business at the bottom of the market.

The net result of Dad's insistence to have a passive, nonproductive stockholder cost him the unity of his family and the succession of what would have been a third-generation business.

Parent leaders should avoid trying to please each of their children with business ownership. Strong leadership is more important than satisfying everyone's desires. The reality of a family business is that it is very rare that everyone in the family will be pleased with how stock is being distributed or how business resources are being utilized. Everyone has an opinion and in most cases the opinions tend to be self-centered. When unity of opinion cannot be achieved, someone must lead, notably mom and/or dad. Focus your energies on leadership that best achieves the overall family business succession goals.

Parents should communicate directly with all family members about strategic business policies that affect them, such as stock ownership. If a parent feels it is mandatory for family harmony and/or business success to have passive owners, so be it. Or if parents believe that only actively employed family members should own stock, so be it. Just take the time to explain your rationale to those affected and forthrightly respond to their concerns. Their thoughts may help you to refine your thinking. They may not like your plans. Nevertheless, the major benefit is that all children will know where they stand, what to expect and who is responsible for the circumstances. There will be fewer surprises and fewer possibilities for projecting acrimony to the improper target, such as a sibling. Any child who is disgruntled about your decision will not be confused as to where to direct their anger. This point may seem trite, but it is very important to long-term family harmony.

Family members should be educated to the responsibilities of business ownership. The discussion should cover the responsibilities, realities and reasonable expectations of stock ownership. While parents are in control of the business, it is reasonable for them to establish parameters for business operation and stock ownership and require children to abide by these rules. In fact, parents have a responsibility to establish rules to protect family harmony. These pearls of wisdom regarding business ownership would include, but not necessarily be limited to:

- Employed family members are expected to be role model employees

- Stock ownership must be maintained in the family bloodline (no in-laws)

- Being a stockholder does not mean a guaranteed job

- Having stock does not mean you will necessarily receive dividends

- There is no such thing as "equal say." The majority vote will rule

- As owners, we serve employees and vendors

- Also of special importance, family members must understand the first family business golden rule: He who has the gold (Mom and Dad) sets the rules.

All agreements and operational rules should be documented. Documented agreements are very important to family business planning, because they provide an element of certainty to a business world replete with uncertainty and further complicated by family emotions. The primary business uncertainty is the financial future. Buy/sell agreements, stockholders' agreements, partnership agreements, stock-redemption agreements, salary continuation agreements and others deal with future contingencies. Agreeing today about how to reconcile future contingencies, such as a death, irreconcilable differences, or divorce converts uncertainty into certainty.

Once the family has agreed - mentally, emotionally and financially -- on what will take place in the event of contingencies, there is confidence, order, and peace of mind. It allows mental energy to be focused on business matters versus personal matters. Endeavor to bring to your otherwise uncertain environment as much certainty as possible through ink, paper and signatures.

Agreements should pursue detail. Do not let your desire for simplicity overpower the need to cover details that can be critically important. The only reason written agreements are made is to preclude disagreements. If you draw up business agreements, take the time and effort to do it right by pursuing as many contingencies and details that you or your advisors can bring to mind.

If details are not addressed adequately, family members will be projected into negotiations, which is a predictably <u>lose/lose proposition.</u>

The Family Business Stockholder's Agreement

Predictably, the family business stockholder's agreement is essential to effective succession planning. This document controls the who, how, and when of stock transfers in a family environment. Here are some of the specific provisions that can enhance your family's business agreement:

1. Provide passive stockholder "puts" that will allow them to require active controlling stockholders who may become insensitive to their needs to purchase their stock based upon a predetermined stock price.

2. To protect against divorces, restrict stock transfers to the lineal descendants of (bloodline) family. Other transfers are subject to first right of refusal by family members.

3. Require spouses of family members to endorse the agreement so that they will have affirmed that they understand transfer- restriction provisions.

4. For banking and/or bonding purposes, designate that any stockholder who withholds a personal guarantee that is deemed necessary by the board of directors to prevent deadlock to tender their stock.

5. To maintain an active family member ownership structure, restrict stock ownership to "qualified successor employees" and define "qualified" as someone who, by age 35, has at least three years of full time employment with the family business.

6. Make sure any agreement is reviewed by several advisors. Different professional disciplines will approach a document differently and their input is very valuable in developing a good working agreement.

Demanding the adoption of stockholder agreements does not mean that children's opinions should not be taken into consideration. Children can and should play a productive role in establishing buy/sell agreements, operating agreements and family business employment agreements. Their perspectives and insights are needed to develop compatible agreements. However, in lieu of bickering, the controlling family and business leaders (parents) should disengage from arguments and use their best judgment to put in place strong agreements that will bring order to what can easily become a disorderly environment. If, as a parent, your judgment was good enough to start and build a business, it is surely good enough to establish a good stockholder's agreement that will control current and future stock ownership.

Show appropriate recognition to employed in-laws who earn key-man status. Employed in-laws also carry the responsibility for setting the standard for effort, attitude and expectations.

They assume a tough role, sandwiched between the upward scrutiny of employees and the downward scrutiny of family.

Additionally, they frequently must withstand distorted expectations of their spouse. Any employed in-law who withstands this pressure and genuinely rises to the top without artificial support should be given key person recognition above the sort of ownership recognition that would normally be given the marital unit. This recognition should be in a form compatible to your feelings. Performance bonuses are a natural. Stock bonuses or stock options are not required and should only be utilized if you feel comfortable -- and then only when accompanied by an ironclad stockholder's agreement that assures that the stock will remain in the family.

Adopt a Family Business Employment Policy (FBEP) describing the employment compensation and benefit criteria for those actively employed children and in-laws, as well as those who anticipate entering the business. It is natural for family members and in-laws to be drawn to a business because of both the environment and the potential benefits. It is also natural that these aspiring businessmen and women have assumptions about where they will start, what they will be doing, what their pay will be and what their title will be in relationship to both employees and other family members.

These assumptions are dangerous. Pre-employment assumptions are a potential source of frustration that can devour enthusiasm, spoil a beginning or even an entire career. Incorrect assumptions can also create family friction that can handicap the prospects of future harmony and teamwork. A Family Business Employment Policy provides family members a clear understanding of employment requirements and compensation to preclude assumptions that can lead to problems. This document gets Mom and Dad off the hook regarding the employment of children and, even more importantly, regarding the employment of in-laws.

The agreement specifies the education and experience requirements for employment. Notably the FBEP states that family members are not entitled to a job but are entitled to an opportunity to earn a job. Initial employment of a family member, just like everyone else, is probationary until their commitment is understood and their talents can be applied to the appropriate job. Further, the agreement states that the initial opportunity each family member gets will be dependent upon how they prepare themselves in their formal education and experience with other employers.

Other important concepts of this unique family agreement are that employment is encouraged elsewhere prior to joining the family business, and the successor child's job record away from the business will impact the opportunities they receive within the family. Why should the family hire someone who flunked out or sandbagged through another business just so she or he can get in with the family and rip them off, too?

This agreement should convey that there are no elevators to management positions in the family business; everyone must take the same steps.

Case History: The Family Business Employment Policy

A few years ago I worked with an automobile dealer who had a very successful business involving three dealerships. He and his wife had three wonderful daughters, none of whom had any interest in the automobile business. The youngest daughter was a teacher married to a football coach; the middle daughter was a nurse; and the oldest was a homemaker married to an attorney. My client called me and said he had been talking to the attorney son-in-law about coming into the business and asked me what I thought.

I responded that it sounded fine, but in the past I had witnessed awkward times when siblings and in-laws entered a business. I further stated that reality could easily be distorted when an attorney entered private business. Attorneys are generally very bright and confident in their training and ability. Attorneys tend to think that they can transition to what they feel is a less demanding career and not miss a beat in their new profession.

I asked my client what he expected would be the employment and compensation criteria for his son-in-law. He responded that he felt he should start as a service advisor and, on six month rotations, work in every segment of the business. He felt that his son-in-law should complete his indoctrination tour in the business office and spend a solid year to eighteen months of a three-year training program learning the ropes of business finance.

When asked how much he expected to pay his son-in-law, he replied, "I will pay him what he is worth in the various jobs he will perform. I know it will probably be less than he is making now, but he will be earning substantially more in four or five years. I can also make some cash gifts to my daughter to supplement their income during this period."

My response was that his plan sounded great, but I would bet one of my mother's fruit cakes that the son-in-law's assumptions of what he would be doing were much different. Although admittedly late, I suggested that he write out his thoughts, send them to me for refinement and I would coordinate with the company attorney the adoption of a Family Business Employment Policy corporate resolution. I advised that he keep talking with his son-in-law, but not finalize any agreements before giving him the document and asking for his agreement. He agreed and, with the attorney, we quickly put together a resolution.

As soon as the corporate resolution was available, my client forwarded it to his son-in-law with a note asking him to endorse an acknowledgment. Daughter immediately called back, accusing her dad of having no respect for her or her husband and that they deserved better treatment. Naturally, my client referred his daughter to me. She called using the same line. My response was, "Save your fire power; let's all meet and work this situation out."

About a week later I met with the client, his daughter and her attorney-husband. I confessed that this was my idea, so I should be the one who explained it. I said that the program was based upon respect; we respected both of them enough to make sure they were properly prepared for assuming a management leadership role. This was a tough business that was very different from the practice of law. Having a legal background would help the son-in-law be a better manager, but it would not make him a manager. Only the son-in-law could make himself a manager by learning the fundamentals of the business and earning the respect of those whom, at some point in time, he will hope to lead.

The daughter responded with, "But our friends are all managers and executives." She was determined to continue with the fairness platform. I was in the process of explaining to her that their friends had initially chosen to go into management in lieu of law, when her husband jumped into the discussion. He remarked that he had substantial reservations about the automobile business, as well as his ability to live up to the expectations of his father-in-law.

The daughter was taken back with what her husband had said; however, she quickly responded by asking how she and her husband were going to live on blue- collar compensation.

Her father responded by saying he could find ways to get them enough extra money to get by for a couple of years; however, as in any situation, achievement would require some level of sacrifice. I added that, as the first-born with two younger sisters, she should be a proponent of a restrictive Family Business Employment Policy.

I asked her what she would think if her husband had paid his dues and had followed her dad as the dealer, only to have two other brothers-in-law come along and demand manager jobs. Not only would they put a financial and managerial strain on the business, but they would also provoke friction between sisters. If her husband skipped the steps, she would have no valid argument regarding her brothers-in-law sliding into the business.

There was no further argument. Evidently, that thought got her attention. She recognized the precarious example she could be setting, and we went on to work out the details of her husband's training program. That was five years ago. The attorney son-in-law is now the general manager. I suspect any day now I'll be hearing from dad, wanting me to begin developing retirement plans. Over this five-year period, one of the other sons-in-law came into the business and dropped out after six months because he "did not like the long hours." To be sure, if that son-in-law had entered as a top-level manager, he would have found a comfortable spot and ultimately become dead wood to the business.

Compensation Programs

Compensation programs should be adopted for family member managers. Compensation of family members is a common cause of controversy. Anyone who has ever had a brother or sister knows without explanation that family environments are competitive. This competition can be very healthy; however, selfish emotions can convert healthy competition into petty backbiting or, even worse, nasty struggles.

A compensation program takes the politics out of how much family members are paid. A compensation program establishes the parameters of compensation for the various management levels that family members progress through. The parameters include both salary and incentives. Although a parent may enjoy the short-term thrill of giving a child a fat salary or a discretionary bonus to support their lifestyle, this short-term joy can turn into a long-term headache when the child comes back to the well looking for more, or when another family member questions the fairness of the bonus.

The headache intensifies when siblings and/or cousins begin making petitions for a higher bonus than their brother or sister.

Compensation programs and pay plans keep parents out of harm's way.

There are three major schools of thought on family member compensation: equal, reflective and a combination of the two. Under the equal approach, family members are paid the same regardless of their contribution, so that no one will feel unappreciated. Under the reflective approach, each child is paid salary and bonuses reflecting the contributions she or he makes, which resembles the environment parents experienced when the business was getting started. The third program is a compromise hybrid of the first two: equal salaries with bonuses that reflect the specific contribution of each family member.

All three programs have their obvious advantages and disadvantages. The reflective program is the generally accepted method for compensating family members. This approach to compensation is more in line with the proverbial theorem of life that "you will reap what you sow." The equal pay program looks good on paper and sounds good in the parlor but rarely works in business. It is difficult to sell a communist theory to ambitious Yankee capitalists.

The most important issue regarding family compensation is that a policy is adopted, recorded, communicated and followed. Every child who contemplates working in the family business has a different opinion regarding appropriate compensation, expected responsibilities and perks they should receive. If the plan is not in writing, it will be subject to debate. The specifics of your plan are less important than the fact that you have a plan, that everyone knows what pay to expect and that everyone knows not to gripe, bicker or politic regarding compensation. The only way to be really sure you have a plan is for it to be in writing.

Qualified Employee Benefits

Qualified employee benefits are costs that must justify the expense. Qualified retirement plans are not benefits designed for owners.

With the ERISA discrimination provision, the owners (family) will rarely be credited with a significant portion of the annual contribution. On the other hand if, in lieu of a pension or profit-sharing contribution, the owners took a bonus, the family would receive the majority of the contribution after a 40 to 50 percent tax. In light of simple math, any qualified plan should give you a reasonable return with respect to attracting and maintaining quality employees that can sustain succession success.

An ESOP is an intriguing qualified employee benefit program that is often discussed in succession environments; however, for the most part, ESOPs get more dialogue than action. The reason is simple: ESOPs are qualified plans with heavy administration. Furthermore, employees may become owners. The administration can be an expensive endeavor because of a plethora of rules and the requirement for annual, relatively expensive appraisals of the business. The thought of employee partners usually brings to mind scenes of disaster for families who, over the years, have struggled to manage and motivate less-than-ideal employees. Generally these concerns are well founded, even though the employee ownership is not direct. However, the law requires that vested employees have the opportunity to pay income tax on their accruals and become direct owners of stock. For these reasons, most families are not interested in ESOPs to achieve their succession goals.

> ***When there is no objection, an ESOP offers the opportunity to create a tax-deferred market for stock that can be tax-deductibly funded from the business and remain under the family's control.***

The ESOP can also provide an attractive source of tax deductible estate tax financing. The major problem with an ESOP as a succession tool is that it is a long term government regulated program that is politically vulnerable to the whims of Congress. At any given time, Congress can change the rules, leaving a family with prior assumptions holding the bag.

Non-Qualified Executive Benefits

Non-qualified executive benefits can be worthwhile investments in succession planning. The primary differences between a qualified plan and a non-qualified plan are discrimination, tax deduction timing and administration. Non-qualified plans can be effective succession planning vehicles because the plan can provide benefits for a select group of highly compensated employees, often the retiring parents, a few family members and special key employees. Therefore, succession-oriented benefits for owners and key executives are typically done on a non-qualified basis. In a qualified plan, the corporation receives a tax deduction at the time the contribution is made. In a non-qualified plan, the corporation does not receive a tax deduction until the benefits are paid to the employee. Notably, with a qualified plan there is no annual ERISA administration.

Parents logically can become concerned about their security as they contemplate various aspects of the succession process, such as gifting or turning over control of the business to their children. These security concerns include the continuing ability to draw income and benefits from the business after retirement, or in the event of disability or death. Fortunately, these concerns can be reconciled through non-qualified salary continuation agreements.

These agreements take the form of contracts between the parent and their business. The contracts generally state that, in recognition of the past contributions to the business, the company will continue to pay the parent's salary and benefits in the event of retirement, disability and even death. This non-qualified retirement benefit allows the parent to essentially draw passive income from the company without being required to pay corporate tax. In most succession planning environments, non-qualified salary continuation benefits are a vital aspect of the parent's security package. In a buy-out situation, this can also be utilized to indirectly pay a portion of the purchase price as tax deductible compensation.

Non-qualified benefit agreements can also be utilized effectively with successor children. The successors in a family business typically are not as concerned as their parents about security. Usually, the children's interest is focused on obtaining more equity in the business. Owning more of the business provides long term security by reducing the projected estate tax costs involved in the total transfer of the business.

Non-qualified programs also include various forms of stock ownership incentive plans for successor children. The unqualified nature of the benefits provides (discrimination) the ability to meet the circumstances of both the family and the business. The children's interests are usually focused on stock bonus plans or stock purchase-option plans. Each of these fringe benefit structures allows the children to increase their stock holdings in the family business at a favorable cost. If they are based upon incentives, these plans are also consistent with the parent's interests, as they will require the children to profitably manage the business. As you might expect, any program that benefits a business owner or the children is subject to close scrutiny by the IRS. Consequently, experienced technically competent advisors are mandatory.

Golden Handcuffs

This same form of contractual agreement can have a dramatic impact upon the employment continuity of non-family key managers effective succession planning must address the continuity of supporting key staff.

Non-qualified "golden handcuff" agreements can provide a substantial employment retention incentive to those select key non-family employees whom the successor will depend upon after parents are long retired.

They are effective tools in retaining key managers. There are also many variations of cash and equity golden handcuff benefits that can be utilized to form a "Succession Bridge."

Case History: The Oranges Family

To help you better understand some of the business structuring concepts we have discussed, let's visit a succession planning experience with a substantial citrus grower and fruit processor, Mr. Oranges. He owned 10,000 acres of orange groves, a trucking company and a fresh-fruit packing company. The most notable attribute of this gentlemen was that he had 10 children. He loved each of them dearly and had every intention of bringing each one into the family business.

When I met this gentleman, about half of his children were grown and self-supporting. Half of those grown children, despite his plans, had decided to go into other professions, and half were employed in the family business. Although disappointed that all his children were not going to stay at his feet, he concluded nonetheless that each child would receive an equal interest in the family business, which was worth about $22 million.

In the first aspect of succession planning, we reviewed Mr. Oranges' goals, assets and his existing plans. We pointed out that it was very unusual for a parent to get along well with all children. Regardless of how well he interacted with each child individually, it would be highly unusual for all of his children to have harmonious relationships with each other. We wanted Mr. Oranges to establish realistic family business ownership objectives by helping him accept that it would be nothing short of a miracle if all of his children worked together in harmony. Despite our counsel he reiterated his objective: each child would receive an equal share of the family business, regardless of his or her career choice.

In our continuing discussions, Mr. Oranges also stated that he wanted to keep all family business enterprises under one management structure. I found this bizarre and asked Mr. Oranges how he expected the business to operate with at least 10 stockholders and ultimately, many more as grandchildren began to emerge and assume ownership positions. He responded very succinctly that he expected them to simply vote their stock and the majority opinion would prevail. I commented that, with as many children as he had, his business could resemble a public corporation in just a few years. I continued to explain that although his "majority rules" plan looked good on paper, it had potential problems. Half of the passive owners would be subject to the power moves of the active children.

The concept of majority rule assumes that the minority submits, which rarely occurs in governments and large public corporations.

Unhappy minority stockholders would be heard, by whatever means they felt was necessary. There was also a possibility that, through attrition of actively employed children, the passive family members could obtain control of the business and disrupt the careers of other children. My point was that neither of these contingencies would be healthy for family harmony. It was my recommendation that Mr. Oranges avoid creating a control environment involving 10 voting family members.

Up to this point, I had not influenced Mr. Oranges' opinion. I felt it was time to get Mrs. Oranges involved in our discussion, hoping that she would be more practical. In a discussion on the structure of succession management, her remarks to Mr. Oranges were, "You may think all of your kids are great, but the fact is that you don't really know them. You've been too busy for the last 30 years growing oranges to really understand them. Each one is very different."

"Although they have a common family bond, they have different priorities, talents and values. At any given time, any two of our children could be at odds with one another. What keeps them harmonious is they have no control of financial issues. They are just brothers and sisters. To give the chil-

dren who will be inactive in the business an equal say in control would be comparable to asking all of them to agree on what to have for dinner. If you will recall, to keep them from starving to death, I have made the decisions on dinner for the last 25 years."

"You run the business the same way. You only ask for input from the kids after you have made up your mind. Because of your control, I believe there is reasonable doubt that even the ones working in the business will know how to make the right decisions after you are gone. However, I am sure those who devote their careers and lives to the business do not need critical, uninformed brothers and sisters making their decisions more difficult. It makes no sense at all to change the way this business has succeeded: the operator is in control. If you insist on making all our children owners of this business, at least give operational control to those who are dedicating their careers and lives to the success of the business and try to protect the interests of those who are passive."

Evidently, Mrs. Oranges did not say much about the business; but when she did, Mr. Oranges listened. Based upon her insistence, Mr. Oranges wisely made concessions, and they achieved a unified decision: all children would receive equity in the business, but only the children active in the business would have a management vote.

With the first of two major planning goals identified, our task was now to review and analyze the existing business structure to develop a method of keeping all the business enterprises under one management structure and protecting the interests of the passive owners.

Succession planning structures are not necessarily conformed to objectives. Objectives can sometimes be more flexible than business structures. This theory came to the forefront with the Oranges' family business. The groves were owned by Mr. Oranges individually and by Mr. and Mrs. Oranges jointly. The packing house was a regular corporation with substantial retained earnings that were marked for capital improvements. The fruit brokerage and the transportation company were combined in a subchapter-S corporation.

Mr. Oranges had structured each of his businesses based upon the advice of either his accountant or attorney, depending upon his specific concerns at the time. Notably, none of the businesses were organized with succession as a planning priority. He knew that his current structure presented challenges to the accomplishment of their objectives; however, he confidently reflected, "That's why I called you guys."

Our staff studied this complex situation for a considerable period before we achieved a breakthrough. Our conclusion was that we could accomplish his objectives of equal ownership, central management control, operational control by the children active in the business, and protection for passive family members with the following steps:

- *Organize the orange groves, which were a classic passive investment, into a family limited partnership.*
- *Give the limited partners the right, by majority vote, to select the controlling general partner.*
- *Allocate the orange grove limited partnership interests to the passive children.*
- *Elect Subchapter-S structure for the packing house.*
- *Recapitalize both the packing house corporation and the trucking corporation with voting and non-voting stock. Within dispositive provisions of his trust, direct voting stock to active children and non-voting stock to inactive children.*
- *Adopt stockholders' agreements and restrict transfers in operating companies to only family members who are actively employed in them. Also stipulate the methods and terms through which a stockholder could sell his or her stock or be bought out.*

Organize a new company, Oranges Management, to provide the unified control of the operations of the three independent business entities through management contracts.

I can distinctly remember Mr. Orange's reaction, "Limited what? You are not going to make a tax shelter out of my orange groves!" The impulsive gentleman was infamous for jumping to conclusions. Needless to say, he was not familiar with how a limited partnership could apply to his family business environment. We were not suggesting that he form a tax shelter. We were suggesting the use of a limited partnership to consolidate control of the orange groves into the hands of specific family members, protecting inactive family from operational liability and reducing potential estate tax by millions.

His response: "Why do we have to have make everything so complicated?" He continued at length to say that the last thing he wanted to do was over-complicate the business so that only the attorneys and accountants could make money.

He felt that his children would hate him if they had to depend upon legal and financial professionals to figure out what they were doing from week to week, with business structures that they did not understand. He concluded his diatribe with, "How much estate tax do you think we can save?"

I responded that I was also a fan of simplicity, but the trade-off was the achievement of his goals. The proper distribution of his business interests to all children and the reduction of estate tax exposure required high-tech structures that could easily be confusing. However, we were talking about saving millions of dollars in estate taxes, which might justify spending time to learn about new planning tools, such as a limited partnership.

Mr. Oranges was a good businessman. He simply did not understand the need for the new and complicated structures. I appealed to him that I was a family business planner, not a magician. Although these were new concepts and structures to him, they were very common to the field of business succession and estate continuity planning. Before he discarded these recommendations or amended his objectives, we should meet with his attorney and accountant to solicit their input.

We were talking about millions of dollars in estate taxes, which might justify spending time to learn about new planning tools.

Fortunately, Mr. Oranges' attorney was up to date with contemporary planning techniques. Even more fortunately, he was familiar with Mr. Oranges' cumbersome decision making process. Like every attorney I have worked with, he took exception to some of the design points but agreed with the overall plan concept. He patiently attempted to explain the plan on two separate occasions, with Mr. Oranges responding each time with, "But I don't want it to be this complex."

Finally the attorney was at his wit's end. I was actually pleased to see that I was not the only one who had problems with Mr. Oranges. In frustration, the attorney said, "you've got three options that I, and I'm sure Mr. Rawls, feel you should choose from:

1. Proceed with the implementation of this plan, trusting me to explain it effectively to your children;
2. Change your very ambitious objectives, or;
3. Start over with another succession planner and another attorney."

I was in agreement with the attorney. We had done everything we could to achieve this gentleman's objectives as simply as possible. However, neither his circumstances nor his objectives were simple and it was unrealistic to assume that any practical plan would offer the kind of simplicity Mr. Oranges was looking for.

This meeting concluded with Mr. Oranges stating that he would have to think about it. A week or so later I called the attorney and asked what was happening. He said that Mr. Oranges had called him back a few days later and they got into a heated argument because Mr. Oranges accused him of over-complicating the planning to increase the legal fees. He said, "I hung up on the blockhead. If you want to call him back, be my guest."

I didn't call him back, either. I occasionally visit by phone with the attorney and he hasn't spoken with Mr. Oranges. Evidently, Mr. Oranges cannot accept the inevitable compromise between planning concepts and ambitious objectives.

In summary, it isn't always easy But business structuring is a vital aspect of family business financial planning. Coordination of the business structure, agreements and benefits with personal and estate objectives and plans are imperative for the development of an overall effective succession plan.

Estate Issues

*K*now the value of time; snatch, seize, and enjoy every moment of it. No idleness, no delay, no procrastination; never put off till tomorrow what you can do today."
~ Earl of Chesterfield ~

The Estate Planning Process

More often than not, the uninformed would conclude that estate planning and succession planning are one in the same. Estate planning is indeed an important planning element, but is by no means the essence of succession planning. Business succession planning addresses the transfer and continuity of a business, including tangible assets, intangible assets and the culture that has supported the historical strength, resilience and success of the business. Aggressive succession planning actually encourages the transfer of a business to the next generation prior to the deaths of the parent principals. Unfortunately, this ideal lifetime succession planning achievement is rare because of financial security concerns and tax restrictions. As a result, an effective succession plan must also address the transfer of assets, which usually includes significant business interest, through the estate.

Estate planning supports business succession planning by providing for the efficient fulfillment of your asset transfer goals after your death. Estate planning is essential to succession of the family business to prevent the assets of success from becoming the liabilities of succession. No one has the true confidence that she or he will be blessed with independent cash assets or the lifespan to sell, gift or otherwise transfer the business to the children prior to the settlement of an estate. The passage of a complex, capital-intensive business through an estate can create all sorts of problems for successors, family employees and vendors. The owners of a successful family business have a stewardship responsibility to develop estate plans that will minimize the impact.

To avoid confusion, let's define estate planning. You can better understand the definition of what estate planning is by specifying what it is not. Estate planning for succession is not doing a new will, adopting a trust, buying some life insurance, taking care of the Mrs. or a project.

Estate planning for succession of a family business is not
something that you can take care of and file away for your
attorney to dust off and read to your children when the Lord
takes you home.

Estate planning is the ongoing process of designing, expressing, adopting and refining the documents, structures and programs needed for the achievement of your family business continuity objectives. It is the implementation and continual refinement of the structures and documents necessary for the efficient closure of your affairs and the transfer of assets to your designated heirs. Estate planning is the communication of those plans to the family, partners, key personnel and vendors who will be affected by your death.

In summary, estate planning describes the development and implementation of strategies concerning the transfer, management and perpetuation of an individual's or a family's assets from one generation to the next. Because of the date of application (after your death), estate planning is a truly sacrificial effort that directly benefits your family and beloved employees, and indirectly benefits others. Hopefully, in fulfillment of the spiritual law of giving, estate planning will be one of your most gratifying efforts while on the planet Earth.

Estate planning endeavors to accomplish three ambitious goals. The first is to establish a plan for the continuity of family assets, notably the family business. Secondly, estate planning initiates the transfer of those assets to family members and charities prior to death, to the maximum extent possible. Finally, upon death, estate planning completes the transfer of assets at minimum cost and administrative hassle, according to the wishes of the decedent. Notably, we will be relating estate planning to transferring a business from one generation to the following generation at minimum cost, with minimum hassle and with due consideration to whether children are involved in the business or are seeking other careers.

Estate planning for family business succession can be relatively simple or complex, depending upon your circumstances. On more than one occasion, such as with Mr. Oranges in the preceding chapter, I have been accused of making estate planning too complicated. However, I tried to help my client recognize that the relationships, objectives and circumstances were the real source of complication. Ambitious goals, such as financial independence, total harmony, no publicity and no tax, combined with challenging circumstances such as significant assets, multiple marriages, multiple children, drug abuse, irresponsibility, handicaps, partners, and sibling rivalry demand high tech (complicated) estate plans.

Individual states have also complicated matters by creating administratively burdensome probate laws to protect the rights of decedents, beneficiaries and creditors. Individual states and the federal government have confused matters by levying taxes of up to 55% on property transferred between generations. States and the federal government have developed a broad and convoluted body of laws to control the conveyance of wealth from one generation to the next. Admittedly, estate planning can be a challenge; however, this challenge is not insurmountable. With sufficient time, patience and resources, effective estate plans can be established and maintained.

Depending upon your personality and perspective, estate planning can be a real chore. I have witnessed phenomenal procrastination by business owners. In some cases, unfortunately, they were incredibly successful at avoiding the subject. As you can imagine, the results were frustration, stress and hard dollar loss to family, employees and others. Given those realities, let's identify the essential requirements for addressing estate planning:

- Recognition of mortality
- Recognition of responsibility
- A willingness to give
- A willingness to sacrifice
- A conviction to take action

If you cannot come to grips with your mortality, estate planning will stress you beyond your limits. Unfortunately, mortality is a profound reality. If you feel no responsibility to establish plans to preserve your business and protect your loved ones, you will not have the ability to stay on task to address the details of how to protect and prudently disperse your hard-earned resources. If you are not motivated to give your children the assets that you have earned, you will receive no gratification from the laborious estate planning process and will probably lose enthusiasm before completion. If you are unwilling to pay hard-earned money for professional assistance and to spend valuable time dealing with frustrating details, you will resent the cost of the effort and will probably pull out of the program before completion. Later, you may fail to spend the time and money to keep current. If you do not have the conviction to stop talking and start moving forward, estate planning will always be a great idea that you will never get around to. Estate planning process is about the preservation of a legacy, the spiritual remembrance of your presence here on earth through the continuity of the fruits of your labor. Estate planning provides the opportunity to allocate the time, effort and money to protect the business you have created from the jaws of government bureaucracy, taxation and management challenges.

Estate planning process is also about gifting. This gifting embodies transferring ownership to children or possibly others who have no familial right to the property. The only way they will acquire it is if you want them to have it. Whether transferring during lifetime or after death, you have to want to preserve a legacy and make a gift for estate planning to have motivating significance.

Nevertheless, estate planning is not a morbid experience that dwells on what happens upon death.

Those who have this misconception would rightfully rank estate planning with dental appointments and cleaning the garage. The significant portion of the estate planning effort focuses on very important lifetime activities that anticipate and execute asset transfers. These lifetime transfers serve a variety of functions that support the succession process, enhance the efficiency of ultimate transfer of assets and, hopefully, give great joy.

The process also allows parents or a business owner to evaluate the wisdom of their estate planning intentions and may motivate children to work harder and strive for greater achievement. On the other hand, tasting the power and income of asset ownership can sometimes be disorienting and serve as a deterrent for harder work and greater achievement.

Resentment between brothers, sisters, cousins and other family members may surface. From the other perspective, an apathetic family member may become inspired after being informed of planning maneuvers, such as transfers of the business interest. Notably, when estate and business succession goals and actions begin to be implemented, parents will receive the benefits of a veritable X-ray vision into the strengths and weaknesses of their children and their estate distribution plans.

With the benefit of this information, critical adjustments can be made to estate plans that will defuse and even avoid the potentially disastrous problems that have been identified.

There is another benefit to making lifetime estate planning transfers. In the words of the lady beer wholesaler, "Why wait until you are dead to gift? In the hereafter, I am not sure I'll be able to get the pleasure of seeing my children enjoy what I have been able to give them." In support of her thinking, I have worked with some of the wealthiest people in America and come to the profound conclusion that the greatest joy of having is giving. There is no substitute for joy received in doing something for a child or charity that they likely could not do for themselves. Gifts are like seeds and everyone is fascinated with the potential of the germination process.

Another more tangible benefit of lifetime estate planning is the removal of assets from harms way. With a 55% estate tax hanging over an estate, there is a substantial financial benefit to divest property during a lifetime. The bottom line advantage to Timber Man, Lady Beer Wholesaler and any other individual with substantial assets is a leveraged 55% tax savings on every dollar that is passed along free of gift or estate tax. It is leveraged because the growth or income derived from the gifted asset is also free of the 55% estate tax. Unfortunately, tax exempt gifting restrictions, which are discussed in more detail in the next chapter, prevent the immediate transfer of significant resources. However, over a period of several years, significant assets can be transferred. The idea of preserving or protecting 55% of both the asset transfers and their subsequent growth is a great incentive to pursue gifting.

The two most important steps in the estate planning process are initiation and completion. Getting this job done, in whatever way suits you and your family, is the single most important step. Depending upon your personality, family makeup, advisor group and business circumstances, the steps in the estate planning process may vary significantly. However, 25 years as a participant and student of the estate planning process has led me to several profound conclusions.

Aggressive, state-of-the-art estate planning is an essential facet of business succession planning.

Estate planning in the business succession realm is a formidable challenge demanding significant commitment of time, energy and financial resources.

The steps followed in the estate planning process have a significant impact upon the quality of the final product.

Before you undertake a significant challenge of any nature, it is wise to have a plan. Otherwise, as mentioned above, it is very easy to become distracted, discouraged and to fall short of your initial goal. I strongly suggest you take these time-proven steps:

1. Make a commitment to get started and communicate this commitment to someone who will hold you accountable. Estate planning is one of the most popular subjects to postpone. Procrastination may relieve current anxiety but, long term, the problems will only be compounded. There is no hope for successful completion if you never get started. There is no better way to get started than to authorize someone whom you respect to hold you accountable for your commitment.

2. Select qualified advisors to facilitate your estate planning efforts. Regardless of your personal convictions and confidence in your decisions, the quality of your estate plan will be substantially dependent upon the quality of your advisors. Estate planning is a professional discipline requiring a solid foundation of training, constant experience and ongoing continuing education. There is no reasonable room for generalists. Effective business succession estate planning requires specialists.

3. Establish a time target for the initial implementation of your plans. With the input of your advisors, make a realistic assessment of the time required to design, develop and implement your estate plans. This assessment should provide you peace of mind during the process that you are working within a reasonable time boundary. This assessment should also serve as an accountability tool to assure that your advisors diligently pursue their action items.

4. Close each meeting with a scheduled commitment for the next meeting and a reservation time for the following meeting. Maintaining momentum is one of the biggest challenges during the estate planning process. If you can end each meeting with a commitment for the next one, you'll have reasonable comfort that your planning is moving forward as expected. Scheduling with this diligence substantially relieves one of the greatest challenges, getting all critical parties together in the same room.

5. Develop and understand a schematic diagram of your estate plan before drafting any documents. A picture is worth more than a thousand words. Having a schematic of what you are trying to do is imperative to understanding the far-reaching implications of your plan relating to your business, your spouse, specific children, all children and employees.

6. Prior to drafting documents, develop and refine simple document summaries that stipulate pertinent document provisions. Simple summaries of the proposed documents following the schematic provide better understanding of the structure of future documents. This process will enable you to further refine your thinking and, without wasting legal fees, confirm important provisions such as trustees, executors, guardians, asset divisions and distribution dates.

7. Discuss estate planning intentions with those who will be impacted, such as spouse, children, key managers, franchisers, and lenders. Keep in mind that the estate planning process is a sacrificial effort. You are expending time, energy and money for the benefit of others. Within reason, prior to implementation, it is prudent to discuss your intended plans. "Pandora's box" is not as ghastly as you may presume. Sharing your estate planning intentions may generate a negative remark. However, positive or negative remarks about your intentions will be instructional or educational. Rational, well thought out comments by loved ones may help refine the plan. Irrational, self-centered comments by loved ones can also help you modify or reinforce your plans to deal with resentment or self-centered emotions.

8. Refine plans and document summaries as necessary. Going through the process of refining the diagrams and the document summaries will confirm the virtue or uselessness of what you learned from discussing your plans with your spouse and children.

9. Draft, affirm and execute the documents. Having followed the above steps, the actual preparation of the documents, and more importantly the refinement of those documents, will be greatly simplified. Moreover, you will have avoided substantial confusion over the awkwardness of legal documents. Ideally, this step simply confirms that the documents prepared for execution conform with the previously affirmed document summaries.

10. Conform property and plans with the documents. Generally, after designing, drafting and executing documents, the fun just begins. "Fun" relates to the detailed process of establishing asset titling and beneficiary designations to empower the documents to achieve the estate planning objectives. In most cases, intended gifts or sales also require asset appraisals, asset transfers and the filing of gift tax returns and Crummey notices. This is a very busy step that demands diligence. Usually it will be your CPA and/or attorney that will lead you through this process.

11.Make final review of documents and conform property. This step assumes that something will fall through the cracks. A final review of the executed documents and related property administration is essential to give yourself peace of mind.

12.Make a commitment to periodic review. The shelf life of estate planning is two years on the outside. In the absence of periodic reinvestment of time, energy and financial resources to confirm circumstances and implement needed updates, plans will become outdated and ineffective. It is very important to understand that, in complex family and business environments, estate planning is not in any sense a project, it is a never-ending process.

Case History: The Farmer Family

To illustrate a common misconception about estate planning, let's look at the case of a gentleman, 68 years old, who lived in a small town and, much to my surprise, was very wealthy. He lived with his wife, in a tidy wood-frame, six-room home on a small lot without much grass or any ornamental flowers. He was a very private, close to the vest type, who had achieved the heralded rural art of talking without moving his lips.

Looking at him, one would think he was a tenant farmer. He drove a seven or eight-year-old rust-riddled station wagon, carrying every dirty tool he owned in the back. Presumably all the clean ones were in the small dirt-floor shed behind his house, which doubled as his office.

We met as the result of an estate continuity presentation I had made to the Georgia Timber Owner's Association. He believed in reinvesting profits into his trees. This frugal, hardworking gentleman had developed an impressive estate. I had realized years before that farmers had originated and perfected the art of understatement, but I almost swallowed my Mont Blanc when he told me that he owned a shade over 33,000 acres of prime pine forest, giving him a net worth well in excess of $20 million. After I departed, he must have had a big chuckle, recalling the look on my face when I finally quit saying to myself in disbelief, "33,000 acres."

This was a simple man. A local attorney took care of his property acquisitions and filed his income taxes. He would not use an accountant because he had heard that the IRS could seize an accountant's records. He did not even know an accountant. He owned all his trees in his personal name. There were no corporations or partnerships. The balance of his estate consisted of a couple of hundred thousand dollars in passbook savings, some very light equipment and his home. Mr. Farmer was married and had five children.

Developing an understanding of his situation was the shortest data session of my career. When I inquired about his goals, he said: "Don't wanna buy no life insurance, just want a will to take care of mah wife and chillren."

In my defense, I told him I was not talking about life insurance. I was inquiring about the estate planning goals that he hoped to achieve. His answer was, "Don't wanna marry ya boy, just wanna take care of the Missus and chillren." He did not say very much more beyond "nope" and "yep." When I asked about the children, he said, "You better talk to the Missus, I've got chores to do." Incidentally, the wife and kids had no idea what the "ol' man" owned. One son helped him in the business but was primarily a book-keeper, not a timber man. He had no perception of the difference in owned land and leased land. All the other children had moved to the city.

On later inquiry, the son who worked with his dad said he knew his dad owned a few trees but had never figured he owned an entire county.

I had all the data for this estate on one sheet of paper. My staff accused me of losing my notes. When I convinced them of the simplicity of this situation, we developed a presentation with a dual focus. We prepared what we thought would be a simple plan that he could follow. Our plan called for him to form a limited partnership, to gift as much of the timber to his children as possible (while keeping control) and to make future timber acquisitions through a partnership. We also provided a relatively simple description of a revocable living trust that would convey his property according to his wishes upon his death. It also would avoid a massive mountain of probate administration required for what appeared to be more than 100 separate deeds of timber land.

Having reasonably good hearing, I didn't make any life insurance recommendations, as I assumed he would draw the proper conclusion when he saw the estate liquidity analysis.

I returned two or three weeks later for a presentation of our observations and suggestions. We began our discussion with a review of his current circumstances, highlighting what we considered to be his potential problems and opportunities. These observations were followed by suggestions as to how he could begin taking action to achieve his estate planning goals.

Our first topics were reducing taxation by restructuring his business. We were only a few minutes into our presentation when he abruptly stopped me. He said as emphatically as he could, without moving his lips, "Look here, I hired you to do my estate planning. I don't wanna hear 'bout forming no partnership and making gifts to my children."

I responded with, "Don't worry, we will get to that part quickly." To my statement he responded, "You don't listen very good, boy." He then stood up, walked out of the house, got in his station wagon and left. I was now alone in his office. After waiting and feeling stupid for about an hour, I concluded that Mr. Farmer was not coming back. As innocently as possible, I had really made him angry. He clearly perceived estate planning simply as making plans for the distribution of his property after his death and had no intention of even listening to the value of making gifts or repositioning assets to save estate taxes and probate expenses. The next day when I returned to my office, I tried to call him -- with no luck. A few days later, I received a check in the mail for our agreed fee with a note that said he would not be needing my services any further.

Mr. Farmer did not understand the process of estate planning. I had failed to listen to him properly and specifically try to explain the process of estate planning. His idea of estate planning was limited to expressing his desires as to how he wanted his property divided among his heirs. He was, needless to say, closed-minded to anything but adopting a will. As you would reasonably conclude, Mr. Farmer and I did not develop a close relationship. For several years after that experience, I felt solely responsible for not successfully motivating him to update his primitive estate administration and lower the estate tax bill by millions. Based upon our conservative estimates, his limited understanding of estate planning could have cost his family $10 million in avoidable estate taxes and probate fees.

As time passed, however, I realized I was not totally responsible. Mr. Farmer felt a responsibility to 'take care of the Missus,' but he did not want to give anything to his children. It really was not a major concern to him that the government was going to confiscate 55% of what he had worked all of his life to build. He was unwilling to sacrifice his time or money even to hear about how he could improve the administration and continuity of his estate.

Mr. Farmer wanted an estate plan, but he did not want to get involved in the estate planning process. He did not have a goal for the preservation and continuity of the financial blessings he had received. To accomplish his goal to 'take care of the Missus,' he felt he only needed a will. Almost everyone besides Mr. Farmer has a goal for the proper disposition and continuity of their wealth and prized business assets to their beloved family. I can count on one hand the number of clients and prospects who truly did not care what happened to their property and specifically, their business, after their death. Much to the chagrin of Mr. Farmer and others like him, it is rare indeed when estate continuity and business succession goals can be achieved with just new wills and/or trust agreements. Typically, time, effort and money must be expended in the planning process to dodge the tax bullets that can destroy a business and to divide assets in a prudent, equitable fashion.

Estate Planning Issues

With an understanding of the importance of the estate planning process, let's talk about how it's involved in succession planning. The most common estate issues impacting the succession of the closely-held family business are probate avoidance, asset management, asset distribution and estate tax financing.

Probate

Probate is the general term describing the administrative closure of a decedent's business affairs and the subsequent transfer of assets to heirs according to a documented bequest or to heirs-at-law in the event there is no will. Inasmuch as death prevents a decedent from representing his or her own affairs, the state court of jurisdiction becomes the guardian or conservator for the decedent's assets and assumes responsibility for supervising closure. Specifically, the guardian of the descendant's estate is the probate court and notably the probate judge. The judge's role is simply to protect the rights of the survivors, who include the creditors and legal successors in interest or beneficiaries. "Creditor" is a general term that describes commercial debt as well as debt resulting from income taxes and property taxes with respect to the decedent, as well as inheritance taxes and estate taxes.

Legal successors in interest are those who, in the absence of documented beneficiary designations, have a statutory right to the decedent's property due to marriage (dower) or bloodline. The term "beneficiary" represents the documented intended successor-owners of the decedent's assets. In most states, probate court is administered as a typical public judicial forum with clearly defined rules for the settlement of debt or conveyance of property, which are specified in the state's probate code.

The term "probate" derives from the Latin word, meaning "to prove." The assigned judge of the probate court utilizes an individual, typically known as the personal representative or executor, to organize and administer the affairs of the decedent's estate.

In a probate environment, the Personal Representative (PR) 'proves' to the probate judge that the decedent has expressed his or her asset distribution intentions in a valid will and the makeup of the asset inventory.

The PR then attends to the outstanding financial and administrative details of the decedent. The PR searches available sources to confirm the assets and liabilities of the decedent. The PR then proves to the judge that the decedent's debts are paid.

These debts would, of course, include taxes of all sorts. After specified time allotments have expired, probate administration forms and tax returns are filed. Then, with the court's approval, debts are paid and the Personal Representative submits a final asset inventory requesting distribution, according to the decedent's recorded and approved last will and testament. In the event there is no will, this distribution is according to the state's intestacy statutes. Ultimately, the estate net of debts and taxes is distributed to the rightful beneficiaries and the estate is closed.

The above description is a gross oversimplification of the probate process. As an element of the probate process, the estate tax return (Form 706) must be filed and ultimately accepted by the IRS. There are severe tax penalties for understating values, and the IRS demands proof of value that requires independent appraisal. Assuming there are no protests or challenges, the probate process generally ends nine months after death when the estate tax return is filed. Usually the IRS will not respond to the tax return for nine months to two years. If the Service accepts the return as filed, the estate can be closed. The normal procedure in the family-business succession realm is that the IRS sends notification that they are auditing the estate. In this likely event, the estate remains open until final tax settlement is reached, which generally means several years.

In order to file the return, assets must be appraised by qualified appraisers. And let us not fail to mention that closing the estate requires payment of the estate taxes. In the realm of the multi-million dollar, closely-held family business, this can be a major impediment to estate closure.

Generally speaking, keeping an estate open over an extended period of time can best be described as the retirement funding program for the lawyer and the accountant.

In spite of the above, probate is not inherently bad. Probate provides an independent party, the court, to protect the interests of beneficiaries, creditors and the state. The process provides order and control to an environment that would otherwise be a powder-keg combination of money, emotions, and contention. Undeserving parties could steal assets; creditors could be cheated; and beneficiaries could hold up the process with petty arguments. The probate system has a proven structure for dealing with these challenges and continuing the process of closing out the decedent's affairs. If there is contention regarding creditors or rightful beneficiaries, probate provides a regimented procedure for reconciling these issues. The probate environment may be a bit awkward, but it does serve the public well.

Each state has a probate system that is designed to handle the affairs of its citizens. This probate system treats each estate the same, regardless of the decedent's notoriety or size of the decedent's assets.

Unfortunately, as with any broad-based government system, there are undesirable side-effects for business owners of substantial means who, because of planning, do not need the government overseeing the closure of a decedent's business affairs.

With respect to probate, individuals of substantial means (such as business owners) are unnecessarily exposed to many complications. The exposure is unnecessary because business owners have the resources to avoid the complications of the probate process.

Professional assistance in the form of financial planners, attorneys and accountants who are familiar with this difficult terrain should be retained to help your family avoid as much of the probate process as possible. The cost of these professional guides is not cheap but, relatively speaking, well worth the money. With regard to probate, a dollar's worth of prevention is worth several hundreds or even thousands of dollars worth of cure. Do everything possible to avoid the probate experience and minimize publicity, costs and hassles.

Case History: The Brown Family

Probate and estate planning bring to mind the initial planning events of a family we worked with who owned two beer distributorships. In the planning process with our clients, Mr. and Mrs. Brown, a business succession and estate preservation plan was prepared. They asked me to work with an attorney on the 80th floor in one of the "pillars of commerce" downtown to whom they had been referred, but had never met personally. Our firm provided engineering for the estate documents and presented our recommendations to him for refinement, drafting and technical compliance. As is customary, we continued working with the attorney to coordinate the retitling of assets with the newly formulated plans that the attorney prepared.

One day I received a call from Mr. Brown who said, "Loyd, what's going on? Have you entered into a partnership with this attorney?" I responded, "No, all I have been trying to do is get him to transfer your property to your revocable family trust to avoid unnecessary probate. He has written a great document but is clearly reluctant to move your assets into the trust." Mr. Brown told me he was getting weary of legal bills, and I could understand why. At $375 an hour, he said he did not want me chit-chatting about the weather or politics with the attorney.

I responded by stating that there is a variable and a constant involved in estate planning. The variable is the attorney. You can get quality work for anywhere from $100 per hour to $500 per hour. The constant is that estate planning is not simply a matter of adopting a revocable trust. It involves coordinating your property with your new documents.

I continued, asking, "Have you heard the 'pay me now or pay me later' commercial? Would you prefer to have this opportunity to challenge me and the attorney about the planning cost, or give the attorney an opportunity to charge $375 per hour for whatever little nitpicky job he can find after your death without you looking over his shoulder?" Probate attorneys make a great living relieving widows of estate administration details, which a tenth grader could do.

He did not think about those options for very long, concluding, "If the attorney would send bills like this with me looking over his shoulder, he would be merciless in my absence. Stay on his butt so my family will not have to deal with him after my death."

In addition to the cost of advisors to deal with the regulatory aspects of probate, there are additional considerations. Because probate is administered in a court of law, the process of closing a decedent's business affairs in many states is subject to public review. Public disclosure of the intimate details of a family's business is one of the major concerns of estate planning. The attitudes and actions of competitors, bankers, suppliers and customers could all be impacted by a revelation of the intimate details of a business owner's family and financial affairs. I have witnessed the face of prospective clients washed with terror when they learned that probate could expose their estate to public scrutiny.

Avoiding the publicity of probate has probably motivated more business owners to pursue succession planning than any other factor.

Probate is a formal administrative environment with potentially burdensome checks and balances. Substantial reports, filings and notices must be completed during the nine-month period following death. The probate judge must be consulted for maneuvers such as the sale, leverage or distribution of assets required to bring the affairs of the decedent into order. This administrative structure can drain the mental energy required to operate a family business. The probate passage of time represents a form of financial purgatory for beneficiaries of the estate, during which time they are unable to assume unrestricted control and management of estate assets, most notably, the family business.

Fortunately, techniques are available to capitalize on the good aspects of probate while minimizing the publicity and administrative hassles involved during this process.

An easy way to minimize probate is to establish detailed, easily understandable distribution documents that do not require interpreters (attorneys, accountants) to translate the language and terms for your children.

There is something to be said for precise language with specific legal meaning; however, there is also something to be said for documenting estate distribution instructions with language the common person can understand. You are paying good money for legal services, so demand that your attorney produce documents that are understandable by an average person. The best test for the utility of your documents is to give them to your children and see if they can understand your intentions. Your children will likely need help from your attorney or financial planner in digesting the heavy words; however, if your children need more than basic explanations, send the documents back with instructions to make these documents readable.

Asset Simplification

Another method of minimizing probate is to simplify the structure of the estate. If an individual's assets are complicated during their lifetime, they will be even more difficult to administer in an estate. A multitude of individual business interests, properties or accounts will require more administrative effort to attend to the reporting and compliance details. Multiple corporations may be a convenient way of segmenting business interest. Yet unnecessary corporations will only complicate probate.

Dissolving unnecessary corporations or merging compatible businesses will simplify probate. Consider blending various independently owned parcels of commercial real estate into a partnership. Also, consolidating investments and liquidating undesirable assets and businesses during your lifetime will make probate more efficient, saving both time and money in the estate.

Joint with Rights of Survivorship

Avoiding probate is further facilitated by retitling personally owned assets into a form of ownership that will survive the decedent's death. The mandate of probate is closure or termination of a decedent's business affairs, including the transfer of personally owned assets to the rightful heirs. If there are no individually owned assets, the decedent's ownership and the form of ownership do not require closure and the process of probate is minimized. The most popular technique for establishing a form of ownership that will survive the decedent is joint, with rights of survivorship (J.T. WROS). Upon the death of the first joint tenant, the asset becomes automatically titled in the name of the surviving joint tenant. There is no personal ownership for the court to terminate and reestablish in the name of the heir. J.T. WROS can be utilized with bank accounts, security accounts, real estate and most other assets, including stock in the family business. Although an effective means of avoiding probate hassles, J.T. WROS should be utilized only by direction of your technical advisors. J.T. WROS can create an estate asset flow that is actually contrary to the intentions of your wills and trust requirements.

Revocable Living Trusts

Another effective method of avoiding probate is the adoption and funding of an intervivos, or revocable living trust (RLT). The terms "intervivos" and "living" mean that an individual creates a trust for him/herself during lifetime. Usually, the grantor serves as the initial trustee so as to retain total control of assets. Because the assets will need management after the grantor's death, the document designates successor trustees to assume this responsibility upon the death or disability of the grantor.

Assets that are intended to be protected from probate are transferred to the RLT during the grantor's lifetime. Upon the grantor's death, a change of title is not required because the assets are in the trust's name and their ultimate disposition is determined by a beneficiary designation.

After the grantor's death, the ultimate distribution of RLT assets to the designated beneficiaries is not under the purview of the probate court.

Notably, the revocable living trust can also provide for the continued management of the assets within the trust under the time period and terms suitable to you, the grantor.

After the death of the grantor, management is provided by successor trustees. Continuation of asset management is provided for within the trust according to the detailed stipulations of the trust, just as a will would, if utilized properly. The living trust can become a form of asset ownership that survives the death of the grantor and avoids probate for those assets owned within the trust. The trust continues as the owner of assets after the grantor's death beyond the probate process, avoiding most of the administrative hassles of probate, such as terminating title and transfer of title to rightful heirs.

After the grantor's death, the ultimate distribution of RLT assets to the designated beneficiaries is not under the purview or supervision of probate. In most states, the last will and testament is placed on file at the probate court and therein becomes a matter of public record. Therefore, probate can expose the asset distribution plans of a family to public scrutiny. When you are the owner of a successful business, privacy of estate distribution plans is a BIG DEAL. In contrast, trusts such as the RLT, which avoid probate, remain private and are not readily subject to public scrutiny. The use of an RLT as your estate asset-disposition instrument can privatize this very personal and intimate aspect of your financial planning.

Trusts

To further consider the subject of trusts and how they impact estate planning, there is a common saying, "You cannot control beyond the grave." For the most part, this is a true statement.

In estate planning, to a limited degree, trusts do allow a decedent to control the management and disposition of assets beyond the grave.

A trust, as mentioned earlier under probate avoidance, is a legal entity taken from English common law, created by an individual or institution that delegates specific management authority over the assets within the entity.

Trusts come in various forms as defined by the nature of the management activity and the laws of the location of the trust. There are grantor trusts, such as the RLT, beneficial trusts and testamentary trusts. A grantor trust is an asset management entity that is created for the benefit of the grantor. A beneficial trust is an asset management entity created for a second party. Living trusts, as described earlier, are created during the lifetime of the grantor. Testamentary trusts are created after the grantor's death by their last will and testament. There are revocable trusts and irrevocable trusts. As the names imply, some or all of the terms of an irrevocable trust cannot be changed, whereas the terms of a revocable trust are changeable by the grantor or a party the grantor may designate within the trust. Within the parameters just described, there are an infinite number of utility trusts carrying titles that describe their function. Limited only by the creativity of estate planners, the list of utility trusts includes, but is by no means limited to:

- Voting Trust

- Term Trust

- Qualified Terminal Interest Property Trust

- Blind Trust

- Life Insurance Trust

- Key Man Capital Replacement Trust

- Skip Generation Trust
- Disclaimer Trust

To be recognized and binding, trusts should be, and in some cases must be in writing and executed with the same formalities as a will. However, there is also an oral or parole trust. In other words, one party can say to a second party "You are my trustee," and if the second party agrees and acts like a trustee, then this may be a legally recognizable trust. This may seem far-fetched, but I worked with a woman who had massive land holdings that she planned to divide among four children. Being in poor health, she told her oldest son, her attorney and one other child in my presence that the oldest son was to be the trustee of her estate and responsible for dividing the property among himself and his three brothers and sisters. She further asked the attorney to start drawing up the necessary legal documents to formalize this arrangement. The oldest son began administering the estate on behalf of his mother. The woman died before a written trust could be funded.

Later, one of the children became disgruntled with how the older brother was dividing the property and brought suit, contending that no trust existed and that all of his mother's estate must be administered through the probate court. Needless to say he also petitioned to have himself appointed executor. Much to my surprise, a trial and several appeals affirmed that the probate estate had no control over the assets because the woman had verbally and legally formed and funded a trust. Although it is interesting to note the versatility of a trust, formally adopting a written trust document and transferring the title of assets to the trust is a safer, simpler, and less costly procedure.

The purpose of a trust is to provide asset management and administration. The authority for trust structure, management and taxation is found in state and federal statutes. The trustee or co-trustees are designated by the trust as the parties responsible for asset management. The authority and responsibility of the trustee are specifically described in the trust and generally in the state and federal fiduciary statutes. Depending upon the wishes of the grantor and the discretion of the drafting attorney, trust documents carry varying authority and responsibility of the trustee.

From both a general asset management and a family business
succession perspective, a trust should be as specific as possible
to protect the grantor's intentions.

If you question whether the trustee will do what you want done, give specific instructions.

Prudent, on-the-spot judgment is the vital asset that a trustee provides. Specific intentions regarding the management of an asset, especially a family business, or the distribution of an asset, must be supported with specific instructions within the trust document. Otherwise, the best judgment and subsequent actions of the trustees may be contradictory to what you feel is prudent.

A trust is the classic instrument to provide for the continued management of estate assets. Most business owners develop substantial assets independent from the business through retirement plans and personal investments that need competent, if not professional management. Confident and competent business owners often question why I recommend successor asset managers. However, the reality is that a business owner's death is usually preceded by an extended period during which husband, wife or survivor are not capable of meeting the demands of asset management because of a lack of health or mental acuity. In addition, the spouse who manages the assets could die first, leaving the surviving spouse with the dilemma of asset management.

One or more of the children who are beneficiaries of the estate may also lack the knowledge, experience or maturity to deal with asset management. Addressing asset management contingencies is a very important estate planning issue, for no one wants hard-earned assets to be squandered.

When technical skills, experience and maturity are not present, it is the responsibility of the parent to provide management through trusts. Responsible estate asset management is very important to the achievement of estate distribution and business succession goals.

If you have no doubt whatsoever that a spouse, son or daughter
can manage the assets allocated to them, designate them as
trustee of the trust account that you provide for them.

Give them the power to select co-trustees to help manage the funds or the power to terminate the trust and take free and clear ownership of the assets, reflecting your total confidence in their good judgment and financial acumen. Do not complicate their lives by requiring that they work with a trustee or even maintain the trust.

Under any other circumstances, with less than total confidence, provide a trustee or a co-trustee for asset management assistance. Trustees can be individuals or institutions. Being a trustee is a significant responsibility, so pick someone who can deal with this assignment. Also, be realistic as to the capability of a potential trustee to manage your family's assets. Just because an uncle or a close friend is a good guy does not mean he is a qualified asset manager. Just because your attorney is a whiz bang litigator does not mean he is qualified to manage a portfolio. Remember, if you designate your attorney as trustee, a conflict of interest may require him to hire another attorney to represent the trust.

When you do not have confidence in a qualified individual, select a responsible, bright individual to serve as co-trustee with an institution that has a good track record of success as an asset manager. This individual will keep the institution in touch with the important issues of the beneficiaries and serve as a balance to the bureaucracy and personnel turnover of the bank or trust company. The institution will take care of investing the funds and providing the accounting. As the beneficiaries of your trust reach age 25, allow them to serve as co-trustees with the institution. They will learn a great deal about financial management that will be of significant value when the trust is distributed.

In the event that it is necessary for you to utilize an institutional trustee, do not burn any brain cells trying to pick the best institution. Financial management is a dynamic profession, subject to ebb and flow because of turnover of talented personnel, mergers, changes in corporate policy and change in location of the beneficiary. Today's great institution could be an awkward arrangement or real loser in 5, 10 or 15 years.

In lieu of designating a specific institution in the trust document, empower the co-trustee, beneficiary or, in the case of a minor, the guardian of the beneficiary to appoint an institutional trustee at the time of need. Equally important, give this same individual the ability to discharge the trustee and select another one if they see fit. I assure you that, with this "portability provision," the institutional trustee will return calls faster, be more conscious of trust expenses and spend more time in genuine communications to keep their customer satisfied.

Family businesses have a unique culture and are, for the most part, not compatibly managed by an uninvolved third party such as a corporate trustee. A corporate trustee or an individual trustee who is given responsibility for business management should be familiar with the culture of your industry, your business and your family. Otherwise, giving the trustee responsibility for anything other than supervising the liquidation of your business could prove disastrous. I would not even recommend utilization of a corporate trustee or an independent third party trustee to sell the business on behalf of your beneficiaries. They often do not understand the unique nuances of business valuation. Do not overestimate the capability of corporate trustees or third party trustees to serve any important role critical to your business or your family's value in your business.

There are an abundance of trust management needs for family business interests. Children may be minors or unprepared to assume a responsible role in ownership or management. Financial security and/or deferral of estate taxes may dictate that the business interests be maintained in a trust for the benefit of a surviving spouse during their lifetime. Circumstances, such as the lack of estate liquidity, may dictate that family members who are not active in the business receive interest in the family business.

Under all reasonable circumstances, control of the trust holding the business should be directed to a responsible person knowledgeable about the family's business, respected as a leader and motivated to achieve optimum business operating capability.

In most family business environments, at least one child will demonstrate both the desire and capability to be the business leader. Hopefully, during your lifetime you will give this child the opportunity to assume the control of the business through transfers of stock, voting proxies or the adoption of a stock purchase agreement. Lifetime transfer of control will give you the opportunity to experience the fruit of your succession efforts. If, for any reason, you are reluctant to transfer control and you are anticipating holding the family business in a trust, such as a marital trust, specific business management-control instructions should be stipulated. Assuming capable, mature family succession, the shorter the trust holding period, the better the chances your business will maintain optimum performance.

Within the confines of your best judgment, provide for the distribution of a family business out of a trust or as soon as possible. Your document should address which child or children will receive the family business and who will have operating control.

Do not leave a 50/50 ownership with two prospective successors unless you're willing to accept your business failing because of <u>lack of leadership or power struggles.</u>

Provide someone the ability to lead without the threat of reprisal or a deadlock. Remember, it is your stewardship responsibility to provide for a succession of leadership.

Unfortunately, there are circumstances when a trustee and/or a responsible, capable family member is not available to manage the family business on behalf of the surviving widow, minor heirs, passive heirs and in-laws. If your successors are neither capable nor mature, your challenge is dramatically increased. The reconciliation of these circumstances is, at best, challenging. The classic response is to minimize risk and find a buyer as soon as possible. In the absence of confidence that family successors can operate the business, the trust should authorize the adoption of a Succession Bridge as discussed in a prior chapter or require the sale of the business.

Against the laws of logic, I continually encounter situations where, even without a competent family manager, a Succession Bridge or the outright sale of the business are not acceptable solutions. Under this acknowledged handicap, the prospect of succession is not good, but a vestige of hope can be achieved through a very special colleague and an advisory committee of trustees. A very special colleague or key person would be a trusted non-family member who is capable of running the business. This individual should have the experience and resourcefulness to independently and effectively manage the business on behalf of the passive beneficiaries.

In advisory committee consists of family members and/or a trust department's representative who serve together as fiduciaries under the trust document to oversee the designated business managers. Members of this advisory committee should consist of knowledgeable, responsible business persons who serve as a covering to the designated manager with the power to regulate activities and, if need be, name a replacement. It should be pointed out that a supporting advisory committee usually does not come cheap; however, the cost may be justifiable in light of your determination to keep the family business going.

This management arrangement also comes with greater hazards of disorganization, self-dealing and a lack of tenacity when dealing with difficult issues. If this structure is your only way to resolve your problem, go for it; however, keep in mind that this should be an intermediate term solution at best. Long term, if no family members line up to handle management roles, or if there are no key managers with the incentive of a Golden Handcuff Succession Bridge, the growing obstacles to succession become insurmountable.

Empowerment of a Successor Manager is a critical estate planning issue. Other succession related estate-planning maneuvers are in vain if this subject is not addressed effectively. A Succession Bridge is an excellent alternative to the profound handicap of management by an inexperienced, uninvolved trustee. As mentioned in the prior chapter, the concept of a Succession Bridge is too broad to address within this book. However, the following experience should illustrate how one of the varieties of a Succession Bridge played a significant role in estate planning.

Case History: The Bingler Family

Tom Bingler was a 42-year-old, second generation auto dealer. He and his wife, Sandy, had two children, a 15-year-old son and a 12-year-old daughter. Sandy was a full time mother with good business judgment, but no first hand experience in running an automobile dealership. Tom's son professed that his dream in life was to become an automobile dealer just like his dad and granddad. Tom's charge to me was to find a way to provide estate liquidity for Sandy and his children, as well as continue the business for the next 15 years in the event of his death. He felt that, if his son was not ready to take over the business at 30, then he never would be.

In discussing the situation with Tom and Sandy, I learned that their general manager, Larry, was 50 years old and had been working with Tom for over twenty years. He was capable of managing the dealership and both Tom and Sandy trusted him without question. Larry was a perfect candidate for a Key Man Contingency Succession Bridge.

As a result of my urging, Tom asked Larry if he would continue to manage the business on behalf of his family if something happened to him. Larry reluctantly agreed. I suggested that in the event of Tom's death, we plan to utilize a trust to hold the business, designating an advisory committee consisting of Sandy, her brother who was a local business attorney, and one of Tom and Sandy's close friends who owned a dealership in a neighboring community. Sandy was given the right to remove and replace either of the other advisory trustees. In the event of Sandy's death, the other two members would choose her replacement.

The trust agreement stated that, in the event of Tom's death, within fifteen years, Larry, assuming he was the general manager, would be sold 25% of the dealership. He would report to Sandy as the representative of the advisory committee and meet with the full committee once a month. Larry's continued ownership of the stock was stipulated in the trust in an accompanying Stockholder's Agreement, to be contingent upon his continued employment until age 65.

To facilitate the purchase of the stock and to provide a continued employment incentive, we organized a life insurance trust and purchased a million-dollar policy on Tom's life within the trust. The trust specifically stated that, in the event of Tom's death, within fifteen years the proceeds of the insurance policy would be utilized to purchase the 25% interest in the dealership for Larry. The Stockholders Agreement also stated that if Larry became a stockholder, his stock would be redeemed at age 65 to provide him a very generous retirement benefit.

If Tom lived beyond fifteen years, the general manager's interest in the irrevocable life insurance trust would lapse, and Tom's two children would become the replacement owner/beneficiaries of the pure life insurance. We arranged for payment of the $20,000 annual premium on the $1,000,000 policy on Tom's life by the corporation on a split-dollar premium loan basis to maximize cash value buildup. We dedicated the cash values of this policy to fund a Supplementary Executive Retirement Plan for Larry in the event Tom lived another fifteen years, as expected.

The net result of the structure was that we provided locked-in successor management that would help Sandy and her son to continue the business in the event of Tom's premature death. This was accomplished by empowering Larry to the purchase 25% of the business as compensation for assuming the responsibility of managing the dealership for Tom's wife and children. In addition to 25% of the equity, Larry would have the operating incentive of participating in profits through Subchapter-S dividends. The Contingency Succession Bridge also provided the general manager a "thank you" incentive if Tom lived, and the stock purchase was not activated in the form of a golden handcuff salary continuation program funded through the cash values of the life insurance policy funding the buyout.

It also bears mentioning that other benefits included guaranteed estate liquidity for Sandy and the children. If Tom died within fifteen years, they would have a million dollars cash in exchange for 25% of the business; and if Tom lived beyond fifteen years, the irrevocable trust retained the policy's death proceeds for the direct benefit of Sandy and the children.

Prior to formalizing this successor planning arrangement, we submitted our plan to the proper successor dealer administrators at Buick Motors. The franchisor's primary concerns were the qualifications of Larry to be the successor dealer. Due to his experience and good standing with factory managers, he was quickly approved. Their secondary concern was the *actual structure of the documents. Buick's attorneys reviewed the docu-ments and confirmed that Larry, not Tom's wife, would be in control of operation and that Larry would own stock in the corporation to provide him a vested interest.*

It bears mentioning as another important estate planning issue that fran-chise organizations such as General Motors, Ford, Anheuser Busch, Miller and McDonalds consider the franchise as the delivery arm of their business. In most cases, the franchise agreement stipulates requirements for the suc-cessors of that franchise. The manufacturer/franchiser realizes the critical importance of highly qualified managers for the delivery of their products and services. They are very serious about their requirements regarding the qualifications, attitude and, in most circumstances, vested interest (owner-ship of a portion of the business) of the designated successor franchisee, dealer, wholesaler, etc. In most circumstances there is too much downside risk (loss of the franchise) to assume that your general estate plans and spe-cific trust provisions have complied with the contractual requirements for franchise succession.

It is highly recommended that you and your attorney read and understand the succession provisions of the franchise agreement and conform your estate plan to these provisions.

Then you can send your franchisor an explanation of your plans and and request their approval in writing. Any other course of action is equivalent to rolling the dice for the family jewels.

Asset Distribution

The next major consideration of estate planning is asset distribution. This is classically the area of greatest concern to business owners, because the distribution of the business among the children is one of the most important family and business issues. The business is generally considered a family heirloom and usually makes up the bulk of the estate. Strong emo-tions are usually present regarding the control and succession of the business through the estate. When there are children who are not active in the business, the complexity of asset distribution increases dramatically because of the potentially conflicting goals of doing what is best for the business and what is fair for all the children.

An Omaha, Nebraska auto dealer described estate planning very succinctly a few years ago. His daughters were inactive in the business and his son, as the general manager, was positioned to take over management and ownership of the business. We had been deliberating with attorneys and accountants about estate tax financing and probate avoidance "ad nauseum" when, after an unusually technical meeting, he made a very appropriate observation. To paraphrase what he said, "This estate tax planning is a philosophical quagmire that has bankrupted my patience. I hired you to figure out a way to solve and to lower my estate taxes so I can transfer this business to my son. You appear to have solved those problems, but in doing so you have uncovered a bigger problem with my children: treating my daughters fairly and keeping them out of my son's hair."

As a result of the volatile circumstances that develop with the mixture of family, pride, business, money and competitive children, addressing the issue of asset distribution is one of the major hurdles of estate and business succession planning. Under the stress of a family dividing the fruits of a recently deceased parent, it is common for a child to say that their brother/sister "got the mine and I got the shaft. I do not care what you think is the right. I want to own a portion of the business because it will make me feel like a member of the family. I want a portion of the stock for me and my children because Dad made this company, and I feel like I am keeping part of him."

In the realm of estate planning for business succession, estate distribution of the business follows one of two paths:

- All assets, including the family business, are divided equally among the children irrespective of employment status; or

- The business is equitably allocated to the children who are directly or indirectly (in-law) involved in the business.

Equal Distribution

There are three alternative methods of estate distribution. The default reaction to dividing assets between children is the equal approach, share and share alike. Equal distribution among several children of an estate containing a family business looks both simple and natural on paper. This appears immediately fair at the surface, as it allows the parent to say "we are treating everyone equally." There are no valuation issues for the family business or business related real estate, because it is share and share alike.

93

If all children are active in the business and if they all have equal responsibility and ability, equal division of assets may work very well. However, that is a lot of "if's."

In most families, the decision to share and share alike does not work well because the career motivation and management capability cards are not divided equally among children. In these situations, it is not perceived as fair for active family members to be required to deal with inactive family members for the duration of the their working careers. Passive stockholders challenge intrafamily harmony.

> *When inactive, passive owners begin trying to influence business operations, attention usually changes from business management to turf management at the cost of both* <u>*profitability and harmony.*</u>

It is also not perceived as fair to divide management control equally when one child is shouldering all of the management responsibility.

Equitable Distribution

The most popular and, based upon my experience, the most effective estate asset distribution technique is equitable asset distribution. This approach allocates assets to children according to career choice, interest, aptitude and experience while endeavoring to provide each child a share of equal value. Even though this technique is more challenging, it is popular because parents can provide equality and can also aspire to appropriately allocate specific assets such as the family business to the children who have a special interest in those assets. There are complications in equitable asset distribution because of the potential variations in business valuation that impact the "equal distribution."

The valuation of a family business is a very subjective matter. History has proven that it is difficult to get valuation experts to agree on a business value, much less family members. Business values also are subject to major swings because of economic cycles and changes in marketing demographics. Another complicating aspect of valuation is that, in most situations, one or more of the key managers who create value in the business are also children who are participating in the division of value.

The challenge of an equitable estate distribution plan is not in determining equal value, but is in determining what is an equitable or fair distribution of assets between children. Unfortunately, there are no formulas for determining what is equitable. This is a subjective decision that is based upon your feelings and circumstances. All you can do is evaluate your feelings and the feelings of your children, take into account everyone's circumstances, and trust your judgment. Considering the importance of this decision, I suggest you share your decision with those that it will impact. An explanation of how you determined "equitable" will generally be very helpful. A child may disagree, and depending upon their maturity, may even get their nose bent out of shape. However, if you state that you are trying to be as fair as possible to all concerned, children generally will accept the equitable decisions of parents.

No matter how difficult it may appear to be to discuss the valuation of your business for estate purposes with your children, the benefit of your sharing your thoughts and feelings is profound. The potential of future conflict over valuation will be dramatically reduced just by opening the subject up for discussion. You, the decision maker, can very likely convince a disgruntled child of the fairness of your decision.

On the other hand, after your death, a child who may appear to have been favored by a parents' asset distribution decision will have little to no chance of defending his deceased parents' decision. The most pathetic course of events in estate planning is for parents to make equitable decisions in private and never communicate those decisions to children. Then, after the parents death, the siblings become adversaries over issues that were not under their control. There will be far less likelihood that brothers and sisters will come into conflict with one another if you discuss plans openly and regularly. This will avoid letting your decisions create walls between siblings.

When valuation is an issue in asset distribution, I advise the parents to specify within their estate documents that the value of the asset, such as the family business for estate division purposes, will be those values confirmed by the I.R.S. for estate tax computation. Using any higher value would unnecessarily inflate estate taxes. The I.R.S. indirectly represents family members who are not receiving any interest in the business, since the service has substantial revenue motivation to establish the highest possible value for the business.

We will discuss valuation of the business in more detail in the next chapter under the heading of estate tax; however, a few thoughts are worth mentioning here. If you are endeavoring to depress the value to lower future estate taxes, obtain the assistance of a qualified business appraiser who has successfully defended previous valuations of your type of business from I.R.S. challenges.

According to the tax code, the estate tax collectors are not bound by inter-family valuations that they interpret as mechanisms to lower estate taxes. The I.R.S. is naturally suspicious of any business valuation agreement among family members. Consequently, do not make any hard or inflexible estate or business succession plans based upon a value that is not a realistic reflection of the business value. You will only be setting yourself up for disappointment and complications down the road.

> *Be cautious about establishing a valuation technique that might elevate the business valuation above what the I.R.S. might otherwise accept.*

As an example, a child active in the business frequently agrees to buy a portion of the family's estate. The purchase puts ownership and control in the hands of active employees and puts cash in the parents' estate that can be distributed to children (brothers and sisters) who are not active in the business. If the purchase price established for the sale is greater than the value the I.R.S. would accept for estate tax purposes, the I.R.S. will use the higher value as stated on the agreement or documented in a prior transaction. Without even a thank you, they will ignore any attempts to justify a low value relying on the precedent at hand to validate the higher value which creates higher estate taxes.

After determining the value of the business, an evaluation can be performed to determine how the valuation will impact the members of the family who will not receive stock in the family business. If the valuation of the business seems unfair to those who will not pursue careers in the business, do not automatically increase the value of the business. In lieu of inflating estate taxes, ask your advisors how more assets can be created for non-successors without increasing business value. There are a variety of ways assets can be created which your advisors can describe, including life insurance.

Another important estate planning issue regarding asset distribution is, "When should income and principal be distributed to beneficiaries?" A simple answer to this question is to distribute assets as soon as a child or beneficiary can effectively manage the assets. The age when heirs should be prepared to assume personal control of assets, including business interests, ranges from age 18 to never, 18 being the earliest technical age of responsibility. Some people never develop the capability or maturity to manage assets; however, most people achieve sufficient maturity to manage assets or select professional management assistance sometime between the ages of 25 to 50.

Based upon my experience, the younger the children, the earlier the desired distribution date. When Johnny and Susie are 8 and 10, Mom and Dad generally feel that by ages 25 to 30 they should be able to handle any form of estate distribution. Predictably, when Johnny and Susie become crazy 15 and 17 year-old teenagers, Mom and Dad feel that maybe 30 to 35 would be a more prudent age. Then, when Susie marries a blockhead and Johnny alienates half the employees, Mom and Dad consider lifetime trusts.

Income produced by trusts is generally dispensed at the discretion of the trust up until the beneficiary reaches age 21, and then is paid directly to the beneficiary thereafter. Because of the taxation of trusts for individuals over age 21, there is compelling justification for not paying out all income to a beneficiary after reaching age 21. However, to avoid tax at the trust level, assuming beneficiaries are reasonable and competent, all income is usually paid to the beneficiaries after age 21.

When addressing the timing of your estate asset distribution, follow your instincts, not your memory. You may remember that at 18 or 21 you were independent and capable of making business decisions. But here is a news flash: times have changed. Business is more complex.

If you feel your spouse and/or children do or do not have what it takes to responsibly manage money or assets, let those feelings dictate the management and distribution provisions of a trust.

Also, be conservative. If their capability is debatable, be protective and allow for errors only on the conservative side.

The consensus is that assets should be distributed in installments beginning when successors are around age 30 and completing at around 40. Distribution is usually in two or three installments, such as 50% at age 30 and 50% at age 35. With the advent of the "generation skipping" provisions of the tax code (to be discussed in the next chapter), more families are allocating a generation skipping portion of their estate which is never distributed to children. The children get income from the generation skipping allocation, but the principal is held in trust for grandchildren until they reach ages of maturity. Also, it is common for trusts to provide that principal distribution can be made for a child to purchase a primary residence or open a business.

Life Insurance

Life insurance is an important element of estate planning because life insurance produces a valuable commodity: cash. Although life insurance is often criticized for various reasons, no one ever criticizes the cash product. Even with the worst dividend and premium related investment criteria, life insurance can be considered an outstanding investment when an unexpected death is quickly followed by cash.

As you certainly appreciate, the subject of life insurance carries negative baggage. The negativism is based upon the facts that the cash is related to a death. Some people have problems with the concept that others (insurance salesperson and family) will profit from life insurance. If you feel you may need life insurance, ask a third-party professional (insurance salesperson) to evaluate your need for life insurance. It would be a rare circumstance in the family business succession arena for life insurance not to be a valuable commodity for either estate tax or key-person indemnity.

Case History: A Question of Value

A few years ago, an attorney referred a client to me to offer a third party opinion as to whether or not he needed life insurance and, if so, how much. After analyzing his situation, I reported to this business owner in letter form what I felt he needed to achieve his specified goals. A few days later he called me and questioned my recommendations. I shared my background rationale, but most of it was repetitious of what was in my letter. In spite of the simple logic, he continued to seem uneasy. The source of his concern came to light when he asked me how much commission the agent would make. I gave him an estimate, and he started to gripe and moan that he was being ripped off.

My response may help you in your concern about life insurance salesman compensation. I admittedly was bold with this gentleman because I was being paid a fee and was not participating in the commission. I reflected to Mr. Bob that I thought he was short-sighted. If he were to remove the salesman's commission from the life insurance pricing, the long-term cost would drop approximately 4%. I continued to express that I was familiar with his business and I knew that 4% was lower than his gross profit margin. I also knew from his attorney that he had been working with the life insurance salesman for two years, and he had motivated him to the point that he was taking estate liquidity seriously. Although the commission may seem substantial as a lump sum payment, by the hour, the agent is being paid very reasonably.

I further stated that Mr. Bob was a 70-year-old cantankerous, frugal, insurance prospect who had a critical need for estate tax liquidity. In the absence of a substantial incentive, his current insurance representative, like the many who preceded him, would have said, "I don't deserve this abuse. I'll find someone else less contentious to deal with."

Mr. Bob was not quick to respond to my rather brash comments. Then, true to form he asked "What about no load insurance? Can you help me with a no load policy?"

My response was, "Yes, but I do not recommend it." I explained that he did not appear to be a person who would enjoy being on hold for a 1-800 number trying to get policy information. "Don't expect your kids to do that after your death, either. They will hire the attorney or accountant to work the 1-800 number." I continued to express my opinion that the best situation was to have a servicing agent who had a renewal commission incentive to keep him happy and provide professional guidance in admin-istering the policy.

With that final "in your face" response, the tone of his voice changed. He thanked me for my input and concluded the conversation. I later heard from the attorney that, contradictory to his wager, Mr. Bob did purchase a policy. The attorney said the only thing his client mentioned was that he did not want to deal with an 800 number.

As in life, so too in life insurance, there is no such thing as a free lunch. Life insurance is a service-sensitive financial instrument. You are going to need information about the performance of your policy, need for premiums, change of address, change of owner, change of beneficiary and the status of the company as you move forward. When considering a no load life insurance product or asking for a commission rebate, remember that you will be needing service, and quality service has its price. Something for nothing in the insurance industry usually translates into a financial enema. Commission paying life insurance policies create a relationship wherein your agent has an incentive to respond to ques-tions and provide ongoing policy service. Trust me, you want your agent depending upon renewal commissions when you call for service.

I have also dealt with people who objected to life insurance because they felt life insurance companies were making obscene profits and ripping off the public. If you think life insurance companies are getting rich, check the recommended insurance company's percentage of surplus (initial capital plus retained earnings) to assets. Also ask for information about the dividend paying history of the proposed company against other companies with outstanding ratings. You should discover that they are only rich enough to support the asset structure and give a reasonable cushion for hard times. Depending upon your unique circumstances, if this surplus to asset ratio is above 12%, you may have a legitimate concern about the company's willingness to pass profits through to policyholders.

Surplus is needed for insurance companies to withstand economic downturns to grow and invest in customer service programs.

Without the peace of mind that an insurance company has sufficient surplus to survive in hard times, life insurance is not <u>*worth owning.*</u>

The life insurance business is very competitive, and the quality insurance companies are paying out all the dividends they can prudently justify in order to attract business. A more reasonable concern is that competition is making an insurance company pay out too much in dividends at the cost of prudent surplus.

Another criticism is that life insurance is a poor investment. Life insurance may be a poor investment as compared to hot real estate, growth stocks or a family business; however, life insurance does things that other investments cannot do, such as pay tax-free death benefits. The key to life insurance is understanding the place for this planning tool in the greater financial universe. Life insurance is a systematic vehicle for building a cash reserve to cover possible or inevitable financial liabilities created by a death with the actuarial potential for substantial gain in the event of the unfortunate death prior to life expectancy.

Life insurance originated under the fundamental concept of setting aside a few dollars today to meet a very big dollar need in the future. In operation, the life insurance contract represents two opposing wagers that generally do not give a prospective buyer "the warm fuzzies." The insurance company is betting the insured is going to live, and the prospective buyer as policy owner is betting the insured is going to die. With medical justification of insurability and administrative justification of delivery expenses, the premium represents reasonable consideration for both wagers. The pooling of thousands of insureds who share the same need of providing cash upon their death provides the affordable economy.

Regardless of your personal opinion, do not let investment concerns prevent you from responsibly addressing death contingency cash needs that can be satisfied by life insurance. We are talking about contingencies such as security of dependents, payment of debt, estate tax financing and/or key man indemnity. Rest assured that if you purchase a quality permanent life insurance product (whole life or universal life) under the worst case investment scenario (the insured lived to age 100), you will have paid premiums equaling approximately 30% of the death benefit. Under these circumstances, investment in life insurance on a present-value basis should compare favorably to passbook savings. On the other hand, under the best case scenario (the insured dies immediately) the investment considerations could be phenomenal.

The actual cost of utilizing life insurance to fund a financial need is a function of the time value of money that a sharp calculator operator can readily compute. The life insurance company, with its understanding of the value of money, the medical history of the insured, administrative expenses and actuarial probabilities, projects the life expectancy of the insured and prices the insurance accordingly. The policy owner, with a knowledge of financial and personal circumstances, evaluates the premium cost in relationship to the psychological value of protection and business benefits of having a guaranteed death benefit to meet a certain need. Notably, an insurance policy does not have to pay a death benefit to be a good investment. Just having the peace of mind resulting from life insurance protection based upon perspective can be perceived to be a value.

The healthiest eventual result of a life insurance policy is that both the reasonable return expectations of the insurance company and the policy holder are fulfilled.

In application, life insurance is a current cash flow sacrifice (premiums) for future payment of specified capital. As a product of pooling mortality risks with a large group, affordable annual insurance premiums today can provide impressive, otherwise unaffordable large sums of cash upon death in the future.

Most parents do not have any problem with the concept of sacrifice, because sacrificing is a fundamental aspect of parenthood. Some people, however, do have a problem with the concept of sacrificing through a life insurance premium. They think they have sacrificed enough for their wife, children or business and it is silly to pay life insurance premiums so their survivors can live "richly ever after." There is no simple solution for these emotion-based paradigms beyond this advice: forget the richly ever after and focus on the end-product or specific benefits of life insurance, such as saving the business from taxes or debt. If the benefit of saving the business from taxes or debt does not justify the means, drop the subject of life insurance and move on. However, if your rationale is flawed with insecurity and resentment of your own mortality, be prepared to readdress the subject because your family's legitimate needs will continue to haunt you.

Regardless of emotional mindsets, life insurance is unique as it provides cash when an insured is no longer able to do so.

One of the most important aspects of purchasing life insurance is the selection of the life insurance company. With the advent of creative accounting and computer-based policy illustrations, insurance products have been elevated on the complexity scale to that of rocket science. Your only hope of understanding the financial mumbo-jumbo, without spending an enormous amount of time climbing the learning curve, is to deal with people you trust. Even with people you trust, make sure your insurance advisor is knowledgeable. The blind-leading-the-blind is a formula to disaster in the insurance business. A check and balance between your advisors is also an asset in addressing life insurance issues. Specifically, be leery of advisor teams (attorney, accountant) provided by the insurance salesman. This environment could create too much professional courtesy and not enough check and balance.

Purchasing life insurance is similar to buying a car or a mortgage in that shopping around pays. If you look at only one company, you are in double jeopardy. The agent may sell you the wrong product and/or the life insurance company may stick you with an expensive medical rating. You should consider three or four highly rated competitive companies when making an insurance buying decision. This comparison should keep underwriters competitive and give you peace of mind that you are not making a major financial decision based upon blind faith. However, unless you enjoy dog fights and confusion, do not try to deal with three or four insurance salesmen. If you want to get confused and frustrated above any level you can imagine, get two or more salesmen making pitches to you with computer illustrations and company sales literature. You will waste an incredible amount of time hearing puffery about the promoted company and accusations about the competition. The most productive and civil course of action is to deal with one salesperson with the professional standing as a Chartered Life Underwriter and Chartered Financial Consultant who will represent your best interests in dealing with several companies as a broker.

To further enhance your purchasing environment, ask your insurance agent for information on the recommended insurance companies, including historical data, structure of the company, comparative financial data and ratings by the various rating services. Steer clear of companies that are not rated, because they are probably hiding substandard financial statements.

Also, ask the insurance salesman to provide current financial information on the suggested company to support his or her recommendation. Simplified layman's financial data is available to insurance professionals through independent software companies. Spend time reviewing and analyzing the information just as you would look over your own financial statements or a new business acquisition. You do not have to be an expert insurance analyst to make good conclusions from financial data designed for the consumer.

Ask practical questions, such as, "How profitable is the company?" and "Has the company met past dividend projections?" Do not expect an insurance broker or salesman to do the analysis for you. Life insurance always represents a very important acquisition that merits your attention. Relying on your good judgment will bring positive results in the insurance market. Relying solely on your agent's recommendation may bring disappointment.

Structuring Life Insurance

Structuring of life insurance is very important. Estate tax laws make the federal government the beneficiary of 55% (the highest estate tax bracket) of much of the insurance in force today. This may come as a shock to those who have assumed life insurance death benefits are tax free.

Life insurance is income tax free, but death benefits of a decedent who directly or indirectly owns the policy will be taxed in the decedent's estate.

Parents who own their life insurance subject the death benefits to a 55% estate tax. The estate tax can be deferred by passing the benefits to the spouse under the marital deduction, but upon the spouse's death the taxes become due. When a corporation owns life insurance, the death benefits inflate the value of the corporation which, in turn, inflates the value of an estate and increases estate taxation. To make the situation even more frustrating, the estate tax laws are changing daily through legislation and judicial decisions inspired by the I.R.S. that make it more difficult to protect life insurance from taxation.

My profound conclusion is that life insurance is no bargain when receiving only 45 cents on the dollar of the death benefits. Quality advisors are the key to avoiding 55% estate tax in the death benefits. Because of the aforementioned complexities, estate planning has become a recognized accounting, legal and financial planning specialty. To make sure your insurance is structured properly, you must rely on qualified, experienced advisors who can back up their advice with technical training, research experience and omissions insurance. In a 55% tax bracket, there are just too many tax dollars at risk to casually approach purchasing life insurance with anyone other than professionals who are at the top of their game. We will discuss sheltering life insurance from estate tax in more detail in the next chapter.

Periodic Review

The process of estate planning can be annoying, discouraging, and frustrating; however, to the diligent, the persistent, and the pro-active go the spoils. Those who are willing to pay the price of involvement will have the achievement of goals and succession, and the gratification that a legacy will continue.

The families who regularly readdress estate distribution and asset management assumptions will be the best prepared for the challenges they will confront when endeavoring to settle a large estate with specialized assets such as a family business. In far too many cases, the estate planning effort is limited to drafting a will and/or trust agreement and locking it away until something happens to cause it to be reviewed. Unfortunately, when this happens there is usually profound frustration and gnashing of teeth as a result of outdated documents and financial assumptions. With the complexities of family relationships, taxation and business, effective estate planning is an ongoing process, not a one time project.

The good news about estate planning is that, with few exceptions such as irrevocable gifts, estate plans are flexible and can be changed. The allocation of assets, the management of assets and the dates of distribution can be changed as individuals and circumstances change. A periodic review is imperative because of the constant changes that occur in the dynamics of families and circumstances which we generally classify as the "Four F's": feelings, finances, the federal tax law and family. Time spent reviewing your estate planning and considering changes in the succession environment will bring rewards of peace of mind to you and the reward of an enhanced estate and business continuity to those you love.

Estate Tax Avoidance

Addressing estate taxation is a fundamental succession planning concern. The best wills and trusts that distribute business interest, real property and personal property will be vulnerable to potentially catastrophic problems unless provisions are made for the payment of estate taxes. Paying estate tax is the focal point of administering a substantial estate, such as one that would hold a business interest, because, for the most part, assets (the business) cannot be distributed to successors until the estate administration is closed. The estate cannot be closed until the estate taxes are paid. No family business succession plan can be complete without a realistic plan for financing estate taxes.

> *Unfortunately, business capitalization in the public's eye continues to be defined as wealth, which is taxed heavily as it passes from one generation to the next.*

There was a point in the development of our society when working capital and wealth were synonymous. Families who owned businesses were considered wealthy because they literally lived out of their businesses. The larger the business, the better they lived. In the nineteenth and twentieth century, circumstances have changed. For revenue collection purposes, the IRS has been given tremendous technology and power. Accordingly, the IRS has seen fit to use this technical power, to redefine wealth -- with the blessing of congress -- by restricting the use of business resources for personal needs. Consequently, the definition of wealth today has been redefined as sufficient personal income-producing capital to support the good life. Working capital has become the essence of business life as blood is the essence of life. Working capital is the liquid resources (apart from machinery, inventory) that the business depends upon to carry out its day to day operations. Without sufficient capitalization, a private enterprise cannot make payroll, cannot buy inventory, cannot pay rent and ultimately cannot survive.

This money cannot be readily withdrawn from the business. Simply put, our businesses will fail without adequate working capital. Business working capital is not wealth.

Welcome to the opportunities, challenges and demands of doing business in the new millennium. Because of inflation, the investment demands of high technology and the consolidation of otherwise comparable competitors by public companies, the working capital requirements of private business have dramatically increased. Without generous business capitalization, your business could be just one bank reorganization, economic downturn or technology leap from being "new millennium road-kill." Unfortunately, the increased demands for working capital have inflated the value of businesses. And ultimately, the increase in business value will inflate the value of the taxable estate. The net result is predictable increases in estate tax before the business passes from one generation to the next.

Estate taxation is a forced extraction of resources from that business, purportedly for the betterment of society. If you believe that, I have some hot stock tips for you. A more realistic social explanation of what occurs is a spreading of the purported wealth, which, as explained above, is not an excess of cash, but resources that essential to business continuity. Inevitably, estate tax on a family owned business causes the extraction of working capital, which, in turn impacts the operational capability of the business. Cash reserves are spent, assets are sold or stock is redeemed to pay the tax. Or, when cash or liquidity is not available, debt is incurred, jobs are cut and expansion is curtailed in order to keep the doors open and pay off the loan. In some unfortunate cases, the businesses are sold or liquidated. As a result, estate tax has been a significant obstacle in the path of the sustained growth of our economy and the succession of a family owned business.

What impact will estate taxes have on your family business? This question is especially important, in light of the confusion our fast-talking, slight-of-hand legislators have created with the publicity and Swiss cheese, estate-tax repeal legislation. Amidst this puffery and confusion, many question if estate tax financing can continue to be a critical aspect of business succession planning. Perhaps the best way to predict the future is to examine the past. Let's take a brief review of the history of death transfer taxes.

An estate tax is an excise tax on a decedent's right to transfer property from his estate to children or other non-charitable beneficiaries. The estate tax, like the income tax, is graduated to have less impact on those whom the government has arbitrarily determined do not deserve the privilege of paying as much estate tax.

Each U.S. citizen currently receives a credit against estate tax and a limited amount of gift tax that effectively establishes a threshold for those who have the privilege of paying any estate tax at all.

The first form of federal estate or death tax was employed in 1862 to help finance the Civil War. The tax initially applied only to personal property, but was later extended to real property as well. The rates were quite low and the tax was repealed in 1870, presumably after the war debt was paid. The first income tax enacted in 1894 treated personal property received by gift or inheritance as taxable income. Fortunately, this first income tax was held unconstitutional the next year. In 1898, not to be denied, our irrepressible Congress adopted a mixed inheritance and estate tax. The tax showed unfortunate creativity, being both progressive with the size of the estate and graduated with respect to the relationship between the beneficiary and the decedent. There was an outcry of discrimination among the wealthy, but the law was upheld in Knowlton v. Moore as a pure inheritance tax. Fortunately, this obviously unpopular tax was repealed in 1902 because of pressure from the business sector. Congress acquiesced because the revenue was negligible.

Congress knew it was on to something with estate tax that could create more tax revenue to fund the growing federal appetite and gain political favor from the working class, which was resentful of those who accumulated wealth. As the voting base expanded in the early 1900's, Congress recognized the estate tax to be an appealing method of raising revenue at no apparent cost to the common laborer. The roots of the current federal estate taxes are in the Estate Tax Law of 1916, adopted for both revenue and social purposes.

Revenue was needed to help finance World War I. From a social perspective, the industrial revolution had produced numerous high-profile, extremely wealthy families-- such as the Fords, DuPonts and Rockefellers -- and a ground-swell of political support emerged to prevent the evolution of large blocks of wealth into a perpetual royal class, as had been experienced in Europe.

Substantial political support emerged for preventing the continuity of large blocks of wealth from one generation to the next.

The estate tax, as adopted on September 8, 1916, by the 64th Congress, ranged from a low of 1% to a top bracket of 10% on estates in excess of $5 million. These relatively low rates, and the rarity of taxable wealth within the working class, created little resistance to our country's initial effort to extract revenues from the highly successful to help finance government.

It would appear that the rationale was that a highly successful individual was only partly responsible for his or her success. The society, the consumer, the market and the government were also major contributors. Therefore, the government at some point in time should get back its contribution to an individual's success. Death was considered the most convenient time, because the post-death ownership of the assets now would be in question.

Five years later, Congress was held to task again for trying to recover its share of its citizens' success in New York Trust Co. v. Eisner. Unfortunately, the Supreme Court held that the estate tax was a valid excise tax and, as such, did not require apportionment among the citizenry. However, as we would expect, the tax paying citizenry of that time were no fools. To avoid estate and inheritance taxes, property owners pursued the available loophole by making gifts of property. Not to be outwitted, Congress subsequently adopted the Federal gift tax in 1924 to protect falling estate tax revenue. Facing an uproar of opposition, a more sensible Congress in 1924 repealed the gift tax. The temptation of more revenue overcame good judgment and the gift tax was reinstated in 1932. Thereafter, as the congressional black hole for tax revenue expanded, Congress increased both the estate and the gift tax rates, which reached a high of 70%. In 1976, the estate and gift tax tables were merged into a Unified Estate and Gift Tax Table.

In addition to the federal estate tax, most states also impose an inheritance tax in some form. The state death tax is levied on the taxable estate, prior to computation of estate tax. Therefore, this tax is a deduction to the higher Federal taxation.

The state's inheritance tax is a tax levied on the beneficiary's right to receive property from the decedent. Inheritance tax rates vary from state to state based both on the size of the inheritance received and the relationship of the beneficiary to the decedent. The closer the family relationship (a spouse, child or sibling), the greater the exemption and the lower the tax.

Most states recognize that taxing the assets of a decedent is very unpopular and avoid creating more local ill will with an inheritance tax. These states have simply elected the credit estate tax that allows them to receive a portion of the estate taxes collected by the federal government.

As if the inherent technical aspects of the law were not a sufficient challenge, the latest in a long line of estate tax reform legislation, adopted in 2001, has pushed the level of confusion off the scale. This insult to the intelligence of the public creates a sliding scale for the increase of estate tax credits (but not gift tax credits) and a decrease in the estate tax brackets, with total estate tax repeal scheduled for 2010.

However, in order for the repeal to be sustained beyond 2010, our revenue ravenous Congress must affirmatively vote that they do not need/want the projected $30 billion to $50 billion dollars in revenue that the estate tax would generate. Assuming Congress did not change the existing legislation, give thought to how popular life support systems will become in 2008 and 2009. For sure, everyone with a substantial estate would be revoking Living Wills.

I assure you that Congress cannot keep its hands off this political hot potato for 10 years. Facing a significant loss in revenue (Congressional operating capital) I personally guarantee you that estate tax will be in the headlines again, again and again. At the maximum, I contend that the current estate tax will just be renamed for political purposes to an inheritance tax, capital gains tax or disguised income tax. After this inevitable political mishmash occurs, I have no confidence that the business owners who purportedly have all this wealth in their business will be any better off from an ownership transfer tax perspective.

Anyone who holds hope for estate tax repeal as described in the "Pollyanna" Estate tax reform act of 2001, should bear in mind that, in the absence of an estate tax, there will be no estate tax credits refunded to the states.

Consequently, the majority of the states stand to lose billions of dollars. Being unable to sustain deficit spending, the states will have to replace this revenue and will certainly be inclined to reinstate inheritance taxes. Governors and state legislators are going to put intense pressure on their congressional delegations not to put them in this very difficult position.

Unfortunately, as the owner or potential beneficiary of a successful business, which, according to the law until 2010, will be subject to substantial estate tax, you must have an estate tax strategy or you run the risk that this quirky legislation will nuke your succession plans. Logic would support the conclusion that a wise person would rather regret having done unnecessary stock maneuvers than regret having lost the business to estate tax.

The bad news is that the tax is real and potentially devastating to the unprepared.

In 1987, the estate and gift tax revenue was $7.5 billion. In 1995, it rose to $15.1 billion. In 2007, estate and gift tax revenue is projected to be $35.3 billion.

Unfortunately, this tax revenue comes from a very small element of our population. Although this small group (1.2%) is vocal and politically connected, the estate tax payers have insufficient political clout with elected school teachers and social workers. The probability that a government under pressure to lower income taxes and desperate for revenue to support ever-expanding social programs will give up $35.3 billion in revenue in response to the outcry of less than 3% of the population is very low. I personally believe estate tax rates will increase.

The good news is that our federal government will not nationalize your business in lieu of estate taxes. However, the IRS will pursue whatever means necessary to collect what it feels is rightly its own -- including putting a tax lien on your business. And if the need arises, when there appears to be no other reasonable way to collect the tax, the IRS will directly or indirectly require the sale and/or liquidation of the business. Fortunately, as described in the chapter on estate tax financing, with proper planning, reasonable means for the payment of estate taxes can be developed.

Take a few moments to examine the estate and gift tax table in detail. Do not dwell on it for too long because, as I mentioned, it could change at any time. However, I feel comfortable in reaffirming one of my most profound beliefs: "The more things change, the greater the probability they will remain the same." Consequently, estate tax financing will always involve three considerations: tax avoidance, tax deferral and tax payment.

2004 Estate and Tax Rate Schedule						
If the amount with respect to which the tentative tax to be covered is:				The tentative tax is:		
Not over	$10,000	18% of such amount				
Over	$10,000	but not over	$20,000	$1,800	+ 20% over	$10,000
Over	$20,000	but not over	$40,000	$3,800	+ 22% over	$20,000
Over	$40,000	but not over	$60,000	$8,200	+ 24% over	$40,000
Over	$60,000	but not over	$80,000	$13,000	+ 26% over	$60,000
Over	$80,000	but not over	$100,000	$18,200	+ 28% over	$80,000
Over	$100,000	but not over	$150,000	$23,800	+ 30% over	$100,000
Over	$150,000	but not over	$250,000	$38,800	+ 32% over	$150,000
Over	$250,000	but not over	$500,000	$70,900	+ 34% over	$250,000
Over	$500,000	but not over	$750,000	$155,800	+ 37% over	$500,000
Over	$750,000	but not over	$1,000,000	$248,300	+ 39% over	$750,000
Over	$1,000,000	but not over	$1,250,000	$345,800	+ 41% over	$1,000,000
Over	$1,250,000	but not over	$1,500,000	$448,300	+ 43% over	$1,250,000
Over	$1,500,000	but not over	$2,000,000	$555,800	+ 45% over	$1,500,000
Over	$2,000,000	but not over	$2,500,000	$780,800	+ 49% over	$2,000,000
Over	$2,500,000			$1,025,800	49% over	$2,500,000

Individual Lifetime Tax Credit (Unified Credit) Against Federal Estate and Gift Taxes (2003)

Individual Estate or Gift Tax Credit - $345,800
Tax Credit Property Equivalent - $1,000,000
Individual Annual Gift Tax Exemption - $11,000 per Recipient

We will first review various methods of positioning an estate to avoid taxation. In the next chapter we will address the various methods of deferring and paying estate tax in a manner compatible with the continuity of the business. Wherever applicable, reference will be made to the provisions of the 2001 Estate Tax Reform Act. Inasmuch as we are dealing with an approximate 50% tax, estate tax avoidance will be given significant attention.

State of the art estate tax financing involves three considerations: tax avoidance, tax deferral and tax payment.

My goal is not to make you an expert in estate taxes but to prepare you to work effectively with your advisors as an informed, motivated member of a succession planning team. You must consult your succession planner, tax attorney and/or certified public accountant for the application of these ideas to your unique planning environment. There are too many fronts in the estate tax war for a business owner to become an expert at estate tax avoidance. Even the experts have trouble keeping up with this fast moving body of knowledge.

The estate tax has historically been the highest tax in the land simply because the decedents have not been around to scream about this inequity. Even with all the bugaboo about estate tax reform, I do not expect this to change because of the inherently deceptive and spineless nature of politicians. A simple description of estate tax is confiscatory. The common characteristic of the family business succession environment is the presence of a major non-liquid asset (the business) that will create significant estate taxes. Recognize that the IRS has a contingent lien on your prized asset equivalent to 45 to 50 cents on each dollar of value.

Your estate-tax avoidance and reduction strategy brings with it the gratification that, for every dollar of the business or estate that is removed from harm's way, heirs will save approximately 50 cents in estate taxes.

Upon the death of the business owner, the personal representative, with the assistance of the attorney, accountant and appraisers, organizes the financial data of the decedent for the filing of the Form 706 estate tax return. An inventory of assets is listed, with the current fair market value for each asset. Dispense with the thought that you can determine the value of your business or that it is valued at "book." Your advisors will insist that fair market value appraisals accompany the 706 estate tax return to verify value and, hopefully, preclude the IRS from engaging in extended (expensive) debates about asset value.

Nine months after the date of death, the estate tax return is filed with values that can be defended and the taxes are paid. Print does not do proper justice to the statement, "the taxes are paid." Yes, after paying combined income taxes approaching 50%, the precious capital asset that has been developed is taxed again at approximately 50%. These four short words, "the taxes are paid," describe the traumatic act of handing over hard earned working capital, the product of countless years of hard work and family legacies, to the federal and state governments for the privilege of a family continuing to pay employees, produce goods and contribute to the income tax coffers.

The first estate tax planning axiom is to not pay any more than necessary. Prudence, capitalism and common sense say to do everything reasonable (compatible, affordable and legal) to reduce the ultimate tax bill to the bare minimum. Judge Leonard Hand, in 1947, set the tone for Americans with his ruling for the defendant in the tax appeal case: Commissioner of the Internal Revenue Service v. Neuman.

> *"Over and over again, courts have said that there is nothing sinister in so arranging one's affairs as to keep taxes as low as possible. Everybody does so, rich or poor; and all do right, for nobody owes any public duty to pay more than the law demands: taxes are enforced exactions, not voluntary contributions."*

There are many other more earthy descriptions of taxation, but Judge Hand does provide us with a classy graphic description with "enforced exactions."

To provide further support to the notion of enforced exaction, chapter 14 of the Internal Revenue Code has sections written specifically for the family business. Among other things, chapter 14 states that the family business will be valued for estate or gift tax purposes on an arms length, third-party basis. A binding buy/sell agreement with a non-family member or an independent appraisal reflecting arms length consideration should satisfy this requirement. Loving arrangements by parents to transfer assets to their children at family-friendly prices is in direct conflict with this portion of the law.

Speaking from years of dealing with the Fellows of the Leonard Hand Society, I give you this assurance: If you snooze when you should be planning the avoidance of estate tax, your family will tragically lose hard-earned capital, and maybe your business. Opportunities are available to reduce estate tax exposure, but they will not jump in your lap; nor will an IRS agent make suggestions as to how property should be structured to cut the government out of its right to your property. In order to pay the minimum estate tax, you must be prepared to get help and zealously work at reducing taxes.

> *"Nobody owes any public duty to pay more than the law demands: taxes are enforced exactions, not voluntary contributions." Judge Leonard Hand*

Minimizing tax exposure begins with challenging your attorney, accountant and financial planner to come forth with the latest, most creative ideas and recommendations for the avoidance of estate taxes. The general theme of their recommendations should be that estate taxes can be avoided by reducing the value of your taxable estate as it will be appraised by the IRS.

If they give you a blank stare, it is time for you to make some telephone calls. The provisions of chapter 14 that require verification of estate value by a third party can work to your family's advantage. You should take comfort and even joy in knowing that the socioeconomic jealousy that motivated the adoption of chapter 14 has backfired on the career bureaucrats and regulators. The fair-market value mandate has created many very effective techniques for avoiding taxation.

For your clarification, the term estate tax avoidance does not mean tax evasion. Tax evasion would refer to such activities as failing to report assets in the estate, failing to report pre- death gifts, or placing erroneous values on assets. Tax evasion is against the law and naturally carries severe penalties. The IRS has seen every trick in the book. They zealously audit estates from which they expect to exact substantial tax. Their natural audit attitude is that the taxpayer is trying to cheat. Consequently, the auditing agents are trained to look in the cracks and crevices and ask incriminating questions. The IRS has time-tested methods of finding bearer bonds, jewelry, gold bullion and unreported gifts made many years earlier.

You should take comfort in knowing that the socioeconomic jealousy that motivated the adaptation of chapter 14 has backfired on the career bureaucrats and regulators.

It is noteworthy that estate tax auditors are not like income tax auditors. They are well-trained and well-educated in the dynamics of business and the appraisal of assets. Most are actually young attorneys who are attempting to find out how the enemy operates before entering private practice. The estate tax auditors are coached to read local newspapers and business magazines to learn who has assets and the value of assets that are changing hands. The Service also has a great spy system of resentful, jealous citizens who squeal on neighbors, acquaintances and even friends who they believe are taking unfair advantage of the system. Finally, IRS auditors are not chumps. They know the value of assets and they know that you have to pay attorneys and accountants to defend positions that they assert. And do not think you will roll over them with your hot shot attorney. The success of the IRS, to a substantial degree, is a function of their zealous social motivation to gather wealth from beneficiaries.

Estate tax avoidance reduces tax exposure while following the rules. Estate tax avoidance may take an aggressive position on a gray point of law, but tax avoidance does not knowingly violate the law. We are simply joining the Leonard Hand Society and pursuing the use of every possible opportunity to reduce estate taxes within the letter of the law. Tax avoidance addresses the numerous opportunities within the tax law to lower the valuation of an asset and therein reduce estate taxes.

Before discussing specific tax avoidance techniques, let's review three very important fundamentals:

- Don't let the tax tail wag the dog. Tax avoidance is important, but not more important than peace of mind or personal financial security.

- Do not feel compelled to gift. The only thing you owe your children is your love and respect. Furthermore, do not tolerate attitudes of entitlement from your children.

- Don't set yourself up for disappointment with respect to assumptions about how much the recipients, notably your children, will appreciate the gift. Remember, that which is easily obtained, is often, lightly regarded.

- Be careful gifting to your children's spouses. Make no assumptions about the ultimate disposition of a gift to an in-law.

- Work with technically competent tax advisors experienced in planning estates, and negotiate with the IRS for settlement of estates. Extra dollars spent with experienced planners, specialized advisors and tested appraisers will prove to be a great investment, both in saving taxes and avoiding trouble.

In light of the potential devastating impact of estate tax, leave no stone unturned to avoid estate tax.

Gifting in its various forms would generally represent the most effective business succession estate-tax-avoidance technique. Any assets that can be transferred out of an estate will avoid the bite of estate tax. The most fundamental form of gifting is tax exempt gifting. Unfortunately there are limitations to anything that is exempt from the claws of taxation. As of 2003, each individual can gift at least $11,000 per year (adjusted for inflation in minimum $1,000 increments) to any individual exempt of gift or estate taxes. This means that a husband and wife with three children as of 2003 could gift $11,000 to each child for a total of $66,000 per year. This is an annual "use it or lose it" exemption. If you snooze you lose. The maximum estate tax avoidance potential of a gift of $11,000 to three children would be the estate tax on $33,000 per year for the husband and the wife, plus the tax savings on the compounded growth of the $66,000 in the children's estate.

Estate tax avoidance can also be achieved with gifts above the annual exemption. Of course, these gifts are subject to gift tax. Fortunately, in an effort to lessen the impact on smaller estates, Congress has seen fit to provide each individual with gift tax credits that further facilitate estate tax avoidance planning.

Using these credits is dependent upon having estate tax. So, if you are transferring all of your assets to a spouse under the marital deduction or transferring all of your estate to a charity, these credits will be of no value to you. However, if you are planning to make transfers of assets to children or other individuals, there will be taxes and the credits will have value. Asset transfer tax credits represent a lifetime allowance that each individual can use to wash out the taxable gifts or estate transfers up to the limits established. This allowance is growing according to current (and no doubt future) legislation that theoretically counteracts inflation. If these credits are used for gifts, they are not available in the estate. If the credits are not used for gifts during your lifetime, they become estate tax credits. The schedule shows the credits increasing from $1,000,000 in 2003 to $3,500,000 in 2009, but do not bank on this schedule because it is sure to change when Congress determines that it is time to tinker again. Also, remember that the "unified credit" no longer applies, because Congress has seen fit to limit the gift tax credits to the equivalent of $1 million, while allowing the estate tax credits to prospectively grow to $3.5 million.

However, do not bank on full growth of the estate tax credit to $3.5 million because, between now and 2010, Congress will surely tinker further with the law.

Estate Tax Exemption Schedule				
	Top Rate	Estate Exemption	Estate Credit	Gift Exemption
2004	48%	$1,500,000	$555,800	$1,000,000
2005	47%	$1,500,000	$555,800	$1,000,000
2006	46%	$2,000,000	$780,800	$1,000,000
2007	45%	$2,000,000	$780,800	$1,000,000
2008	45%	$2,000,000	$780,800	$1,000,000
2009	45%	$3,500,000	$1,455,800	$1,000,000
2010	0%	$0	$0	$1,000,000*
2011+	55%	$1,000,000	$345,800	$1,000,000

*In 2010 a modified carryover basis rule immediately goes into effect. $1,300,000 of basis will be permitted to be added to certain assets and $3,000,000 of basis will be permitted to be added to assets transferred to a surviving spouse. Gifts in excess of $1,000,000 will be subject to a gift tax equal to the top individual income tax rate at that time.

Why consider using the available gift tax credits if I can let my heirs use them in my estate? Although deferring the credits to your estate is simpler, there are several good reasons to consider using them during your lifetime. The first reason is that estate tax avoidance is not all about death. Assuming you have the resources to make gifts without impacting your personal financial security, there should be fun, joy or gratification in making gifts to your family and having the opportunity to see them use and even enjoy the new-found resource. From a family business perspective, I suggest that it is helpful to evaluate (while you are alive and reactive) how children will deal with the responsibility of substantial gifts. You can also learn how you children will deal with each other when the subject of gifts arises. If you do not like what you see, your reasonable reaction may be to adjust your estate distribution plans.

Another reason more in keeping with the context of this chapter is the brutal impact of estate tax on the predictable growth in value of family assets such as the business and real estate associated with the business. Inflation, retained earnings, mortgage satisfaction, and appreciation are taxed regardless of the liquidity or marketability of the asset. Therefore, considering the prospective penalty on growth in value of a family asset, it may make sense to use the credits as soon as possible to remove the potential growth from your estate. In other words, if your assets are growing in value faster than the rate of inflation, deferring the use of the gift tax credits for estate transfers will dilute their value. To appreciate the potential impact of tax credit gifting to avoid estate taxes, just look back 10 years at your business assets and determine the value of the growth. Then multiply 50% times the growth in value. The number you come up with will be the approximate amount of estate tax, attributable to growth that could have potentially been avoided with gifts that utilized estate tax credits.

Example

As an example, let's consider using credits to gift real estate or stock in a family business. Let's assume that the gifted stock generates an 8% return over the balance of the donor's life of 15 years due to appreciation, retained earnings or debt retirement. A combined husband and wife $2 million gift would have grown in value to $6,344,000. In recognition that the original $2 million gift would have also been free from tax if it remained in the estate, the prospective gain is the avoidance of estate tax on the difference of $4,344,000. Consequently, under these assumptions the combined one-time $2 million unified credit gifting could avoid estate tax of approximately 55% of $4,344,000 or $2,389,000.

Any form of gifting in a family business environment is challenging. From a technical perspective, the IRS is after revenue and has a vested interest in policing your gifts. Congress has established gifting parameters and requested that the IRS establish regulations to ensure that the citizenry abide by legislative intention. Consequently gifting to avoid estate taxes requires competent technical advice. Notably, gifting to family members requires a qualified third party validation of the value of the gifted asset. The IRS just assumes that all red-blooded Americans are trying to follow Judge Hand's precedent and avoid estate taxes. Therefore, the IRS constantly audits gifts and estates to assure that all state gift values can be backed up with legitimate expert appraisals.

From a practical perspective, strategic gifting in a family business environment involves the volatile combination of complex business interests and overactive family emotions. Consequently, effective gifting to avoid estate tax requires forethought, preparation, patience and diligence or your good deed can be spoken evil of. It is usually not easy to gift substantial assets, especially when it is a piece of the family business. Questions always accompany gifting, such as:

- When should I begin gifting?
- How do I establish a gifting program?
- Can I get the asset back if I need it?
- What should be gifted?
- What happens if there is a divorce?
- What happens if I decide to sell the business or the asset that was gifted?
- Will this gift make my child lazy?

These questions and others are legitimate concerns. There are reasonable answers to these questions that will be addressed later in more detail. The answers focus on two concepts. Notably, it's important to respect your feelings and not do anything that contradicts them. First you must develop an understanding of the various methods of guarding against gifting mistakes. This research will affirm that you can develop structures that will allow you, the donor, to retain control of the gifted asset. Transfer restriction contracts can be developed that prohibit the transfer of asset as a result of divorce or bankruptcy. A buy/sell contract can provide for the gifted asset to be held in escrow or trust to facilitate efficient, emotionless recovery (for reasonable consideration) of the gifted asset in the event there is even a threat that the asset will be transferred to an undesirable party.

Due to the tax-exempt gift limitations, the success of a gifting initiative can only be determined over the long haul. Therefore, it is important to establish a disciplined program as soon as possible that will be a catalyst for using the annual exemption as well as the gift tax credit. Usually, the best catalyst is an advisor, who systematically pushes you to address annual gifting.

With the exception of two circumstances, there is no concern about gifts made in contemplation of death or in close proximity to death. However, I can affirm for you from my 30 plus years of experience, the bulk of significant gifting activity occurs in the shadow of the "grim reaper." Unfortunately, gifts within two or three years of death usually have limited time to significantly transfer growth. The only significant benefit of final days gifting is the potential discounting of asset value through various forms of restructuring, which we will discuss later. However, you can be sure that gifts in close proximity to death are a red flag to the IRS that gives them maximum incentive to closely scrutinize the transactions. In order for you to have assurance that maximum (within your personal financial security comfort zone) estate tax avoidance can be achieved, you must begin gifting early. The sooner tax exempt gifting can be initiated, the sooner the tax-exempt limit and the growth on the asset can be protected from the bite of estate tax.

Furthermore, exempt gifts made at the beginning of the year are out of the estate in the event of a death later in the year. As you have appropriately assumed, the most sincere gifting intention cannot be carried out after death.

As referred to in the previous paragraph, there are two circumstances where gifts made in contemplation of death will be taxed in the donor's estate. In recognition of the value the IRS places on estate tax created by life insurance, federal law states that any life insurance gifted within three years of death is deemed null and void. When the decedent makes gifts of life insurance within three years of death, regardless of who is now the owner and beneficiary of the policy on the date of death, the death benefits will be taxed in the estate of the decedent.

The other exception acknowledges the potential value of taxable gifts, which will be discussed later. Federal law states that any gift taxes paid within three years of a donor's death will be recaptured in the estate of the donor.

Hopefully you have found value in the preceding encouragement to avoid estate taxes through gifting. However, you probably did not need me to encourage you to gift. You probably knew gifting was a good idea, but you just did not know how to go about it. Questions such as those listed above have prevented you from transferring assets to avoid estate taxes. No doubt, what could be perceived as a simple transfer of title can also be complex when you are endeavoring to avoid estate taxes. The complexity arises from the fact that, in order to avoid estate taxes, your gift must represent significant value and significant potential growth. Transferring significant current or future value without creating problems with family, business or the IRS is a formidable challenge.

There are many ways of transferring title of property, ranging from simply transferring possession, executing titles or assigning interests, to forming corporations, partnerships and trusts. Regardless of the form of gift, you should not gift any property that you think you might need later, such as a property providing income security or a primary residence. Therefore, solid, well informed thinking should precede any contemplated gift. The technically most appropriate gifts for estate tax avoidance are those assets with the highest growth potential, which we will refer to as strategic growth assets (SGA.) SGA's, such as discounted interests in the family business or real estate, will not only immediately remove substantial taxable value from the estate due to the discount, but will also remove significant future value that would otherwise be growing in your estate.

In most family environments, the perfect gifts are those that, as parents, you can continue to control. And, you reasonably ask, how can I continue to control something that I have gifted away? The answer lies in how gifted assets are structured. Prior to gifting, property such as stock in the business, real estate, copy rights, patents, publicly traded stocks and bonds and even cash can be structured so that your gift will represent equity, income, or use, but not control. This restructuring through the use of corporations, limited partnerships and trusts separates control as a property right and enables you to gift all or some of the other property rights while retaining control. It is noteworthy that the IRS looks very closely at control to determine the value and validity of gifts. Therefore, if retention of control is important to your gifting plans, you must rely upon your technical planning advisors to lead you down this highly scrutinized pathway. Your advisors will establish the appropriate provisions to stockholder's agreements and partnership agreements that will enable you to retain some form of control without violating constructive ownership rules.

Another important question about gifting is, "What should be gifted?" Although you may not need a consultant to tell you to gift, you may need an experienced advisor to help you address what to gift and how to gift it in order to get the most tax avoidance leverage. From a tax avoidance perspective, the last asset you should gift is cash. Cash is, hopefully, your only asset that is predictably going down in value as a reflection of inflation. Holding on to cash builds financial peace of mind, which is a predicate to an effective tax avoidance gifting strategy. In more than 30 years of business succession consulting, I have never witnessed a client make aggressive gifts who was worried about his or her personal financial security. In most instances, the family business and related real estate are the most predictable growth assets. Of significant importance, the business and real estate can be structured to allow you to retain control of the gifted asset.

This control will also allow you, in the event of an emergency, to control the income from the business or real estate.

Consider gifting growth assets first, including documentation that protects gifted assets from divorce, bankruptcy, and <u>irresponsible transfers.</u>

Tax avoidance also addresses life insurance gifting and structuring. The attractive leverage of life insurance makes it potentially valuable to you, but do not lose sight of the fact that your life insurance is also potentially valuable to the IRS. The impact of properly gifting a relatively small premium that creates a large tax-free death benefit is the feature that makes life insurance important to you. By the same token, the potential loss of the estate tax on the death benefit makes life insurance gifting important to the IRS.

Congress has no major problem with Mom or Dad making a combined tax exempt and tax credit gift of say, $200,000, in cash on their deathbed. The credit utilized will simple be debited from the estate tax credit allowance. Being tax revenue oriented, however, Congress does not allow Mom or Dad to gift policies with a $200,000 cash value and a $1 million death benefit on their deathbed. It stands to lose the tax on $800,000 of life insurance leverage. Congress realizes it is potentially the largest beneficiary (approximately 50% estate tax) of life insurance and does not wish to give up that valuable position. Lawmakers have acknowledged their feelings about the potential power of gifting life insurance by creating regulations that restrict the ability to avoid estate tax on life insurance. As described earlier, the restrictions state that life insurance gifted within three years of death is recaptured within the decedent's taxable estate. The law also recaptures policies that are beyond the three-year recapture period if the parent continues to maintain any direct or indirect control of the policy. However -- depending upon the size of the policy, the feasibility of replacing the policy and your life expectancy -- it may make sense to gift existing life insurance policies out of your estate.

The three-year life insurance recapture rule can be avoided if the next generation is, directly or in trust, the original applicant and owner of the policy. The primary method of avoiding estate tax on life insurance is not by gifting the policy. The three-year recapture rule can be avoided if the next generation is the original applicant and owner of the policy. If the insured never has incidence of ownership in the policy, gifts can only be attributed to cash transferred as payment of premiums. To be sure, life insurance structuring for the avoidance of estate tax is precarious. Specific procedures must be followed in every aspect of the policy acquisition, from signing applications and structuring policies to receiving death benefits. If these procedures are not followed with technical precision, the IRS will have a fabulous incentive (approximately 50% tax on the death benefit) to crush your tax avoidance plans. If you are endeavoring to avoid estate tax, do not take any action on purchasing or gifting life insurance without the guidance of your technical advisors.

Other than gifting, the most active aspect of estate tax avoidance focuses on reducing the appraised value of assets specifically for the computation of estate tax. This is the IRC Chapter 14 reversal mentioned earlier. Estate and gift tax appraisals are not the same as "going concern" appraisals, because tax appraisals consider the structure of the asset and intrinsic property rights. The estate and gift tax valuation process should value the family business the same way any business or asset is valued irrespective of being family, non family, public or private. In the realm of succession planning, the property rights most important to appraisal are marketability and control.

The ability to convert an asset into cash supports the age-old axiom, "It is only worth what somebody will pay for it." Although your goal is not to sell your business, a realistic appraisal must address marketability, which is the ability to convert an interest into cash. As you are aware, no one makes a market in privately owned business with a worth based solely upon all that you know about your business' potential.

A binding stock transfer restriction agreement would be a valuable tool to showcase the lack of marketability of a family owned business. Due to the lack of market for family owned businesses, the true value of your business cannot be readily determined. Furthermore, experience has shown that selling a privately owned business involves the protracted process of putting the business on the market, taking the steps to locate the relatively few interested buyers and trying to convey to them the unique profit potential of the business. Because of the perceived risks and costs of buying a private business, rarely is a buyer willing to pay a price that would duplicate the prior return on equity. Consequently, for estate tax purposes, business assets should qualify for lack of marketability discounts of approximately 25% of the fair market value.

The estate and gift tax valuation process should value the family business the same way any business is valued irrespective of being family, non family, public or private.

Similarly, the technical control of a family business can also generate valuation discounts. Experience has also verified that it is nearly impossible to sell a minority interest in a privately owned business for a value that approximates the prior return on equity. Any prospective buyer of a minority interest fully recognizes that, regardless of prior performance, there is no assurance that the majority owner would respect the new owner's minority ownership interests. Generally, any voting percentage ownership in excess of 50% represents control of the entity. A 50% voting percentage does not provide control, but does provide a protective dead-lock. Any ownership of less than 50% is considered a minority with no control or deadlock ability. The bedrock of the concept of valuation discounts is that a deadlock or minority ownership interest is worth less than a controlling interest.

The most powerful estate tax avoidance practice of a family business owner is to establish documents that restrict transfer of assets to anyone other than family or partners, to always make transfers (gift or sale) of minority interests and never to die with majority. A married business owner can make transfer of minority interests during his or her lifetime, but go to the grave with undisputed control of the business. The business owner can then pass this interest to the surviving spouse under the tax shelter of the marital deduction. Subsequently, the surviving spouse can, at the appropriate time, yield technical control by making minority transfers (sale or gift prior to death) to children or partners. The net result will be that control will be retained, but the total business value will pass through the estate at the most attractive discounted value. This amounts to a reduction in the taxable value of 30% to 50%. In the realm of multi-million dollar businesses, a 35% discount will avoid big time estate tax.

It should be noted that the IRS is not pleased with valuation discounts for estate tax and gift tax purposes. Therefore, the IRC continues the challenge of what they deem as "abusive discounts," which are perceived devices for estate conveyance. Furthermore, they continue to pursue legislative relief that would specifically restrict or eliminate valuation discounts. Therefore, you must proceed in this area only under the counsel and leadership of experienced technical advisors.

Control Contraction via Recapitalization

With businesses worth many millions of dollars, it is difficult to achieve valuation discounts by gifting sufficient minority interests to leave a minority interest in the estate. As an example, if the business is worth $10 million, under the classic stock structure, more than $5 million in stock would have to be gifted in order to leave a minority in the estate. Even after a minority discount of 40% on the $5 million, it may be challenging to gift $3 million, due to income security or equitable treatment circumstances.

A technique for facilitating the achievement of a minority discount is a recapitalization of the corporate stock structure. The purpose for recapitalizing the stock in a succession planning environment is to contract the voting rights of the stock into a relatively small percentage of the outstanding stock. This form of recapitalization is accomplished by diluting the existing voting stock with newly authorized (by amending the corporate charter) non-voting stock. The non-voting stock is then issued by declaring a non-voting stock dividend on existing stock.

Example

As an example, let us assume that your incorporated business has a value of $3 million, and you have issued to yourself 1,000 shares of voting stock. Let us further assume that you want to transfer the majority of your business to your children, but retain control. So, your attorney amends your articles of incorporation and authorizes 9,000 additional shares of non-voting stock. You subsequently declare a nine share, non-voting stock dividend on your original 1,000 voting shares. The capitalization of your business is now expanded to 10,000 shares. (Unfortunately, the valuation of the business has not changed.)

Now each share of stock has just been diluted in value from $3,000 per share to $300 per share. But not to worry, you still own all the shares, so your net worth has not changed. What has changed is that the controlling 1,000 voting shares now only represent 10% of the business value or $300,000. Consequently, in the normal course of estate tax avoidance, you could gift to your children all the voting stock, which would be valued at simplistically (there would be a modest discount on non voting stock) $2.7 million and retain total control. Actually, you could gift away the 9,000 shares of non-voting stock and 499 shares of voting stock and retain technical control.

From a different perspective, if you were burned out and beat up or if you had encountered a terminal illness, this recapitalization would position you to efficiently move control of your business to your children. Based upon our assumed $3 million business valuation prior to the recap, more than $1.5 million of stock would have to be transferred before you or your spouse could claim a minority valuation discount. After a recapitalization, wherein the voting stock has been diluted to 10%, the voting capital would be valued at the same $300,000 mentioned above, plus a modest premium reflecting voting rights. Consequently, control could be transferred through a gift or sale of 501 voting shares valued at $150,000 to $200,000, depending on the voting stock valuation premium. The net result would be that the remaining 9,499 shares would be subject to a lucrative minority valuation discount. It is also noteworthy to recognize that -- if the transfer of 510 shares of voting stock was done in two minority voting block steps of, say 300 shares in one year and 210 shares in the next -- the entire company could be transferred at a lucrative minority discount.

Regardless of the technical complications, the most difficult aspect of achieving minority valuation discount is relinquishing control. This is not a comfortable position for entrepreneurs who achieved success through asserting control over business operations. And let's not mince words, transferring control of your business is a major step in business succession planning. We are talking about the financial security of many families, including your own.

There are also emotional considerations as you may also be concerned that, after transferring control, no one will value your opinion and you will lose your perceived importance. Whether emotional or financial, we are talking about real issues that have to be addressed in a deliberate and forthright manner. There is a right time and a wrong time. Unfortunately we sometimes do not know this until after we have taken the leap. Ideally, the transfer will occur prior to death to enable a significant avoidance of estate taxes.

The most common purpose for recapitalizing the stock in a succession planning environment is to contract the voting rights of the stock into a relatively small percentage of the outstanding stock.

Family Limited Partnership

Another method of avoiding estate tax is through the use of a family limited partnership (LP) or, in some states, limited liability corporations (LLC). These are entities that facilitate transfers to the next generation by dividing the property rights of the assets other than the corporation's. A limited partnership, as you recall from the tax shelter years, has two types of partners. There are the limited partners, who are essentially passive participants. By statutory regulations, limited partners cannot be liable for the business affairs beyond their invested equity, or take part in the day-to-day management of the partnership. The general partner or partners must own at least 1% of the partnership and be designated as responsible for the liabilities of the partnership as well as the day-to-day operation. By statute, a limited partnership interest may not be transferred without the general partner's consent or the partnership will run the risk of being reclassified as a corporation.

This splitting of the responsibilities and control rights within a limited partnership, as well as the restrictions of transfers, is very convenient for attempting to avoid estate taxes. The statutory definition of a limited partnership interest makes a profound case for lack of marketability and lack of control valuation discounts. The splitting of responsibilities and rights with a limited partnership is also a very convenient vehicle for family dynamics when parents want to maintain control with a very small ownership, or there are actively employed family members who are best suited for general partner and/or unemployed family members best suited for limited partner roles. Depending upon the state of jurisdiction, there also are other partnership derivatives, such as limited liability partnerships, that have special features, but generally serve the same purpose.

A limited liability corporation is another planning tool that has emerged because of the liability issues impacting general partners. The capabilities and nature of an LLC are determined by the state of jurisdiction; however, in most instances, the LLC does everything a limited partnership can do, plus it protects the manager(s) and general partners(s) from personal liability for the entity's liabilities. The individual who controls the operation of the LLC is the manager and does not have to be an owner. The owners of the LLC are classified as members. The LLC adoption agreement, as with LP adoption agreements, stipulates the restrictions relating to transferability (marketability) and voting rights (control).

Example

To illustrate the estate tax avoidance capability and the business succession planning compatibility of these structures, let's assume an auto dealer operates his dealership on a parcel of real estate valued at $2 million, from which he is receiving rental income of $200,000 per year. Mr. Dealer owns the real estate personally and, in the event of his death, the estate tax appraisal of the real estate would be the $2 million fair market value, cre-

ating an estate tax of $1.1 million. Mr. Dealer has two children to whom he intends to pass his property after the death of his wife, assuming he predeceases her. His son is the successor dealer who will inherit the family business and his daughter is a homemaker living in another state. Mr. Dealer wants to retain control of the real estate. His stated succession planning goals are as follows:

- He wants to make a current gift to his daughter of a portion of the real estate with minimum gift tax implications, while retaining the bulk of the lease income for himself and his wife during their lifetime.

- Upon his death, he wants to give his son control and management responsibility of the real estate to prevent his widow or daughter from being an awkward partner and landlord.

- Upon his wife's death, he wants to minimize estate tax and pass the income stream of the real estate to his daughter to achieve equitable asset distribution.

- And, of course, he wants to accomplish these goals at the lowest possible tax cost.

Mr. Dealer is advised by a well-informed succession planner to change the form in which he owns the real estate, so that he can divide and disperse the property rights of the real estate to accomplish his multifaceted goals. He consults with his attorney and accountant. They confirm that, if he owns this property as a limited partnership, he can divide the property rights between himself, his wife, his son and ultimately his daughter to accomplish his ambitious assortment of goals.

Mr. Dealer adopts a family limited partnership designating himself in a dual role as a 2% general partner and 98% limited partner. Recognizing the utility of limited partnership interests, he transfers sufficient limited partnership interest to his wife to validate her unified credit. He also makes a 2% limited partnership gift to his son and a 10% limited partnership interest to his daughter. Based upon the advice of his advisors, the partnership agreement states that, upon Mr. Dealer's death or disability, his 2% general partnership interest is converted to a limited partnership interest and his son becomes the successor general partner. His daughter would currently receive 10% of the partnership cash flow to supplement her income and, in accordance with the provisions of the partnership agreement and as a general partner, his son would not have to worry about his limited partner meddling in partnership affairs or losing the interest because of any financial irresponsibility or divorce. On the other hand, his son would be ill advised to *take advantage of his sister because, as general partner, he would have a fiduciary responsibility to manage the partnership for his sister's best interest.*

In order to properly document the gifts to his son and daughter, the dealer engages a security appraiser to value the gifted limited partnership interests. In the valuation analysis, the appraiser takes into consideration many factors, including a fair market value appraisal of the real estate, the lease between the partnership and the dealership, the inherent passive nature of a limited partner and the documented restrictions relating to marketability and control. As a product of the analysis, the appraiser determines that the value of limited partnership interests holding 98% of the $2 million in real estate should be discounted by 45%, due to lack of control and lack of marketability. Accordingly, the 2% interest gifted to the son is valued at $22,000 ($2 million x 2% x 55%). In the event of the dealer's death, the residual 88% limited partnership interest that his widow would own should also be valued accordingly, generating a value of $968,000 ($2 million x 88% x 55%).

Assuming the underlying $2 million value of the real estate did not change, adoption of the limited partnership under these circumstances would remove $900,000 of asset value from tax computation with resulting tax avoidance of $495,000.

This example illustrates the theory supporting the achievement of tax appraisal discounts with limited partnerships and limited liability corporations, and the subsequent avoidance of estate tax. The example should also show the utility of a limited partnership for succession planning. The use of this structure for the conversion of property rights provides the basis for valuation discounts in Mrs. Dealer's estate. The limited partnership structure also facilitates the achievement of Mr. Dealer's other objectives. If he becomes weary of the liability of real estate management during his lifetime, he can resign as general partner and let his son manage the property. Furthermore, he can make substantial transfers to his wife without subjecting her to the hassles and hazards of property management.

As limited partners, the wife, daughter and grandchildren could participate in the cash flow of the real estate without impacting his son's management of the dealership.

He would also have a passive asset that he could begin gifting to his daughter, and even his grandchildren, which would provide them income and not give him concern about complicating management decisions or exposing them to liability. Notably, as limited partners, the wife, daughter and grandchildren could participate in the cash flow of the real estate without impacting his son's management of the dealership. Nor would it create concerns about disposition of the real estate in the event that his daughter divorced or his grandchildren never matured financially.

Charitable giving can also create attractive estate tax avoidance maneuvers. These are under-utilized techniques that wealthy individuals with charitable interests should consider. The fundamental requirement for successfully utilizing charitable giving to reduce estate tax is a desire to benefit a qualified charity. Life-time charitable gifts provide income tax benefits that vary according to the circumstances of the donor and charity. And the asset is removed from the taxable estate. However, in the absence of a genuine goal to help a charity, the actual after tax cost is usually perceived to be too high.

From an estate perspective, charitable interests can be addressed with the indirect benefit of preserving wealth for family members. From the most simplistic perspective, under current law, direct bequests to a qualified charity create estate tax deductions equal to the amount of the bequest. The withdrawal of the asset from the estate will save approximately 50¢ in estate taxes on each dollar donated; however, using simple reciprocal math, every testamentary dollar donated costs the donor or the beneficiary 50¢. Unfortunately, direct testamentary bequests to charities also do nothing to reduce the estate tax on other assets, such as the business. Furthermore, charities generally do not pursue interest in a family business unless there is a device for liquidating the stock.

Through the use of trusts that direct income to charities, an estate tax shelter can be created for specific assets, such as the business or associated real estate, passing through an estate to the next generation. One such trust is a Charitable Lead Trust (CLT) that provides an income stream to a qualified charity for a specified number of years. After completion of a specified period, during which a specific annuity or a specified percentage of the trust value is paid to a charity, the income-producing asset placed in the trust passes to the specified beneficiaries of the trust (children or grandchildren) essentially tax free. The present value of the "leading" income stream payable to the charity is allowed as an estate tax deduction against the value of the property that will ultimately pass to family members. Depending upon the duration of the charitable lead payout period and the amount of income paid to the charity, a portion and possibly the vast majority of the taxation on the transfer of that particular property is avoided.

Example

Let's assume we have a $1 million parcel of real estate that produces $8,000 per month of net cash flow. Let's also assume that, as a product of the estate documents, this property is placed in a CLT which pays the decedent's church $8,000 per month for 20 years. At the end of the 20 years, the trust will revert to the sole benefit of the children and grandchildren. According to IRS approved tables, the present value of the $8,000 per month income stream creates an estate tax deduction of $1 million. The net effect is that the $1 million property being transferred to the successors after 20 years is totally sheltered from estate tax. Furthermore, in 20 years -- assuming 6% appreciation would inflate the value of the real estate to more than $3.2 million -- the growth in value above the original $1 million also passes estate tax free.

Charitable trusts can be very effective gift tax and estate tax avoidance tools. However, these are complex instruments. Charitable giving for estate leverage is a complex undertaking requiring technical competence in both income tax and estate tax law, as well as the ability to generate proformas which confirm compatibility of these structures to your unique circumstances. It is imperative that you consider such estate tax avoidance maneuvers with the guidance of technically adept advisors.

Another estate tax avoidance technique utilizing future value discounts are Grantor Retained Annuity Trust (GRAT) and Grantor Retained Unitrust (GRUT) gifts. Under the heading of succession planning, these techniques involve gifting assets to the next generation by placing the assets in trusts which specify that the grantor will retain income from the gift for a specified number of years. The grantor retained annuity trust pays the grantor a specified annuity as a percentage of the initial asset value. A grantor retained unitrust pays the grantor a specified percentage of the trust value determined each year.

The GRAT is the simpler structure of the two. To fund a GRAT, parents place income producing assets in trust, such as Subchapter-S stock or business real estate, with the provision that the trust pay the parent an annuity for a specified number of years. At the end of the retained income period, the property is distributed to the children as the free and clear owners. When the property is placed in the GRAT, the parents are making a taxable gift to the children. The value of the taxable gift is discounted based upon the amount of the annuity and the duration of the retained income.

The amount of the future value discounts of a GRAT that impacts the amount of the gift depends upon three variables: the IRS discount rate, the duration of the retained annuity interest and the amount of the annuity payment. The discount rate is under the control of the IRS and generally reflects prevailing economic conditions. The longer the retained annuity, and the greater the retained annuity, the lower the gift.

There are two potentially negative implications to utilizing a GRAT for estate tax avoidance. The specified annuity of the GRAT must be paid in order to achieve the discount in the value of the gift. This feature could create challenges in a cyclical economic environment. Also, the transfer is voided if the grantor of the GRAT does not outlive the annuity term. If the grantor has a retained interest (the annuity) in the trust on the date of his or her death, the fair market value of the asset as of that day will be included in the estate without any present value discounts in value. Fortunately, in this unfortunate event, any gift taxes paid when the GRAT was previously adopted will be recovered as credits toward the estate tax on the recaptured asset. Although these are negative features to a GRAT, they are not necessarily deal killing, because, if the GRAT is voided, the grantor is in the same position as having done nothing. Consequently, families that find a GRAT attractive usually conclude that their only risks are the time and cost of developing and adopting the instrument.

Another "retain interest" tax avoidance mechanism is a Qualified Personal Residence Trust (QPRT). A QPRT applies only to the grantor's personal residence or vacation home. In operation, the parent deeds over the home to a QPRT that provides that the parents retain the utility of the home for a specified number of years. Subsequent to this retained interest period, the title is transferred to the children. Just as with the GRAT computations, the gift tax value of the home is computed by determining a present value discount of the current fair market of the home. The discount in value is a function of the current published IRS discount rate and the term of years specified in the trust.

As an example, at an IRS discount rate of 8.5%, a grantor, age 70, could place a $500,000 vacation home in a QPRT for 10 years, at a current gift value of $141,210. This is not a bad deal, especially in light of the probability that in 10 years the $500,000 home will have substantially appreciated in value.

If the grantor has a retained interest (the annuity) in the trust on the date of his or her death, the fair market value of the asset as of that day will be included in the estate without any discounts in value.

On the negative side of the QPRT balance sheet, parents must be able to reconcile that, irrespective of the estate tax avoidance value, in 10 years their children will own their residence or vacation home. This is generally not a big deal with respect to vacation home but a significant issue with respect to a primary residence. Not many business owners immediately warm to the idea of paying rent for the privilege of living in their own residence. Furthermore, similar to a GRAT, the grantor must survive the retention term specified within the trust so that the title can actually be transferred to the children. If the grantor (parent) dies while the home is still in trust, the fair market value will be included in his or her taxable estate. Fortunately, if this occurs, the grantor's estate also recovers prior taxes paid for credit against the new (higher) estate tax.

Another very effective estate tax avoidance technique is an intentionally defective grantor irrevocable trust, more commonly known as an IDGIT. Many years ago, the income tax division of the IRS issued regulations that, if a grantor of an irrevocable trust retained certain powers, such as the ability to substitute property of equal value, then the trust would be considered defective for income tax purposes. Consequently, although the assets would be owned by the beneficiaries, the income of the trust would be taxable to the parent grantors. At the time, those of us in the estate tax avoidance business thought this was petty harassment.

Years later, we were searching for estate tax avoidance strategies for clients who wanted to transfer far more assets than the gift tax credits and exemptions would allow. One of my bright colleagues recognized that a client could leverage the tax avoidance capability by gifting income-producing assets to a defective irrevocable trust. As expected, the asset transferred to the trust would be out of the donor's estate. However, the bonus was that the donor would be allowed by the estate and gift tax division of the IRS (because it was required by the income tax division) to pay the income tax on behalf of their children gift tax-free. Of course when we did this, the IRS screamed bloody murder. However, much to the delight of all of us who have dealt with their petty regulations, the courts ruled that the IRS could not have it both ways. They could not require that the grantor of a defective trust pay income tax and then also contend that the grantor had made a taxable gift. When I became aware of this ruling, I must have had a smile on my face for a week. It was about time that the IRS got a taste of its own medicine.

If you thought the above was interesting, consider another utilization of an intentionally defective grantor irrevocable trust to conserve personal cash flow, avoid estate tax, gift tax and even capital gains tax on the transfer of an income producing business interest to the next generation. To score this "super hat trick," first form a IDGIT and make a gift of cash to the trust equivalent to at least 10% of the value of the business interest that you are intending to transfer.

Let's consider the value of the business being transferred to the next generation is $6 million, so our cash gift to the IDGIT will be $600,000, and, hopefully, will be sheltered by the unified credit. And hold on, do not jump to the conclusion that I am naively suggesting that you give away your security to your kids. Although admittedly bold, I would not step out that far on a limb. The rest of the redeeming story is that you would subsequently enter into an agreement to personally sell to the IDGIT (your children are beneficiaries) the $6 million business interest (stock, real estate, partnership) taking back the previously gifted $600,000 of cash back as a 10% down payment. (I'm not crazy after all.)

Hopefully, you are feeling a little better, now that you got your cash security back. But you may think I am crazy for suggesting that you create a capital gains tax and give away your business income. Not so! Remember you are selling your interest to the IDGI (children), so you are going to get all the income back as amortization on the note to purchase the business interest for 90% of the value. The same income that was previously coming to you as income on the business interest is now coming to you as amortization on the business purchase note. But the real kicker is that you have frozen the value of the business at $6 million with the sale. Meanwhile, the income from the business is methodically reducing the value of the business (note) remaining in your estate. Furthermore, due to the "defective" nature of the irrevocable trust, from an income tax perspective, you are selling the business to yourself. Therefore, this transaction will not create a capital gains tax. Before you pull your hair out with confusion, talk to your accountant. He will confirm for you that the grantor trust regulations state that a sale to yourself is a nontaxable transaction. The net result of this sale to an IDGIT is that, until the $5.4 million note for the value of the business is completely paid off, you recover the gifted cash and the business income and you pay no additional income tax or capital gains tax beyond what you would have paid if you had done nothing at all. Furthermore, in the spirit of this discussion, you have avoided significant estate tax by freezing the value of the business interest and initiating a process that moves an otherwise taxable business interest out of your estate with zero estate tax.

In most family business environments, the development of net worth follows the generation of income. Therefore, a substantive method of avoiding estate tax is through the redirection of income to the next generation. The application of this technique is limited to circumstances where parents unquestionably have sufficient capital to satisfy any security concerns and/or the amount of income they are receiving substantially exceeds need. The parent's income is simply exasperating an already ugly estate tax situation. The redirection of income to children has no negative impact on the current or projected lifestyle parents, and specifically avoids the continuing buildup of net worth and ever increasing estate tax. Furthermore, in order to pursue this tax avoidance technique, there should be confidence that the next generation is capable of handling this income, or asset management mechanisms should be provided to prevent Junior and Missy from blowing all the cash.

A simple method of redirecting income would be the strategic gifting of assets that produce high income. Although you did not need to read this book to learn that point of obvious wisdom, it is worthwhile to consider that most assets that carry high income also carry inflated appraisals for gift tax purposes. Therefore, the scoop here is that tax efficient gifting for strategic income shifting should first consider assets that have yet not reached their full income producing potential. Good examples of these pearls would be leveraged real estate and interests in a high potential business that have not as yet achieved the economy of scale necessary to be profitable. These high potential businesses are generally ringers that are directly related to the family's core business.

Another important aspect of strategic income shifting is the form of the gift. Due to generally accepted valuation discount procedures, if you endeavor to gift all of an asset, the gift tax implications will be much greater than if you gift a partial interest. Furthermore, if the gift is in the form of an interest in a corporation or partnership, which has documented transfer restrictions, the value of the gift will be even further reduced. It also bears mentioning that if Junior and Missy are young, permanently immature, married to a vampire or dumb as a box of rocks, transferring income through gifts of stock or partnership interests will enable you to retain control of the income.

Unfortunately, some families do not have independent income producing assets that can be transferred to children to divert income and avoid unnecessary estate tax. Furthermore, the family business sometimes is a Regular C-corp that does not facilitate the diversion of income through the gift of stock. And, sometimes, it is just not prudent to transfer stock in the family business to unemployed children because of intra family complications or in some cases (such as automobile dealerships, beer wholesalers and liquor distributors,) because either the franchiser or state regulators place restrictions on who can own stock. In these situations, it may be worthwhile to create a management company to divert income to the next generation. In operation, a family management company is a formal pass-through structure, such as a partnership, limited liability corporation or Subchapter-S corporation that is owned primarily by the desired recipients of income. As mentioned above, the donors/parents can keep control of this entity by retaining a voting stock or general partnership interest. The pass-through management company is subsequently awarded a formal management contract that provides generous compensation for the delivery of what hopefully can be justified as strategically valuable services. This contractual relationship, which hopefully is not stretching reality too far, redirects income to the management company. Through their pass-through ownership, the children receive income.

Another interesting estate tax avoidance technique is a tax free spinoff of a business division. In circumstances where the children have already achieved substantial business ownership and there is a division of the business that could, and hopefully should, thrive as an independent business, the division of a single company into two or more companies can have substantial estate tax avoidance leverage. This maneuver is based upon the concept that the sum of the parts of a business is less than the value of the whole. In other words, the value of an overall business would be greater than the cumulative value of each operating division. A TSO legally divides what was a consolidated business. Subsequently, a specific part of the business that is now independent can be sold or gifted to all or specific children to achieve the estate allocation and estate tax avoidance goals unique to your specific situation. Unfortunately, the IRS also fully understands both the income tax and the estate tax leverage that can be achieved with a tax free spinoff of a division. Consequently, the IRS monitors these maneuvers closely to assure that there is a valid business purpose. The facts of your specific situation and the creativity of your advisors will determine your eligibility of a tax free spinoff. Generally, your advisors obtain the opinion of the IRS in advance, due to the potential adverse income tax treatment (taxable dividend) consequences of being denied tax free status.

If debt is being utilized, children can be the borrower of the funds to purchase real estate or start a business just about as easily as the parents.

Example

Let's assume a beverage distributor owns a beer distributorship that is valued at $10 million. He owns 70% of the stock and his son and daughter each own 15%. The business maintains two franchises that are natural competitors, such as Anheuser Busch (AB) and Miller. Let us further assume that AB stipulates to its distributors that they must become single brand distributors. Under this fact package, the wholesaler could possibly spin off the Miller distributorship to his children tax free in exchange for all or a portion of their 30% of stock. Whereas an independent Miller distributorship on the open market might be worth $5 million, as an operating division based upon circumstances, the spinoff value could potentially be substantially less, based on the assumption that the overhead costs of management and distribution would have to be duplicated and the loss of the economy of scale. Ideally, these assumptions are just that, assumptions and not reality. This being the case, a $5 million asset can be transferred to the next generation for a substantially lower number, such as $3 million. With third party valuation substantiation for these assumptions, Mr. Beverage Wholesaler would have avoided estate tax on $2 million of value at a tax savings of $1.1 million.

The tax-free nature of the spinoff is dependent upon validation by the IRS, a valid business purpose for splitting the business. A simple brand mandate by AB may be a valid business purpose, but avoidance of estate tax is not a valid business purpose. Circumstances must be appropriate for this technique to provide estate or gift tax avoidance opportunities.

Taxable gifts can also be an effective method of avoiding estate tax. This is the tax avoidance technique of the truly wealthy. As you may recall, gift taxes and estate taxes are computed from the same table. To our specific interest, there is a major difference between how taxes are computed for gifts and estate bequests. The computation of estate tax is inclusive (of taxation), whereas the computation of gift tax is exclusive (of taxation). What this means is that, when estate taxes are computed, the tax paid is included in the tax computation. In an estate, tax is actually paid on the dollars being utilized to pay the estate tax. That may be confusing, but the hardball message is that estate tax, as compared to gift tax, is double jeopardy. On the other hand, exclusive gift tax is single jeopardy. Gift taxes are only paid on the value of the property being transferred.

The computation of estate tax is inclusive (of taxation) whereas the computation of gift tax is exclusive (of taxation).

Example

Let's consider an estate planning situation where we want to transfer $450,000 to a beneficiary by either estate bequest or current gift. Let's further assume that the unified credits have been utilized and the gross estate is well above $3 million, so we are dealing with a 55% estate or gift tax bracket. An estate bequest of a net $450,000 would require a gross transfer of $1 million, which would create estate taxes of $550,000, leaving the desired $450,000 net for the beneficiary. The total cost of transferring $450,000 through the estate is $1 million.

Now let's presume you wanted to currently gift the same $450,000 to the beneficiary. A gift of the same net $450,000 at 55% would create a gift tax of $247,500. The total gift cost of the same $450,000 transfer would be $697,500. Comparing the gift cost to the $1 million cost of the estate transfer, the gift generates a savings of $302,500. Substantial estate taxes can be avoided by transferring property through taxable gifts.

Why would the IRS allow Mr. and Mrs. Business Owner to save taxes through gifts versus estate transfers?" The answer is mostly practical. First, the law states that the tax paid on any gifts within three years of death is recaptured for the computation of estate taxes. In the above example, the $247,500 tax paid would be added to the taxable estate generating another tax of $136,125. That is not good, but, if you do the math, it is not all bad. The sum of the gift and both taxes equals $833,625, which is $166,375 less than the cost of an estate transfer.

Second, it is a small group of the wealthy who have sufficient disposable cash to carry out taxable gifting. It is a relatively small group who are willing to currently give up a gifted asset, plus pay the government hard-earned cash for the privilege of giving that asset away. Depending upon the nature of the asset given, a future value computation of a gift tax paid may exceed future estate tax. Further, the government needs cash and the tax avoidance opportunity serves as an incentive to attract cash that could otherwise be deferred. Congress realizes that deferred taxes may fall victim to hard times or may be avoided through new asset transfer technology or judicial decisions favorable to estate tax avoidance.

Apparently, Congress puts substantial value on $2.47 in hand today versus $5.50 in the future.

Estate Splitting

Another related method of potentially avoiding unnecessary estate taxes is through paying estate taxes, which we refer to as estate splitting. In some circumstances, substantial estate taxes can be avoided through dividing the taxation of a married couple's estate, between the first to die and the second to die. Under most situations, as we will discuss next, it is preferable to defer the payment of estate tax as long as possible; however, if the estate has substantial values or has a highly appreciating asset, it may be worthwhile to transfer the asset to the next generation sooner versus later. Also, if a husband and wife both die, or could die within a short time frame, paying a portion of the estate tax upon the first to die can avoid taxes.

Estate splitting avoids tax by maximizing the use of the graduated estate tax tables. Referring to the estate tax and tax credit tables, note that the estate tax in 2003 on the first $3 million is $1.29 million, less $211,300 or $1,078,700, and the tax on assets above $3 million is a flat 55% up to $10 million. Comparatively, at 55%, the second $3 million of assets would create a tax of $1.65 million, less $211,300, or $1,438,700. If optimum unified credits are utilized, followed by the maximum marital deduction for maximum estate tax deferral in a $6 million estate, the tax upon the last to die would be $1.29 million, plus $1.65 million, less $211,300 or $2,728,700.

However, if tax is paid on $3 million upon the first to die, and tax is paid on the remaining $3 million upon the second to die, the total tax would be $1,078,700 plus $1,078,700, or a total of $2,157,400. Consequently, splitting taxation of the first $3 million of an estate between two tax brackets can avoid up to $571,300 in estate tax.

The time value of money can limit the benefit of deferring the payment of the net $1,078,700 tax on the first death to save $571,300 on the second death. The current tax savings should be compared to the value of retaining the $1,078,700 in estate taxes that would be payable upon the first death. Assuming asset earnings or the cost of borrowing is 8%, paying the $1.29 million tax -- less assumed unified credits of $211,300 on the first death -- would have an earnings cost of approximately $80,000 per year before income tax adjustment. Dividing the annual loss of earnings from paying tax on the first death into the estate splitting tax savings will provide a general idea of the time frame within which estate splitting can be a profitable tax avoidance technique.

Paying taxes early is a complex consideration that takes into account both financial and emotional risks. Estate taxes deplete cash. Taxes paid on the first death could otherwise be personally spent on items of need or even avoided completely through continuing gifts or new tax avoidance strategies that emerge after the first death. In order for the tax avoidance technique to have any value, the estate must have the cash to pay the estate tax, less remaining credits, without jeopardizing the security of the surviving spouse or the business.

Under most circumstances, holding on to the cash beats giving up hope and having the cash confiscated by the federal government. Tax avoidance through estate splitting should only be pursued after confirming that paying the first death tax earlier than necessary is affordable. Discuss this concept with your advisors and then rely upon them to tell you the right thing to do. Keep in mind the utility of the "Qualified Disclaimer Trust,"which we discussed in the preceding chapter on estate planning. Through the use of the disclaimer trust, the surviving spouse has the option to direct an asset that she or he would otherwise receive to children for estate splitting, while retaining the asset for personal security.

In order for the tax avoidance technique to have any value, the estate must have the cash to pay the estate tax less remaining credits without jeopardizing the security of the surviving spouse or the business.

The methods of dividing and dispersing property rights for the avoidance of estate tax are not limited to corporate recapitalization, limited partnerships or QPRT's. There are other methods of avoiding estate tax limited only by the creativity of your advisors, the patience of the IRS and the fairness of the judiciary process. Real estate can be encumbered with leases and environmental easements. Assets can be sold to heirs with self-canceling installment notes (SCIN - Frane Notes). Although the names and acronyms are different, the theory is the same. The various planning techniques discount the appraised value of estate assets for tax purposes by dividing the various rights of property such as ownership, control, income, equity security or life estate and disperses them to the next generation either directly or at a predetermined point in the future. The result is that Judge Leonard Hand is honored as you strategically avoid unnecessary estate taxes.

Unfortunately, if the past is any reflection of the future, some of the opportunities will be closed by IRS rulings and judicial decisions; however, Yankee ingenuity will prevail. Other opportunities will open as honest, hard-working citizens and their advisors continue to seek methods of avoiding devastating, undeserved, unmerited estate tax. The key is to deal with technically competent advisors who stay up to date with what is happening in the estate tax avoidance arena.

You can lead your family to a substantial avoidance of estate tax by retaining qualified, aggressive advisors and exhorting them to continually bring forth ideas on tax avoidance.

The planning strategies for avoiding estate taxes are critical to the succession of a family owned business. Capital is just too precious to sit like a lump on a log, waiting to be eviscerated by the IRS. The strategies that we have discussed, depending on the circumstances, can save considerable estate tax that, in turn, may be the deciding factor in the continuity of your business. However, these are sophisticated planning instruments that require technical explanation and support beyond the profile of this book. If you have never been exposed to these ideas or concepts, mention them to those who are assisting you with your planning. Ask for an explanation and a reflection as to how these vehicles could fit into your unique planning environment. As a business owner, it is not your responsibility to stay abreast of developments in this highly technical area. Your role is much simpler. You can lead your family to a substantial avoidance of estate tax by retaining qualified, aggressive advisors and exhorting them to continually bring forth ideas on tax avoidance. Also, keep your eyes and ears open at conventions and association meetings. Good news on tax avoidance travels fast. In a 55% or 60% estate tax bracket, you will quickly realize that the tax savings will justify your efforts.

Estate Tax Financing

At the time we printed the first edition of this book, there were no questions about the reality of estate tax. However, with the adoption of the tax reform act of 2001, our congress has at best created significant confusion in an arena that begs for clarity. The adoption of the latest in the certain continuum of tax reform acts received tremendous publicity. After 10 years of economic expansion and income tax surpluses, the act purported to abolish estate taxes in 2011. The publicity alleged that the federal government did not believe the projected $35 billion of estate tax revenue was worth the ongoing political heart-burn in the business community caused by an estate tax. However, while politicians from both sides of the aisle were soliciting praise for their role in this revolutionary tax repeal, the fine print revealed that all they were doing was seizing an opportunity to achieve a short term political agenda. There was no substantive estate tax reform.

On the surface, the new estate tax law looks both simple and reasonable. Over a 10-year period, the estate tax rate declines and the estate tax credit increases. Upon closer inspection the new law becomes complex, unreasonable and almost comical.

Consequently this author feels this new estate tax and unified credit schedule has a republican's chance in a Massachusetts' election to survive for more than five years.

I include a revised schedule here, reluctantly, as groups meeting Washington who are concerned about the loss of federal revenue and the expansion of wealth at the cost of the poor.

As we examine the new law, it is notable that the estate tax rate declines from 55% to 45% over 10 years, and then goes from 45% to 0%. Needless to say, this is a graduated phase-out as Gibraltar is a gently sloping beach. The problem with a realistic graduated phase-out is that Congress would be forced to act to stop the decline in the tax rate at a level they could tolerate. They do not want to have to act, because then we would know their true feelings. In other words, do not hold your breath that the estate tax will take the final step from 45% to 0%. The increase in the estate tax credit does grow impressively to $3.5 million per individual in 2009. But do not get all worked up about making lifetime transfers, because the gift tax credit does not rise above $1 million. However, the most perplexing aspect of this law is the impact of the Byrd Amendment, more commonly known as the "sundown provision." This law was designed to ward off spineless legislatures that would pass tax laws that would not take place until long after they departed from office.

The "sundown provision" states that any tax legislation that does not take full effect within 10 years of enactment must be readdressed and approved by 60 senators or the tax law "fades away" in the 10th year and the old law is reinstated.

As this law was purposely written to be under the impact of the sundown provisions, the scheduled estate tax repeal of 2010 will not occur unless the House of Representatives calls the estate tax repeal back to Congress and the Senate affirms the law with 60 votes. I personally think there is a higher probability of a blizzard in San Juan than a congressional affirmation of estate tax repeal. However, if the long shot does occur, the tradeoff of no estate tax is the abolishment of stepped up income tax basis on assets that pass through an estate. Consequently, if inherited assets are sold, income or capital gain tax will be paid on the gain with respect to the decedents original purchase price. Therefore, for the balance of this discussion on estate tax avoidance we will assume that we have a 45% estate tax bracket that will impact every estate over $3 million.

Most of us have witnessed the death of a friend, business associate or celebrity and the impact estate taxes had upon business assets and family members. As we move forward, we assume that this experience removed any doubt regarding the reality and brutality of a tax on cross-generation transfers. The good news, as we are going to discuss, is that much can be done to avoid estate taxes. However, the bad news is that after exploiting all available and compatible avenues to avoid, minimize and defer estate tax, we must find effective methods of paying the ultimate bill assessed by the IRS. We will address the payment of estate taxes because, in most situations, this is a formidable contingency to family business succession. We are not going to try to make you an expert in estate tax, but we are going to try to equip you to effectively participate in this important aspect of succession planning. Your decisions are going to have a profound impact upon your successors.

An important axiom regarding paying estate tax is: do not pay estate tax until you have to.

Cash is just too valuable and every capitalist who is worth his or her salt believes that there may be another gimmick or loophole that will beat the estate tax trap. Our cyclical political environment could miraculously provide a reduction in the tax rate or depending upon your faith, maybe even a repeal. God parted the Red Sea and He could also bring us a genuine tax reform act, not the political placebo that is currently in place. The pragmatically inclined could also pursue a delicate plan to spend down their wealth to zero on the date of death. Or, from the pessimistic side, a business downturn could reduce the value of estate assets after the first death, such that there is less tax at the second death.

In reality, there is solid support to the theory that a tax deferred is a tax that may never be paid. Unfortunately, the higher probability is that the converse will occur. Assets generally grow in value. Over time, bracket creep generally increases the effective tax rate. Even more depressing, transfer loopholes are continually being closed. However, in spite of these hazards and the potential tax savings of estate splitting between spouses to achieve a lower effective tax rate, deferring the payment of taxes as long as possible is the most popular course of action.

The ever-popular theory of tax deferral focuses on the estate tax marital deduction. With respect to the marital deduction, the tax code exempts inter-spousal transfers through gifts or estate transfers. This is a very convenient flow of estate assets to provide for the spouse's security and defer estate taxes. This way, a business owner can leave his estate to his spouse and totally defer payment of estate taxes until the spouse's subsequent death. If each spouse designates the other as beneficiary, taxes will be deferred until the last to die.

The circumstances of the estate and family environment will determine the virtue of estate tax deferral. Continuing in our consideration of estate tax financing, we face the sobering reality that, in the successful family business environment, totally avoiding estate tax is very rare. There are numerous reasons why assets may be exposed to estate tax. The dream of spending the estate below the estate tax threshold may have fallen short. Death may have occurred unexpectedly before tax deferral or avoidance plans could be implemented. The estate may have been too large for a realistic presumption that tax avoidance could be achieved. In most situations, substantial assets are maintained by the senior members of a family owning a business to assure financial independence, lifestyle and security. Estate tax is generally considered to be a reasonable price for financial peace of mind. In almost 30 years of hands-on experience, I have never seen an entrepreneur who has built a valuable family business subordinate to his or her financial independence, personal financial security and lifestyle to estate tax avoidance. Predictably, parents will not dispose of their taxable estate because they have a dominating concern that they could someday, be dependent upon their children. A reasonable conclusion is "why should I put my financial security at risk?" For these reasons, finding a compatible method of paying estate taxes is a critical aspect of succession planning.

There is some good news regarding the payment of estate tax. The IRS will not assume ownership of your business. They have plenty of problems without the headache of owning a business. The bad news is that they will pursue other means of collecting their money that are equally, if not more, distasteful. There is a separate division of the IRS dedicated to estate and gift tax audits. This is a more sophisticated and experienced crew, consisting primarily of attorneys. They have seen all the tricks, so do not expect to pull off any hood-winks. Before signing off on the closure of an estate and allowing the transfer of your business to your successors, the IRS wants its estate tax. The Feds have the power to place estate tax liens on assets prior to distribution to beneficiaries. They have the ability to be forceful in collecting their tax and they only take cash. They are serious about their business.

*In the absence of a good faith attempt to pay the taxes, the IRS
can cause assets with tax liens to be liquidated to generate the
<u>cash to pay taxes.</u>*

The IRS can even lien gifts made prior to death if, after due process, they determine that the gifts violated laws, regulations or judicial precedent. If asset transfers have been completed and, for some bizarre reason, there are insufficient resources in the estate to pay the tax, the IRS can sue the beneficiaries to extract payment.

In almost all circumstances involving closely held businesses or other assets that do not have a readily available valuation, you can count on the G-Men quibbling and arguing on the amount of tax that is due. Their attorneys are already on the payroll and they realize you have to hire an appraiser and an attorney/accountant, just to argue with them. Estate tax collectors are like all business people, they know when they have leverage and they are not reluctant to use it. When they argue, they realize that they must justify their time. They do not visit to make conversation. They attempt to intimidate and push for concessions that generate tax revenue. The estate tax division of the IRS understands that there is a significant commission (estate tax) on every dollar that they can substantiate to be in the decedent's estate. Their job is to collect taxes that make their supervisors happy that ultimately lead to promotions. Succession planning must deal with an aggressive and knowledgeable tax collector and the subsequent payment of estate taxes. Therefore, the obvious question is, How are the taxes paid?

There are three general methods of financing estate taxes: capital, credit and life insurance leverage. There are important nuances to each of these methods that have a significant impact upon the succession process.

Capital Financing of Estate Taxes

There are two general sources of capital for the payment of estate taxes: family capital or third party capital. Family capital is created by accumulating cash or cash equivalents, specifically for the payment of estate taxes. Some feel that capital is the best source of estate taxes. Stashing cash into savings accounts and liquid investments or earmarking hard assets for liquidation can give peace-of-mind that the problem is being addressed. Investment yields in stocks, mutual funds, real estate and business ventures can also provide impressive capital accumulating capability. The assumed advantage of capital is that this is the cheapest and surest method of paying estate tax.

As you might expect, there are also disadvantages in utilizing capital for the payment of estate taxes. The most notable disadvantage is the inclusive feature we discussed under gifting.

> ### *If the accumulated cash is owned or under the control of the decedent, the cash or liquidated asset utilized to pay the tax is also taxed.*

Assuming a 45% estate tax bracket, that means only 55¢ of each dollar accumulated for tax payment will be available for paying tax. In other words, in a 45% estate tax bracket, approximately $1.90 of pretax capital will be needed to generate each net dollar utilized for the payment of estate taxes on keeper assets, such as the family business. In financial planning circles, this exaggerated cost is unaffectionately referred to as "reverse leverage." Another disadvantage is that the estate is discounted by the value of the estate tax. As an example, a taxable estate of $5 million, consisting of $2 million of capital for the payment of estate tax, will be discounted to $3 million after the payment of the tax.

The way to avoid this tax on the tax funding is to shift the accumulated capital to the next generation. If the beneficiaries of the estate own the capital allocated for the payment of estate taxes, then it will not be taxed in their parent's estate. The next generation could then loan the capital to the estate of their parents or buy assets from their parent's estate. Either way, the capital is injected into the estate for the payment of estate taxes. Tax on this capital is avoided and the estate is not discounted. However, transferring significant capital to the next generation for funding estate taxes is problematic. Notably, the gift tax laws limit the amount of cash that can be transferred without taxation. If you are talking about a few hundred thousand dollars, it is possible. If you are talking about several million dollars, you have a formidable challenge on your hands that will require long-term preparation.

Another disadvantage of utilizing capital to pay estate taxes is that investment yields on capital designated for the payment of estate tax are usually lower than what may otherwise be available. As mentioned earlier, the IRS wants only cash in payment for estate tax. Higher yielding assets are usually less liquid or more volatile. Investment planners rarely feel comfortable investing capital earmarked for estate taxes in speculative or non-liquid investments. More volatile investments may at any time be depressed in price, and therefore be unattractive sources for tax cash. Less liquid investments may require extended time to convert into cash. An extended conversion time usually causes higher liquidation costs because interest begins to accrue on unpaid taxes nine months after the date of death. The inevitability of estate tax liens dictates conservatism when establishing a capital reserve for estate tax payment.

> *Therefore, capital earmarked for payment of estate tax is typically parked in lower yielding conservative investments that are readily convertible to cash at a dependable value.*

Third party capital would come from the liquidation of hard assets, including a portion of the business to raise cash for the payment of estate taxes. In the realm of business succession, this is problematic. The most predictable liquid asset is the business itself. Selling a piece of the rock is contradictory to the theme of family business succession. Now we have partners to deal with and we have lost some of our family business aura. However, if there are no other acceptable means of generating the cash to pay the estate tax, maintaining a majority of the business is better than having to sell out completely. Further, unless the sale of an attractive asset and/or an interest in the business is prearranged and documented through appropriate contracts, there is no certainty that a sale will be consummated for the generation of estate tax cash. Consequently, the advanced thinking, expense and administrative complications of tying down the cash would be considered a disadvantage to third party capital. The sale of a minority interest to a key manager or preferred vendor would probably be the simplest transaction. The adoption of an Employee Stock Ownership Plan would be more complex administratively, but the family could maintain control over the stock as trustees of the plan. If circumstances permitted, an IPO would reflect the ultimate advanced thinking, administration and expense of raising third party capital for the payment of estate taxes.

Debt Financing of Estate Taxes

A second method of utilizing capital for the payment of estate taxes is debt. Utilizing debt to pay estate tax involves pledging assets for the satisfaction of the taxes and the subsequent reliance upon the cash flow generated by the management or liquidation of assets for the repayment of debt. The advantage of utilizing debt for the payment of estate tax is the avoidance of estate tax on the capital utilized to pay the tax. In essence, the use of debt means that the future capital generated by the business is pledged to the cost of transferring the business to the next generation. Depending upon the circumstances, debt can be even more complicated than accumulating cash or liquidating assets. The complexity is due to the inherent implications of being a borrower and the impact debt can have on the succession of a family owned business. Depending upon circumstances, the interest cost and repayment of principle can be a grievous burden to the business. This burden can put the continuity of the business in jeopardy.

The biggest concern about the use of debt for the payment of estate taxes is that there is no certainty that credit for estate tax payment will be available or that the terms of the credit will be acceptable. There are two sources of potential estate tax credit, commercial credit and statutory credit. Commercial lending is a subjective consideration influenced by the attitude of bankers, economic conditions and political circumstances. Invariably, the greater the need for a credit, the more difficult it is to obtain a commercial loan, the higher the cost and the less reliable the renewal. Under the assumption that estate tax is inevitable, availability, affordability and reliability of credit are challenging contingencies to closing an estate. Those of us who have borrowed money understand that credit extended today can be withdrawn tomorrow

Securing a commercial loan to pay estate tax is substantially different from borrowing money for business endeavors such as capital improvements, expansion and operating acquisitions. Each of these forms of borrowing directly or indirectly anticipates underwriting the loan with the cash flow on the borrowed funds that are invested. In contrast, when money is borrowed for payment of estate taxes, the money goes to Washington and not in an investment that will secure the loan and generate cash flow. I have heard parents on far too many occasions express the assumption that their children can borrow the money for estate taxes and repay the loan with sweat and grit. Parents typically reconcile this assumption based upon the conclusion that repaying a debt for estate taxes is cheaper than starting a business from scratch. My common response is that it is unrealistic to commit their children to a course of action that makes them dependent upon a banker. Under most circumstances, it is a formidable challenge for a successor just to carry on a business after the loss of the founder and maintain profitability. A change in leadership caused by a death, creates transition inefficiencies that are costly.

Taking on significant new debt for the payment of estate taxes can create a grievous burden for successors who typically have limited solo experience running a business or satisfying demanding lenders who know they had high ground.

Before you conclude that estate taxes are your children's problem, consider the full implications of this thinking on your succession goals. As a practical matter, parents who are genuinely interested in succession should project a consistent philosophy about borrowing money. In other words, parents should only recommend to their children what they have practiced. Most business owners are conservative and avoid debt whenever possible. They may have borrowed initially, but they remember the burden of the debt and they do what ever is possible to be lenders, not borrowers. They understand the economy is fickle and they do not trust bankers. They do not borrow money unless they have to, and then repay loans as quickly as possible. If this reasonably defines your feelings, do not be so cavalier as to suggest that your children incur debt that you would personally deem unacceptable.

At the minimum, help your children develop an estate tax financing plan that will give you and your family peace of mind that their future career in the business is not at risk to the whims of bankers on the restrictions of the IRS.

If it is your goal that the business succeeds beyond your lifetime, then assume the responsibility of providing reasonable means for your children and/or key personnel to bear the tax <u>expense of succession.</u>

Parents should not realistically expect their children to support the full financial burden of succession goals from future business profitability.

Commercial credit is dependent upon the circumstances of each situation and the attitude of the bankers. In order to recommend a loan, the banker must feel positive about both the business and the successor ability to repay the loan within a reasonable timeframe. On the other hand, the hardship installment payment provisions are a guaranteed source of estate tax credit if certain prerequisites are met. As long as the government feels obliged to seize a portion of a decedent's estate, we presume they are going to have the decency to provide a statutory credit line for the payment of the tax.

The banking crisis of the late 1980's and early 1990's should generate caution about making broad assumptions regarding the availability of long-term commercial credit. To say that bankers are cautious may be an understatement. Regardless of your banker's familiarity, compassion and motivation to help with the dilemma of estate taxes, the bank is no longer in a position to play good guy and bail you or your children out of a debt crisis. Because of very tight FDIC and state regulations, bankers are now essentially asset lenders who only lend on assets that will unquestionably cover their risks after the smoke has cleared and the debris has settled from financial calamity. Do not expect your bank or your friendly bankers to go out on a limb based upon character or longstanding relationships. That is just no longer the nature of banking.

> *In the event of the death of a business operator, the business operator successor will have to work hard just to extend and maintain existing business credit.*

Expanding credit will predictably be a formidable challenge.

When utilizing commercial credit for the payment of estate taxes, bear in mind these thoughts. Paying estate taxes is not a customary reason for a business to borrow money. Regardless of the profitability of your business and the credibility of children, bankers will look at an estate tax loan with skepticism. The successors will be the ones borrowing the money. The probability of a loan will be no better than the next generation's bankability. If successors are going to borrow, they must build banking relationships. If the successors have spent all their time on the loading dock, do not expect bankers to be impressed.

Not only do the successors need to know the bankers, the successors also need to have experience dealing with bankers. Lenders will try to intimidate the naive and inexperienced to achieve the highest markup possible on their product. If the successors do not understand the game, they will make silly, costly mistakes.

If lending is critical to your business, as in many contemporary businesses, successors must learn the banking game as a fundamental aspect of the business, and realize that an estate tax loan will impact business operations.

The successors need advisors who can help them deal with bankers and make up for shortcomings in relationships and experience.

The bankability of the business is also important. If successors will pursue debt to pay estate taxes, current operations, cash reserves and borrowing policies should reflect the possibility that if one, or, at the most, two tender hearts stop ticking, substantial increases in debt will be required. Try maintaining high quality, unencumbered real assets for guaranteeing debt. And foremost, never forget the proverb, "Just as the rich rule the poor, the borrower is servant to the lender." The lending institution that steps forward to rescue your business from IRS liens will surely recognize the importance of its role and throw its weight around. Depending upon the level of need, a lender could disrupt the operating strategy of the family business. Enhance your family's leverage by maintaining a solid balance sheet and several optional lines of credit.

The second source of credit for the payment of estate taxes comes from the federal government. To your good fortune, the IRS developed an installment tax payment program for business owners with substantial non-liquid capital invested in their business. Provisions are in place, to some extent, in the event your successors are disappointed by commercial lenders. The bad news is that estate tax is a socio-political issue that is subject to change with the ebb and flow of the political environment. You would be wise not to become overwhelmed with optimism that the IRS is going to be your friend for the purpose of coming up with the cash to pay the estate tax on the family business. The potential benefit of government credit for the payment of estate tax occurred as an afterthought. When the estate tax code was adopted, Congress did not contemplate the disastrous impact an estate tax would have on the bedrock of our economy, the closely held, non-liquid, family business. They learned quickly that forcing a family to sell a business for the payment of estate tax was very poor publicity. A groundswell of opposition to the estate tax emerged from the politically powerful, tax-paying business community that threatened the lucrative source of additional tax revenue. As a result, in an effort to relieve the potential estate tax liquidity crunch on the family business community, Congress adopted Sections 6161, 6163 and 6166 of the Internal Revenue Code.

As the years passed and inflation highlighted the unfair punitive nature of estate tax, Congress realized that these provisions needed further liberalization. Faced with a continuing buildup of opposition to the concept of estate tax and in fear of losing billions of dollars per year in revenue, Congress again enhanced these provisions under the Taxpayer Relief Act in 1997.

Sections 6166, 6161 and 6163 of the Internal Revenue Code are sometimes referred to as the hardship section of the estate tax code. The sections provide for the payment of estate taxes over an extended period at favorable interest rates. Within this section of the code, the IRS has recognized the obvious. An estate tax levied on a business or other non-liquid assets creates a hardship that threatens the viability of the business and the jobs, productivity and future income taxes created by the business.

The IRC Section 6166 estate tax hardship provisions apply only to estates owning closely-held businesses that meet specific qualifications, which require the guidance of technically competent advisors. As an example, in order to qualify for the installment payment of estate tax, the family business and qualifying business use property, must constitute at least 35% of the adjusted gross estate. Over my career as a succession planner I have seen crazy things happen. On more than one occasions I have seen desperate executors of unprepared estates inflate the value of the business just to satisfy this "35% of gross estate" requirement. You guessed it, the inflation of the business value also dramatically increased the estate tax due.

Also it is very important that you do not misunderstand the application of the installment payment provision.

The installment payment option only applies to the tax assessed on the value of the closely-held business in the estate. The tax on non-business assets such as homes, portfolios, retirement plans, etc. does not qualify for installment payments. Tax is due on these assets nine months from the date of death.

Assuming the 35% test and other tests that may apply are met, IRC Section 6166 allows an estate to pay interest only for five years on the estate tax due on the business. On the fifth anniversary of the estate tax return, the first installment of the estate tax must be paid, plus interest on the unpaid balance. Then, over the following nine years, the total tax must be amortized. There are no provisions if a payment cannot be paid. The presumption is that the unpaid balance is due or that representatives of the estate would explain their circumstances to the IRS and reasonable arrangements for payment would be achieved. Hopefully none of you are depending upon the reasonableness of the IRS in your succession plans.

The interest rate on the tax due is one of the most misunderstood aspects of this section of the tax code. The interest rate on the tax of the first $1 million of taxable assets, $345,000, is 2%. The $1 million taxable amount that is eligible for the 2% interest rate was indexed for inflation beginning in 1997. The balance of the outstanding tax accrues interest at 45% of the floating interest rate that the IRS assesses on any underpayment of taxes. Section 6166 interest (45% of the underpayment rate) appears to be quite favorable. However, Section 6166 interest is not tax deductible for either income or estate tax purposes. Depending upon the income created in the estate, the taxes on the interest can offset most of the benefit of the reduced interest rate.

With respect to non-business assets, Sections 6161 and 6163 give the IRS the option -- but by no means the requirement -- to provide an estate the opportunity to defer payment of estate tax on the non-trade or business assets for up to 10 years. In order to achieve this deferral, the IRS requires the executor to show "reasonable cause" that immediate payment of estate tax would create a hardship on the estate. With approval of a reasonable cause request, such as the inability to liquidate an asset that dominates the estate, taxes can potentially be deferred; but annual interest is due based upon 100% of the underpayment of tax rate. A tax lien would be placed on the property and the IRS would have first call for lien satisfaction on cash created by sale distribution. Needless to say, there is no prepayment penalty on the estate tax.

There is no doubt that 6166 represents an attractive estate tax financing option. However, as one would expect, there are some negatives. The federal government wants the tax, not a 15-year lending relationship. While credit is extended, Uncle Sam remains nervously at risk, and appropriately acts the part. If the tax causes the business to fail, Uncle Sam could lose his prospective tax. Consequently, the IRS can rain on the parade of succession by preempting business decisions that the IRS believes may jeopardize or even delay collecting its estate tax. In other words, they can make your heirs patch a hole in the roof of the business in lieu of replacing a sieve that perennially costs big bucks.

In an extreme case, the IRS can even force liquidation of assets, including a business, to produce the cash for the payment of estate tax.

As an example, the IRS may overrule additional business borrowing or capital expenditure, business expansion or acquisitions. The IRS takes its role as a creditor very seriously. Unfortunately, the IRS is not as experienced, polished or patient as most commercial banks.

For insight into the intent of the IRS, let's reflect on the language of Revenue Ruling 75-365, which states that Section 6166 "was not intended to protect continued management finance, income producing properties or to permit deferral of the tax merely because payment of the tax might make necessary the sale of income producing assets, except where they formed a part of an active enterprise producing income rather than income solely from the ownership of property." In light of this supporting rhetoric, it is reasonable to state that loose assumptions about utilizing Section 6166 for deferral of estate taxes could be met with disappointment.

Unfortunately, too many business owners do not understand the implications of utilizing Section 6166 as an estate tax financing tool. The less attentive will hear 15 years and 2% over a gin rummy game at the club and, without an appropriate investigation, conclude this will be their family's salvation from an impending liquidity crisis.

To all the naive or uneducated (prior to reading this book), make note of this profound truth: Borrowing money from the federal government is serious business.

Extensions of time to pay estate tax can be a mixed blessing. The IRS is not out to enhance its public image or win market share. The IRS simply wants your money. When the IRS is a creditor, a family will need its attorney and accountant to answer telephone calls, respond to letters and fill out reports. In most cases with outstanding unpaid estate taxes, the estate of the decedent remains open. An attorney and accountant are needed to deal with the IRS and the probate court. It is imperative that you ask your attorney and accountant about the implications of utilizing IRC 6166 before making a commitment to this form of estate tax financing.

Case History: The Construction Family

Several years ago I was referred to a prospect who, with his daughter and two sons, owned a very profitable single family home construction company. Within their family business, they owned several very valuable, large tracts of land that were in various stages of development. The father was 72 and in poor health. His wife was deceased, and he owned about 60% of the company valued in excess of $15 million. The daughter and sons owned the remaining 40%, having received a portion of the business from their mother's estate as well as a unified credit gift of stock from their dad. With little or no other asset transfer options, we were faced with the question of how dad's estate taxes would be paid.

After evaluating the situation, I recommended that the family begin raising cash to deal with this inevitable estate tax problem. The market in 1987 was great for single family homes. Neither dad nor his kids could justify retaining profits for future estate taxes. All I heard was, "Buy more land. We need more inventory." They called me "DD" as in "double dumb" for suggesting that they sell one of their prime tracts to build up cash reserves. Their reply to my advice was, "Get us life insurance or we will use 6166."

There was no way I could get any significant life insurance on Dad. He had been run hard and put up wet. As an alcoholic diabetic with two bypass surgeries under his belt, he was only insurable through "Eternal Life." Section 6166 was their fallback solution. Recognizing the potential problems of this option, I solicited the assistance of the attorney and accountant to help highlight the problems that might develop. I even asked the family banker to come to a meeting and explain how he would react as the primary business creditor if the IRS put a lien on the business for the projected $5 million tax. I will never forget the banker's response and, certainly, neither will the children. "Not to worry," he said as nonchalantly as Crocodile Dundee. "If the IRS becomes a pest, we will take them out. You are a preferred customer. You have a great business here. We've got money to lend. We need loans and Uncle Sam needs their taxes. This is a perfect situation for our team."

The following year Dad's body threw in the towel. All was well and smooth through the filing of the estate tax return in 1988 and even the audit in 1990. Dad's total state and federal tax, after extended arguments for valuation discounts, was approximately $4.3 million. With the filing of the estate tax, the children utilized $1.5 million of cash on hand to pay tax on the non-business assets and elected Section 6166 to defer payment of the $2.8 million balance. The son and daughter called their friendly banker and, quick as a snap, borrowed operating funds to replace the $1.5 million cash outlay for the initial tax payment. The legal and accounting administrative fees were significant, but the children counted these as a bargain compared to losing the business.

In late 1989 and early 1990, the real estate business really slowed down. In response, the children quickly made the necessary adjustment to overhead. Although their profitability dropped, they continued to make enough money to service the interest to the bank and to the IRS. They were hanging tough, anticipating that the market would change.

One memorable morning, the banker came calling. The bank had acquired substantial real estate through foreclosure and was on the "FDIC Watch List." The banker was now singing a different tune about lending and preferred customers. His supervisors realized that the five-year interest-only period of Section 6166 was coming to a close, and they were concerned that my client would not have the profitability to make an installment on the tax bill. Although the bank's existing liens would be superior to a tax lien, the frustrated banker stated that management had no stomach for even the possibility of more foreclosure proceedings. His simple statement was, "Much to my disappointment and because of corporate reasons beyond my control, we will not be renewing your credit line."

My clients were shocked beyond words. They quickly realized that they did not have time to be emotional, and immediately hit the streets looking for new lenders. The responses they received were unanimous, "We are not interested in a lending position subordinate to the IRS."

Unable to secure a replacement lender, my clients experienced the double jeopardy of being unwelcome bedfellows with both a bank and the IRS.

With no substitute lender, they negotiated a continuance with the current lender on the condition that the properties would be placed on the market and sold as soon as possible to satisfy debt.

Under intense pressure from the banks, the premium properties were sold first at heavy discounts. As the proceeds from each property were generated, the bank grabbed the funds to satisfy their liens. The loss of these prime properties quickly reduced business profitability. Tension mounted over pressure to sell at depressed prices, with the bank ultimately electing to foreclose. My clients hired a covey of attorneys and sued the bank. The legal fees began to further burden the business.

The end result was nothing to look upon with a full stomach. My clients were able to scrape together the cash to pay off $2 million of the estate taxes. However, as the pressure began to mount on son and daughter, they began to point at each other to reconcile how they got in this predicament. As harmony deteriorated, so did profits; and they found themselves unable to make interest payments on the outstanding $800,000 of tax owed. The IRS moved to enforce the tax liens and the business disintegrated like a satellite reentering the atmosphere.

After the IRS was paid off, the bank continued action to recover their loan. Unfortunately, there were not sufficient assets. The RTC had taken over the bank and, as expected, they pursued personal judgments against each of the family members. Most tragically, the pressure and stress of these circumstances caused the children to walk away hating each other. To this day, they do not speak to each other.

In the wake of this horror story, take heed to these recommendations. The IRC 6166 option for financing estate taxes can be an attractive method of financing estate taxes, but it can also come with problems. There is negative baggage to any course of action that involves either debt or the government. The combination of debt and government is very unpredictable. A plan for the succession of a family business should not include servitude to the IRS. If there are no other options than borrowing from the government, relentlessly pursue options to pay them off, or at least be in a position to do so if circumstances deteriorate.

Life Insurance for Estate Tax Financing

The third method of financing estate taxes is life insurance. As discussed in the previous chapter, life insurance provides cash upon the death of an insured as a product of the cooperative sharing of risk by a pool of parties having similar need. The segregation of reserves, investment returns on the premiums, accurate projections of mortality, predictable forfeitures from policy lapses and efficient administration provide the financial resources to provide cash death benefits to those participating in the insurance pool.

The pooling and sharing of risks through a life insurance contract provides a structure for establishing a tax-efficient, pre-death reserve for funding a post-death liquidity need, such as estate tax.

The basic requirements for life insurance are reasonable health, defined as insurability, and a cash premium to fund the reserve. Do not confuse reasonable health with good health, because individuals with impaired health can also get insurance. The cost is simply higher, relative to the risk of the health impairment. The simple purpose of life insurance is leveraged cash, either for payment in the event of a death or for the assurance that the cash would be paid if death occurred. Financing estate taxes with life insurance is attractive, because cash will solve almost all problems created by estate taxes. Life insurance is an attractive estate tax financing tool to individuals and families who place high value upon the removal of the uncertainties regarding the source of cash to pay estate taxes. As we have reviewed, these uncertainties include:

- Accumulating sufficient cash

- Liquidating assets

- Securing credit

- Maintaining credit

- Maintaining business profitability

- Maintaining family harmony

Business owners buy life insurance for estate tax because of the peace of mind they receive with the elimination of estate tax uncertainties from business operations and their children's future.

Life insurance is an attractive estate tax financing investment for a variety of reasons. At the top of the list is the fundamental feature of providing the needed cash upon a death that will cause significant estate taxation. Life insurance avoids the complexity of managing cash reserves earmarked for the payment of estate taxes. With the peace of mind that life insurance is covering cash needs upon death, mental energies can be spent upon the needs of living and capital can be spent for never-ending business needs.

Life insurance premiums are also relatively affordable in relation to the potentially devastating lump sum cost of estate tax that will be due upon death. The relatively affordable premiums that provide a disciplined method of funding the death benefit reserve accommodate a multitude of concerns from avoiding gift taxes to satisfying corporate budgets. Life insurance premiums can be flexible and therein adapted to varying cash flow availability. The premiums can be amortized over a specific term of years or over the life of the insured. Because of the relatively affordable annual premium in relationship to death benefits, ownership can be shifted to children or trusts to avoid estate taxation on the life insurance benefits.

A unique feature of life insurance is that death benefits are payable to a stipulated beneficiary. The beneficiary payout provision allows death benefits to be efficiently directed to the desired party(ies) independent of the complications of a probate estate. No one knows what the future holds, but history says we can count on death, taxes and life insurance death benefits. Unfortunately, life insurance does not share the certainty of death or taxes, but it does provide cash about as predictably as any investment vehicle available.

The use of life insurance as an attractive estate tax financing tool presumes that the anticipated cash will arrive at the time of need free of estate taxes. Do not assume that a life insurance policy is naturally free of estate taxes. The source of confusion is that life insurance death benefits are free of income tax. However, an insurance policy from a general perspective is a financial instrument, such as a stock or bond. However, unlike most other financial instruments, a life insurance policy requires premiums and has both an owner and a beneficiary.

From an estate tax perspective, the IRS is not particularly concerned about the beneficiary. They assess estate tax based upon who owns the policy.

History shows that these multiple features make life insurance a magnet for confusion and complicating circumstances, such as an outdated beneficiary, gift taxes and estate taxes. To successfully utilize life insurance as an estate tax financing tool, you must methodically address the details of ownership premium payment, beneficiary and taxation. Incorrect assumptions in any one of these areas can disrupt the utility of life insurance as an estate tax financing tool. You should retain competent advisors to give you assurance (backed up by Errors and Omissions Insurance) that the structure of the death benefits will accomplish your intended estate tax financing objectives.

The cost analysis of life insurance should reflect a reasonable return on the reserve (premium payments) and provide less future stress on the business and family. This assumption is supported by the historical performance of quality life insurance companies that confirm the payment of death benefits when called upon. Historical performance also confirms that death benefits represent a fair return in exchange for the premiums paid. Permanent life insurance as an estate tax financing tool for an individual who is in good health represents a pre-death installment method of funding the tax with reasonable assurance that the cumulative premiums will not exceed 40% of the ultimate tax bill.

I constantly hear from clients and prospects that, "Life insurance is a terrible investment." My response is always, "As compared to what?" My clients are business owners with aggressive personalities, so they typically lean forward, point a finger at me and say, "Listen, I know if I invested my money in my business instead of some greedy life insurance company, I could earn 15%, 20% or even 30% on my money." At this point I usually bring my hands together to signify a time-out and acknowledge that life insurance, as a classic investment, does not compare favorably with rein- vestment into the business or even other highly touted investments in stocks, bonds, mutual funds, or real estate. I also point out that under some circumstances (early death) reinvestment into the business, stocks, bonds, etc. do not compare favorably with life insurance.

However, if life insurance is compared to long-term very conservative investments that could predictably produce cash at any given time, such as a Treasury Bill, then the comparison is more favorable.

From a pure investment perspective, some life policies have self directed investment accounts that can be positioned in almost any form of investment available on the market. However, regardless of whether policy cash values are invested in the conservative general account of the insur- ance company or directed by the policy owner into an exotic portfolio mix, the life insurance mortality charges handicap the capital accumula- tion ability of a life insurance policy as compared to a classic investment, such as a mutual fund. However, the perceived investment handicap of the mortality charges is the resounding asset of an insurance policy that gen- erates tax-free death benefit. The fact is that life insurance is a unique financial instrument that cannot be compared in every aspect with any other investment.

If death of the insured occurs 15 minutes or 50 years after the policy is put in force, the death benefit will be paid and the investment return will be, at worst, good and, at best, phenomenal.

The potential leverage of premiums and the predictability of death benefits puts life insurance in a class of its own. Anyone seeking high return should not be considering a life insurance policy. By the same token anyone seeking assurance of tax-free cash upon the death of an individual should. If you are considering methods of building capital that do not carry a death contingency, pursue the classic investments of CDs, stocks, bonds, or real estate. If you are considering methods of building capital to fund a need for cash upon a death, consider life insurance. The clear demarcation is the death contingency. Do not assume that stocks, bonds or other investments are directly comparable for both lifetime and death considerations. This is an apples and oranges issue. Compared to a long-term high quality bond, a treasury bill, or a deferred annuity, investment in a life insurance death benefit will compare favorably. My dad's logic applies here: "anyone who does not believe in life insurance deserves to die without any."

Regardless of how ideal the circumstances to justify life insurance, if the prospective buyer has a hangup about death or a prejudice against life insurance companies, the purchase of a policy is inappropriate. While not facing the financial burdens of an imminent death, it is easy to take exception to the investment caliber of life insurance.

Acknowledging that hindsight is always 20-20, I have never experienced a recipient of a life insurance death benefit who did not feel that life insurance had been a good investment.

To evaluate your circumstances, address these questions:

- Will cash be needed upon or after the death?

- Is the need for cash at the time of death critical to anyone's security or to the continuity of the business?

- Does the projected estate tax exceed the cash on hand or cash that you are certain to accumulate?

- Is it important that the liquidity utilized to pay the estate tax is protected from estate tax?

- Is there a likelihood that there will be an important purpose for accumulated cash besides the payment of estate tax?

- Is there a need to efficiently direct estate tax liquidity to a particular person or entity?

- Are you too busy or unqualified to manage asset accumulation and a secure, high yield investment management program?

If you answered yes to three or more questions, you are a candidate for life insurance as an estate tax financing tool. If you answered yes to all of them, life insurance is the only complete solution to your need.

Life insurance is a long-term investment that requires understanding and experience. There are numerous forms of insurance that have optimum application to unique circumstances. Contemporary insurance is a byproduct of the computer and the evaluation and comparison of competitive polices is at best complex. Life insurance medical underwriting is very competitive and outstanding results can be achieved if addressed properly. However, getting the lowest price for a given set of medical circumstances is a tricky process. And estate taxation is a high stakes arena that draws the close attention of the IRS because of the potentially lucrative windfall tax revenue generated by a 45% estate tax on life insurance death benefits. No doubt you could become an insurance expert, but during that period of learning and experience, your business would probably fall on itself.

The best course is to deal with a professional insurance broker who has the advanced technical credentials (CLU, ChFC, MSFS, CFP) to work responsibly in the estate tax financing arena. This life insurance professional should have the ability to represent a group of insurance companies who will compete for your business. He should have references from technically demanding planning environments similar to yours. These references should speak to the life insurance professional's experience in estate tax financing, ongoing willingness to provide service and character. It is imperative that you get professional assistance that you trust.

Your attorney and accountant should also be involved in your consideration to purchase an insurance policy. If your attorney is not competent in estate tax matters, get one that is.

Do not make any decision, sign anything or pay any premiums until at least two of your advisors agree that you are doing the <u>*right thing.*</u>

A seemingly minor technicality can have devastating tax implications. With this in mind, be cautious of close relationships between your attorney or accountant and the insurance professional. Also, you should be cautious of dealing with your accountant or attorney as your insurance representative without other independent, knowledgeable professionals holding them accountable. With the blending of professions, attorneys and accountants who sell products are becoming more common. Allowing your attorney or accountant to sell insurance could be like asking the cat to watch the canary.

Always retain a copy of the "as purchased" illustration for future comparison to the actual performance of the policy. Keep all the supporting footnotes and marketing materials. In 10 or 15 years, they may be a valuable reference when you are trying to evaluate how the policy is performing. This illustration can also be very helpful to your survivors. It is not unusual for the insured or the policy owners to be unable to obtain critically needed information from their selling agent for any number of reasons, including death, retirement, etc.

Making a buying decision should be an analytical process, not a process based upon emotions or relationships. Do not buy life insurance because you are so pleased that some company will offer you a policy The hard, cold fact is that some companies are more optimistic than others.

Life insurance is a conservative investment that should always be based upon realistic long-range premium and dividend and/or interest rate assumptions.

The structure of the insurance policy and the quality of the insurance company should be dominating factors in your buying consideration. The financial statement analysis is complex for the average insurance buyer. However, the financial nature of the company can be revealed through the ratings by the various independent organizations that evaluate life insurance companies, such as Moody's, A.M. Best, Duff and Phelps.

Also, regardless of how "bulletproof" an insurance company may appear, prudently consider diversification of your insurance investment between two or more carriers. The past turmoil in the banking and insurance industry only confirms that it can happen again. Furthermore, the deregulation of the financial sector that allowed banks, insurance companies and brokerage houses to merge only makes each financial sector more vulnerable. Insist upon diversification in life insurance just as you would with a stock portfolio. Writing two, three or even four premium checks per year is a small administrative effort in relation to the peace of mind that diversification can give.

The business owner has a variety of sources for premium payment. In order for death benefits to be free of estate tax, children or partners must be the policy owners and pay the premium. A complex ongoing issue is, "Where will children get the cash for payment of premiums?" The big death benefits required to finance estate taxes in the family business environment usually require large premiums. The source of premiums is a very important topic to life insurance planning, because annual tax-exempt gift limitations may exceed the annual premium.

I generally suggest that children use some of their money to pay premiums. They should have a vested interest in the succession of the business and there is nothing that will create interest faster than for them to invest some of their hard-earned money. The prospect of a little current sacrifice to achieve succession may generate reactions that give valuable insight into motivation and sincerity.

Unfortunately, in the real world of capital-intensive family business, children can rarely independently afford sufficient premiums to fund estate tax on the remaining business stock in their parent's estate. The simplest approach is to gift the premium.

The leverage of life insurance is a very worthy use of the annual tax-exempt gifting capability, or, when necessary, strategic <u>unified credit gifts.</u>

Insurance bonuses are also a simple method of providing children and in-laws income for paying insurance premiums.

I believe the income from previously gifted assets, such as subchapter-S stock or real estate, is the best source of cash flow for estate tax financing life insurance premiums. Not only is the gifted asset out of the estate, the income from that asset protects other assets through life insurance funding. The corporate business entity can also provide interest free loans for premium payment through a tried and proven technique known as "split dollar." This technique is a well-proven method of utilizing corporate, partnership or even parental dollars for the payment of premiums on insurance policies owned by children, partners or an irrevocable life insurance trust. However, split dollar premium funding, as we might expect, also brings along technical compliance issues that require supervision by your insurance representative, accountant and attorney. And finally, there are the premium-paying gimmicks devised by insurance salesmen that purportedly provide income tax-free sources of premiums. Be careful! When investing in conservative life insurance to provide critically needed death benefits, do not use an unproven income tax scheme that can put your succession program in jeopardy.

Effective estate tax financing with life insurance requires specific attention to how policies are owned. The ownership of the policy determines whether the death benefit is subject to estate tax. The IRS recognizes that its prospective 45% share (estate tax) of life insurance death benefits is dependent upon issues surrounding policy ownership, so it has developed a litany of regulations to determine who is the substantive owner of the policy. The concept is "substance over form." In operation this means that, regardless of the form of ownership, numerous other factors of substance, such as policy control and the source of premiums, will determine if the life insurance death benefits will be taxed in the insured's estate.

There are a few basic rules that should be kept in mind when considering life insurance ownership and estate taxation.

In order to protect the death benefits of current policies, the ownership of the policies must be transferred to the next generation.

Due to the obvious loss of estate tax revenue, the IRS requires a three year "in contemplation of death" waiting period before gifted insurance policies are exempt from estate taxes. To avoid this potentially costly administrative detail, children should be the original owners/applicants of future policies. If policies are owned in irrevocable life insurance trusts, in order for the gifted premium to be exempt of estate tax, the beneficiaries must be notified of the transfer of cash to the trust (Crummy Notices) and given an opportunity to withdraw the cash for a reasonable period of time, such as 30 days.

In order to avoid gift tax and even estate tax challenges with the IRS, a record must be kept of these gifts and the children's withdrawal waivers.

The final important consideration is the impact of these death benefits upon estate administration. It is important that life insurance solves problems and does not create problems, such as disproportionate or unfair estate asset distribution. Life insurance owned outside of an estate cannot be utilized to directly pay an insured's estate tax because, according to IRS regulations, any cash used to directly pay the tax of a decedent is subject to tax in the decedent's estate.

The most technically effective estate tax financing with life insurance occurs when the policy owner, (children or irrevocable trust) purchases assets from the estate.

The net result of this transaction is that the estate obtains tax-free liquidity for payment of estate tax and the policy owner obtains estate assets free of estate tax. Notably, the ownership and beneficiary designation of the life insurance creates substantial assets in the name of the policy owners. If the estate is not being divided equally among all beneficiaries, the ownership of the estate tax financing life insurance should follow the intended estate division. Otherwise, the life insurance will have a significant impact upon the ultimate division of assets among the intended estate beneficiaries.

Example

Let's assume that parents had made gifts of more than $1 million of family business stock to their son during their lifetime. The balance of assets that they were relying upon for security was their home, retirement accounts and investment accounts. They did not feel comfortable gifting these assets to the daughter to achieve parity. Therefore, in order to achieve equality for their daughter, the parents decided to distribute 75% of their remaining $4.8 million in estate assets to their daughter, and 25% to their son. To finance the estate taxes, these parents adopted an irrevocable life insurance trust holding a $2 million policy, with the son and daughter as equal beneficiaries. As you might imagine, the outcome of this uncoordinated estate tax funding is that "the son gets the mine and the daughter gets the shaft." The $2 million of estate tax on the $4.8 million in taxable assets would create a residual net estate of $2.8 million. The daughter would get 75% of the $2.8 million net estate, equaling $2.1 million, plus 50% of $2 million, equaling $1 million. The $3.1 million total would represent only 65% of the gross $4.8 million estate, not 75% as her parents intended. The $500,000 distortion of intended estate division was caused by the lack of coordination between the estate tax financing life insurance and the plan for estate asset division.

Coordination of estate tax structures (life insurance) with estate distribution intentions is very important. You should request assurance from your financial planner, attorney and/or accountant that the ownership and beneficiaries of estate tax financing life insurance is compatible with your overall asset distribution goals. Prudence dictates that you also realize that, because estate tax financing life insurance is usually held in irrevocable life insurance trusts (you cannot change ownership after adoption) changing how you want to divide your estate after the irrevocable trust has been funded, can be problematic. Changes can be made in how you divide your assets, but you cannot change the ownership structure of the irrevocable trust. Further, predicable changes in the value of your estate will increase or decrease estate taxes, which, in turn, can dramatically impact the equitable division of your estate. These points are not made to frustrate your planning enthusiasm, but to encourage you to make every effort to understand the impact that estate tax financing life insurance has on your estate allocation and to illustrate the importance of good advisors and regular review.

In summary, anyone who is not living in a dream world and can do simple math should understand that estate tax financing is and will continue to be a critical factor in the succession of the closely-held, family business.

Grand dreams of succession can quickly fade to calamity if provisions have not been made to liberate the business from the inevitable draconian bite of estate taxes.

Realistic forethought is needed to acknowledge, avoid, minimize and defer the impending expense of estate taxes. Decisiveness is needed to determine the best way to address the capability of estate taxes to suck the blood out of your dream for family business succession.

Management Issues

𝒯wo stonecutters were asked what they were doing. The first said, "I'm cutting this stone into blocks." The second replied, "I'm on a team that's building a cathedral."

~ Anonymous ~

Succession Success

Success is a fundamental prerequisite to succession. The fruits of business success cover a broad spectrum ranging from joy and happiness to personal chaos and family disaster. As the assumed cure to all ills, the subject of business success dominates both business and social conversation. Based upon the universal popularity of success, one would think that it could be clearly defined and easily achieved. However, this is not the case. A precise definition of business success is difficult because of the variety of perspectives.

To be sure, success is not guaranteed by simply making lots of money, as I have personally witnessed highly profitable businesses crumble. I have also encountered many business owners who annually struggle to achieve profitability, but are, in the total perspective, fabulously successful.

Success is generally defined as the progressive growth of a business toward the achievement of well thought-out, stated objectives.

The degree and form of this process is the foundation for determining business value, whether the business should be sold for top dollar, sold to avoid failure or continued as a family asset.

Perceived business value creates the motivation for business owners and their successors to seek succession of their business. Successful businesses are generally described as financially profitable, satisfying customer and vendor needs, serving the community, satisfying employees' needs and satisfying owner needs.

From the most common perspective, success must create sufficient financial resources to adequately address these issues and others.

So why all this theoretical mumbo-jumbo about success? If you do not have sufficient strength and momentum, you are no more a candidate for succession than a couch potato is a candidate for running a marathon.

If there is no reasonable expectation that the business will continue to be strong and viable into the extended future, succession planning is at best, academic folly and at worst, a <u>waste of time, money and emotional energy.</u>

No doubt, business success supports and/or determines business disposition options and more specifically, business succession opportunities. It would be imprudent for you to consider many of the succession concepts that will be discussed in later chapters, unless you grasp those concepts that are, for the most part, dependent upon a form of success. There are no second places in the succession challenge. This is a potentially cruel test -- you either make it or you don't.

A fundamental goal of succession planning is to provide for the continuation of a valuable enterprise because it characterizes one or more attractive attributes of success. These attributes would obviously include profitability, cash flow, financial security, recognition, community respect, political power, perpetuation of family position and industry interaction.

The achievement and realization of these elements are what motivate most of us to pay the day-to-day price for independence in an ever-challenging business environment. The perpetuation or harvesting of any one or more attributes of success is what motivates business owners to spend the time, money and energy on succession planning. In most instances, succession planning is directly dependent upon the implications of business success.

Succession planning addresses a disposition decision that establishes the ultimate fate of the business: close out or succession. Closeout, as the name implies, involves the sale or liquidation of the business. Business close out is accomplished by selling the assets of the business to the highest bidder or by selling the operations for absorption into a totally new ownership culture. The motives for business closeout cover a broad spectrum. There may be offers that cannot be refused or owners may no longer be able to handle the everyday pressures. Common to all business closeouts is a lack of motivation to improve the levels of business success because of a a lack of confidence that the success can be sustained and continued.

The other disposition alternative is succession, which involves the continuation of the existing culture of a business enterprise. There are several succession alternatives that address who will continue the business -- independent buyers or existing partners, key personnel and/or family. For purposes of this book, we will consider family business succession as continuation involving partners, key personnel, family members and/or a combination thereof. Common to all realistic business succession endeavors is a motivation to continue the business success as a family asset and the confidence that the success can be continued.

There is a difference between a successful business and a "golden goose." A successful business is generally considered to be one that generates attractive, even coveted, profits for the owners. From the outside, the perspective of the general public would support that, if the owners are in the money, the business is successful. I certainly would not argue that point. However, I would remind you that success can be a subjective achievement and profits are not the only criteria for success. More specifically, for the purposes of this discussion on succession planning, successfully producing profits does not make a business a golden goose.

This statement begs the obvious question, "What is a golden goose?" As described in my book entitled, Your Golden Goose, it is an enduring, highly valuable family business asset. Contradictory to the farmer's tale in Aesop's fables, a golden goose in the business realm does not spontaneously evolve. Hard work, sacrifice, patience, prayer and good fortune are all necessary elements to these rare assets. Golden geese vary in shape and size. Further, from my experience, you can find a golden goose in almost any form of business. Although each golden goose is different, they all have one profound, common trait, Succession Success.

The fact is, a higher degree of success is required for family business succession than for the sale of a business to a third party.

An additional dimension of success, which I refer to as a Success Margin (margin of error), is needed to endure the probable, if not inevitable challenges to success during the ownership and management transition process. Unfortunately, history has recorded many business circumstances where, in hindsight, prudence would have been preferred over bravado, because the family pursued succession of a questionably successful business that subsequently failed in the hands of a hard working but unfortunately ineffective next generation.

In the absence of an extended commitment to succession preparation, family successors generally do not have the skill sets and sense of urgency to assume operational control and maintain profitability, customer satisfaction, employee harmony or vendor good standing. Due to the unavoidable enabling environment that is a by-product of family nurturing, successor family members typically require a hardening period to develop the experience, tenacity and urgency required to maintain or regain the success momentum of an existing business. This reasonably predictable success dip of family business succession requires a Success Margin that can withstand a reduction in profitability. Let's review an experience in which the Success Margin became the central issue.

Case History: The Brainy Family

This family was in the retail boat business, notably one of the largest boat dealers in the United States. Dad Brainy had been retired. However, due to tight cash flow, he had come back into the business to help his son. They were very proud to be known as the nation's largest boat dealer. Mom Brainy and their two daughters were not active in the business. Dad and Mom Brainy were in their early 70's. Unfortunately, they were also separated and contemplating divorce. Son Brainy was 38. His two married sisters were in their early 40's and apparently not doing very well economically.

When I first met Dad Brainy, my initial reaction was that he neither looked happy or healthy. By his own admission, he had been "run hard and put up wet." His medical history must have funded the retirement plan of several surgeons. Mr. Brainy was worried about his health and was desperate to retire. He was convinced that the only way he could have retirement security was to sell the business to his son.

I asked why he could not consider transferring the business to his son by gifts or through his estate. His reaction was that he and his son did not work well together. His son apparently was a KIA (know-it-all) who was not receptive to coaching or supervision.

Maintaining an amazing sense of humor, he said he wanted the trifecta; a divorce from his wife, his son and his business. He contended that, if he made gifts of stock to his son, he would have to stay involved in the business to maintain the income he needed for his retirement and alimony to his son's mother. He also shared a concern that, if he made gifts and passed the balance of the business to him through his estate, there wouldn't be any assets to make equitable distributions to his two daughters. Evidently, his daughters and wife had expressed concern about him treating every one equally. His charge to me was to help his son borrow $5 million to fund the son's purchase of his stock. I told him that I was not a mortgage broker or a miracle worker, but I could possibly help his son build a loan package to take to his bank.

Naturally, I was anxious to review the Brainy Boat financials, which, upon review, proved less than impressive. A few rivets were loose and this boat was taking on water. The Brainy business may have been the largest retail boat dealer, but it was clearly not the most profitable. Of significance, working capital was minimal and the debt load was burdening. The business owned the dealership real estate and improvements that were worth several million dollars. Their infamous sales volume was being purchased at a hefty price: corporate profits.

After reviewing the financials, I interviewed Son Brainy and several of the key employees. It did not take me very long to understand Dad Brainy's feelings about his son. He was a nice young man, but not a dynamic leader who could inspire his employees to higher levels of success. He was high on confidence, but there was no substantive history of achievement or vision for success. His greatest shortcoming was that his vision of success was to continue to be the nation's retail boat sales volume leader. He never mentioned profits, debt or working capital!

When I asked the key employees how Son Brainy could improve as a manager, they said he was doing everything right. The operating statement reflected some significant shortcomings in management's interpretation of Son Brainy's leadership ability. It was apparent to me that these key employees were feathering their own management nests and did not represent a realistic appraisal of the son or the business.

Interaction with Mr. Brainy, his estranged wife and their family covered many exciting issues. Our initial planning issue was to address Mr. Brainy's expressed disposition goals. Having developed an understanding of their circumstances, I broke the news to Mr. Brainy that he was in a very difficult situation. His goals were reasonable and his rationale was sound. Further, with the real estate as collateral, his son could probably borrow $5 million. However, because the appraised value relative to the desired loan was so close, I projected that he would have to guarantee the loan. I also expressed my opinion that his son was in over his head, primarily because his chosen supporting management team was either stupid or sinister. I represented to him that there was an insufficient Success Margin to pay debts in the event of a business downturn. Subsequently, due to the low degree of success, he should consider either selling the business to a qualified, financially capable third party or postpone his retirement. I suggested that there should be limited motivation to sell the business to his son, as there was a remote chance that he might have to bail out a bad loan.

After Mr. Brainy's banker validated my prediction, Mr. Brainy recognized the impact that the modest level of business success was having upon his succession plans. As a result of this realistic evaluation, he did not sell *the business to his son. Contrary to his initially stated goals, he followed my suggestion and re-involved himself in the business management. He then fired two of his son's supporting managers and hired a strong general manager with a proven success history.*

I designed a succession plan for him that would get him out of the business via succession or sale within a maximum of five years. He was not happy with the time frame, but ultimately accepted my conservative estimate that changing his business would require some time. We began by making gifts of minority stock to each of the three children. We then adopted an incentive plan for Son Brainy that provided him stock bonuses, predicated on the business making at least $1.5 million per year for three out of five years. We also structured a stock purchase option stipulating that, after Son Brainy (assuming he got his act together) achieved the profit triggers and stock bonuses, he could purchase the remaining 55% from Mr. Brainy for fair market value. It was made perfectly clear to Son Brainy (as in "read my lips") that, if he were unable to reach the reasonable profit potential of the business, he would not receive the stock bonuses and the business would be sold to the highest bidder.

Dad Brainy found he was unable to retire and put space between himself and his son based upon the timetable he initially established. He had to swallow his pride and go back to work long enough to establish the Success Margin that would give him the bank and the boat manufacturer's confidence that this business could achieve succession.

Fortunately, Son Brainy grew a brain and heard his father when he said, "it's my way or the highway." He subsequently humbled himself and learned the basics of management from the new general manager. Together, they worked very hard to elevate the degree of business success. Seven years later, Son Brainy owns 100% of the business, Dad Brainy is financially independent, his daughters are financially enhanced and his estate is positioned to treat each of his children equitably. Even better news, Mr. and Mrs. Brainy have reconciled their differences and are living happily ever after.

An experience such as Mr. Brainy's could be very disheartening. The later into your business career that you discover or come to grips with the reality that your business does not appear to have what it takes to achieve succession, the more traumatic the experience. Your alternatives are to stick your head in the sand or realistically evaluate your success and determine if it can be maintained by your successors. Then follow Mr. Brainy's lead and make the best decision. Unfortunately, facts and circumstances about success cannot be ignored or edited to meet your business succession aspirations. If you are not sure of your circumstances, go through a preliminary self-evaluation answering these questions:

- Is the success of my business based upon location? If so, what is the likelihood that demographics will change and I will no longer have the competitive advantage of my location?

- Is the success of my business based upon timing? If so, what impact will the chronology of economic cycles have upon the long-term viability of my business?

- Is the success of my business dependent upon being the exclusive or otherwise specific provider of a unique product? Would my business be viable if the product fell out of favor?

- Is my business dependent upon the creativity and productivity of a special person (me or key man)? If so, what is the long-term viability of my business if my successors are just wonderfully average?

- Is my success a product of some form of political achievement? What will happen if the political tide changes.

    If the answers to these questions do not affirm confidence in your succession process, you should have an acute interest in the subject of Succession Success.

What is "Succession Success?"

Succession planning protects, builds and sustains value. It effectively addresses the various challenging factors of succession planning and builds value for you, your children, your employees and your franchises. Succession planning is just an academic exercise if there is no confidence that the business will survive and continue under the management of future business owners. The fundamental challenge of succession planning is achieving Succession Success. Family business success is derived from a variety of sources. The degree of success depends upon the sources and therefore can vary significantly.

Succession Success is a very specific term describing the nature and degree of success required to support the transition of business ownership and management.

Succession Success requires a Success Margin sufficient to endure predictable challenges in the transition of business ownership and management.

It is both individual and aggregate high achievement among the sources of your business' success. These sources, which we refer to as "success factors," are the critical issues that determine the stability, resilience and profitability of a business. The challenge of succession is best supported by a broad base of strong success factors providing the stability and resilience of profits needed to withstand predictable profit erosion during ownership and control transition.

Evaluating Your Potential for Succession

To help you understand the concept of Succession Success, the following evaluation illustrates the various factors that characterize the Succession Success of a business. I believe that there are 25 factors that impact the Succession Success of a business. This evaluation quantifies Succession Success by estimating "Success Positioning" relative to "Success Potential" for each factor.

Success Potential is a one to 10 (10 being the best) appraisal of what a business could achieve in each success factor based upon the given circumstances of the business. The first step in this evaluation is to determine how good your business can be in each category considering the limitations that are beyond your control. Success Position reflects your one to 10 evaluation of how well you that believe you and the business are doing in relation to the previously determined potential. Based upon our experience, we have generally concluded that a current Succession Potential of 70% or more is a threshold for Succession Success, or the foundation needed to realistically begin building a succession plan.

Succession Success Evaluation

Please insert a 1 - 10 evaluation of the Success Potential of your business. To the right of the Success Potential evaluation, please insert a 1 - 10 evaluation of where your business is in relationship to its potential.

Success Factor	*Success Potential best being 10	Relative Success Position
1. Personal Financial Planning		
2. Business Location		
3. Business Community		
4. Business Structure		
5. Industry Positioning		
6. Manufacturer Relationship		
7. Product Diversification		
8. Business Capitalization		
9. Business Profitability		
10. Economic Timing		
11. Community Involvement		
12. Successor Management Talent		
13. Successor Management Experience		
14. Successor Management Confidence		
15. Successor Management Talents		
16. Customer Satisfaction		
17. Management Synergy		
18. Family Owner Synergy		
19. Family Owner Harmony		
20. Employee Satisfaction		
21. Family Member Training		
22. Credit Continuity		
23. Estate Documentation		
24. Estate Tax Financing		
25. Owner Humility		

Relative Succession Success: Totals_____ divided by 250 = _____%
*Due to circumstances beyond your control, your success potential for any given factor may be less than ten.

A Relative Succession Success (RSS) of 100% is idealistic. There are probably some businesses that are at this level, but I have not had the pleasure of meeting them. At 100% RSS, they have correctly concluded that they do not need to talk to me. On a more realistic level, our experience has also led us to conclude that Relative Succession Success of 90% or more is needed to have confidence that your business has the momentum to withstand the challenges of succession.

In the real world, we generally evaluate new clients to have RSS scores of 75% to 85%. This evaluation highlights what is usually very obvious, that they need help. Our counsel is that, with a concerted effort to address deficient factors, we can pull scores up above 90% and bring peace of mind that succession is a realistic goal. This evaluation is also a good tool to periodically confirm that a succession planning program is staying on track.

How do you achieve Succession Success?

Succession Success is a significant achievement that requires nothing less than a significant effort. As stated above, this is a higher level of success and a broader form of success.

Succession Success begins with a commitment to excellence and an unwillingness to accept mediocrity in any of the preceding success factors.

Does this mean you will be a 10 in each of the categories? No, because there are some circumstances beyond your control. This does mean that you are willing to make the commitment necessary to achieve a 10 in each of the success categories. This is a commitment of time, energy and financial resources to enthusiastically go for the brass ring.

A commitment to Succession Success also requires a well-planned and well-orchestrated effort. Succession Success is achieved by optimum performance in a broad base of factors. Effective succession planning does not allow you to be great in some factors and lousy in others. You must be good in all and great in as many as you can. Therefore, your succession effort should be well planned and closely supervised by someone who can assure performance on a broad front. For the typical family business, we have determined that there are 25 success factors. However, for your unique business, there may be as few as 15 or as many as 35.

Regardless of whether you are on the high or low side of this spectrum, staying on top of progressive action or maintenance is a big job. Inasmuch as this is a specialty that I have enjoyed for 25 years, I assure you that this job is bigger than any individual who otherwise has a full-time job, such as a family member. The best course of action is to identify an advisor to assume this responsibility. The ideal course of action is to retain a succession specialist who not only understands the concept of Succession Success but also has an organizational structure for dealing with multi-agenda programs.

The final prerequisite to achieving Succession Success is to be realistic. Self-evaluation is not an easy undertaking. Depending upon whether you are one to see the glass half full or half empty, self-evaluation brings great vulnerability to being overly critical or overly optimistic. Either mistake can cause big problems. We live in a subjective world. In order for you to achieve your goals, you must make every effort to make realistic valuations. Realism is achieved by understanding the makeup of your personality and exercising appropriate caution. Of great importance, get third-party objective help. Seek the advice of those you trust who will not tell you what you want to hear, but will tell you what you need to hear. If you don't know anyone you trust in assessing the various success factors, be extra careful, because that indicates the voice that you most respect is your own, which is hardly objective.

There is a reason for every succession story. Success does not just happen, it is always achieved though capitalizing on opportunity. In the family business realm, the reason is either luck or preparation. Luck can bring many good things, but it is not a form of success on which one should risk the family business. The most prolific form of luck is being in the right place at the right time. However, times change and luck does not endure for the long term. The only reasonable basis for risking the fruits of a lifetime of achievement is comprehensive preparation. One of the most fundamental forms of preparation is to pursue a high degree of Succession Success.

Case History: The Wise Family

About 12 years ago, I was called to work for an automobile dealer who had been diagnosed with terminal cancer. Mr. Wise had been told by his physician that he would be able to fight this affliction for only another year and a half or so. He was an icon in the New England retail automobile arena and was very proud of his lifetime career achievements. He was a widower and was operating a single point, multi-product dealership with his 28-year old daughter.

His question: What should he do with the dealership? It was his pre-sumption that the dealership needed to be sold, because his daughter was relatively inexperienced and business failure would be unfair to his other daughter, who was not involved and had no interest in the dealership. He wanted to know whether it was best to sell the dealership now or from his estate. He knew some prospective buyers but was not sure how the busi-ness should be offered to realize the highest net proceeds.

In my normal fashion, I spent a considerable amount of one-on-one time with Mr. Wise, developing a detailed understanding of his goals relating to the disposition of the business, the division of his estate between his daughters and the administration of his estate on behalf of his family. I closely examined the financial structure of the business, the management structure, and the performance history to develop an opinion of value. By interviewing all the key managers and long term employees, I also devel-oped an understanding of their management culture. I concluded my data gathering with a lengthy interview of Mr. Wise's daughter to determine her background and goals.

In my initial planning review and evaluation with Mr. Wise, we covered many issues that could impact his succession planning. A summary of my observations included:

- *Your business has a very solid base with three attrac-tive franchises.*
- *Your business has a history of impressive financial performance.*
- *Your business has a strong capital base with an impres-sive operating capital.*
- *Your support managers have an impressive team attitude and a long history of dedicated, out-standing performance.*
- *Your daughter is inexperienced, but she loves the automobile business, is well educated and under-stands her limitations.*
- *Your managers respect your daughter's attitude and work ethic.*
- *You have achieved an impressive level of Succession Success.*

His reasonable response was, "What is Succession Success?" I gave him the lengthy answer and summarized by saying that this business had "the right stuff" to continue his legacy as a family asset. I then asked Mr. Wise why he was not giving serious thought to succession planning. His reply was that he simply had assumed that his daughter lacked enough experience to be a dealer. My response was that he was correct, although the other factors of his success more than compensated for this temporary short suit.

There was strong motivation to perpetuate the family's 50- year legacy in the automobile business. The business was highly diversified with a good location, good product lines, a good market, strong capital base and an out-standing management support culture.

I added that his daughter was well regarded by the employees and management and her dream was to continue the family business legacy.

From my perspective, the only weak link in this succession picture was his daughter's experience. I qualified my position by saying it was very rare for me to make this recommendation, but under these circumstances, I would recommend that he plan for business succession. If his daughter were to receive any cash from the sale of the business, it was her intention to reinvest in another dealership, so why go through the cost, trouble and disappointment of selling this great operation?

Mr. Wise took my recommendation under advisement. He was a very responsible man and was compelled to try and do the right thing. He has now passed away and his daughter is a successful dealer in her mid-thirties. She rents the dealership real estate from her sister. Three of her key career managers have purchased the 25% interest her sister would have owned in the dealerships. This family legacy was maintained for the betterment of the family, key employees and entire community because Mr. Wise had achieved Succession Success.

It wasn't all a bed of roses, as Ms. Wise did encounter predictable chal-lenges. However, the strength of her management organization and, moreover, the historical degree of success gave her the margin to withstand those challenges. By achieving Succession Success, the Wise Family was able to survive the success dip of family business succession and achieve their family goals.

Successor Manager Development

The development of capable successor managers is a critical factor in family business succession. There are notable examples in every community and industry where family businesses have declined because the successor children could not maintain the management standards of the family predecessors. Successor management capability ranks second only to family harmony as the greatest area of parental concern. This concern is directed not only toward children who will be assuming ownership and control of the business, but also toward the staff who will support those children in their management efforts.

History has proven several facts about family business management. A family successor does not have to be a genius or even an expert in the field to successfully manage a business. Just as important, successor managers of a family business are not made overnight, but over time. And the quality and dedication of the support staff is just as important as the quality of the family manager; it takes a full team to excel in business.

From a practical standpoint, I cannot begin to describe the countless number of multi-millionaire country boys I have met in my career who professed to being just a little slow. Admittedly, they were not the sharpest knife in the drawer, but they were savvy enough to recruit and maintain good help who enabled them to run very successful businesses. In keeping with these facts, we will review preparation and integration of successor family members and supporting staff into the management succession team.

Developing family successor managers and recruiting support staff, like any other worthwhile venture, depends greatly upon leadership. The direction of management development and recruiting efforts is established by determining the specific management skills, or core competencies, needed for the various business management positions. Dr. Wayne Burroughs, Professor of Industrial and Organizational Psychology at the University of Central Florida and Dean of The Family Business Resource Center in Orlando, says that the conscious or unconscious application of the appropriate core competencies is behind every business success. It is critical for business leadership to identify the appropriate core competencies so that the appropriate management skill-sets can be recruited and developed to support the mission of the business.

These skill-sets are similar across various industries. As an example, a manager in retail automobile or wholesale beverage requires a management skill-set similar to those needed in plastics manufacturing or software development, but the technical contexts in which the skills are practiced are very different. Context usually determines the weight or importance of skills within the set. According to Dr. Burroughs, these core skills include, but are not necessarily limited to:

1. Customer focus
2. Commitment to quality
3. Team orientation
4. Adaptability to change
5. Attention to detail
6. Entrepreneurial interest
7. Effective communication techniques
8. Willingness to delegate
9. Leadership ability
10. Organizational ability

In addition to skills, certain other characteristics are also important. These include:

- Assuming responsibility
- Taking appropriate risks
- Exhibiting high energy and motivation
- Maintaining optimism
- Being sensitive to others

And lastly, a high level of the specific business knowledge must exist within the organization. This knowledge must be accessible to all who need it, so that it can be leveraged.

Establishing the target skill-sets and effectively evaluating the potential skill-sets inventory of managers and management candidates can substantially reduce the heartache of pounding square-peg family members into round management slots. It also eliminates much of the expense of hiring management mules to fill race horse positions. In some circumstances, identifying needed skill-sets is easy. The more complex the business, and the more dollars subject to management risk, the more difficult this process becomes.

Skill-set evaluation determines the compatibility of a management candidate's abilities to the specific requirements for a management position. Evaluating a skill-set does not mean determining the child's ability to be a manager. It is assumed that family candidates and existing staff are capable managers, or at least have that potential.

It is highly recommended that an independent third party evaluate skill sets of family members and existing staff because long standing personal relationships can pollute the objectivity required for skill set evaluation.

A very important concept for parents or older siblings to remember is that there are several different personality profiles and each personality approaches management in different ways. When a new personality comes into the management structure of a family business, it quickly becomes apparent that there are many dramatically different approaches to management.

Many industrial management consulting firms provide methods for examining personalities and determining the compatibility of these personalities to certain management positions. According to Wilson Learning Corporation, personalities can be divided into four types:

1. Driver personalities who are bottom-line oriented with tendencies to keep tight control

2. Expressive personalities who are recognition oriented with tendencies to rely upon relationships

3. Amiable personalities who are people oriented with tendencies to please people

4. Analytical personalities who rely upon organizational detail

Each of these personalities, although strikingly different, can succeed equally well as a manager, but each will approach goal achievement and problem solving in a different way. Optimum compatibility of a marriage usually comes from the combination of two different personality styles. Similarly, in family business, a successor rarely has the same personality profile as the parent.

There are no stereotypical behaviors for a successful manager. Supervisors, trainers and especially parents need to have understanding and patience, allowing different personalities to undertake their challenges in a way that is most suitable to each individual's natural personality. A contrastingly different personality can be a complementary asset in a family business. Ignorance criticizes a family member for not doing their job in a specifically predetermined way; wisdom accepts that different personalities can be just as effective at accomplishing a task. This is an important concept, because families are usually comprised of a combination of strikingly different personalities.

A combination of personality strengths is needed to form a strong management team.

Let's assume you understand the core competencies for your business and have identified the optimum management skill-sets for achieving your business goals. Let's also assume that you have a reasonable understanding of the prospective skills of aspiring family managers and existing staff. A determination has also been made that the candidates have the existing management resources and the potential to get the job done.

With these givens, let's address one of the greatest responsibilities of a business owner: the identification and development of successor managers. The major difficulties in selecting future business leadership typically stem from the realization that a child will not manage in the same way as their parent, or that a child does not have the aptitude or the attitude to lead the business through the next generation. Addressing these tough, emotionally charged situations is a critical challenge.

Parents who want their business to continue as a family enterprise carry a responsibility to select and prepare successor managers. The responsibility of their decisions will impact many, including:

- Family members who want to work in the business

- Family members who indirectly are receiving benefits from the business

- Employees and their families

- The greater community served by the business

In recognition of the impact of this decision, parents must approach selecting successor family leaders with respect and conviction to do the right thing. Meeting this responsibility involves taking appropriate action to evaluate and understand the skill-sets of family members. Call upon consultants, colleagues and respected friends to assist with this evaluation. There is solid technology within industrial psychology that can relieve much of the burden of this responsibility. Get help to make the right decision just as you would do if you encountered a production problem that was over your head. Do not fall victim to these stereotypical conclusions:

- He's my oldest son, so he will be the next boss

- Running a business is no place for a woman

- He's an attorney, so he will make a good manager

- You are our only namesake, so you will be the next president of this business

If there are several capable children pursuing a career, irrespective of age, sex or birth order, each may be best suited for a particular role in the business. If there is only one family candidate, do not assume that your child is capable of filling any slot. However, there should be a productive slot for this child.

Regardless of the number of candidates, the most challenging decision is determining if any family member is qualified to be the next chief operating officer and business leader. The brutal question is:

What do you do if your son, daughter, or nephew does not have the personality or skill-sets to be the chief executive and successor leader?

Or, if you do not have any children active in the business, what are you to do?

These questions make up what I commonly refer to as the "Succession Dilemma." The simple answer may be to sell the business. Turning your business over to someone you know is inferior is not an acceptable way to address your stewardship responsibilities toward the aspiring successor, other family members, employees and vendors. There is a good market for the sale and purchase of businesses. If you have achieved an impressive level of Succession Success, you will have buyers knocking down your door. A more complex, but potentially far more gratifying answer is to use one of the various forms of a Succession Bridge. Providing you qualify, you could discover a new world of gratifying succession opportunities through the utilization of a non-family, key manager Succession Bridge. The payoff for the pursuit of this admittedly complex option is that, even without a qualified family successor, your family business could continue as a family asset.

The answer to the Succession Dilemma is based upon my discovery that, under the proper circumstances, non-family managers can lead and family members can follow. There are several classic methods where a Succession Bridge can utilize a non-family manager to achieve succession goals. In each case, great care must be taken to document the responsibilities and authority of management and ownership.

An in-depth discussion of the dynamics of a Succession Bridge is too broad for explanation within the confines of this book. For a more detailed explanation of the Succession Bridge concept, please refer to my companion book, *"The Succession Bridge - Key Manager Succession Alternatives for Family Owned Businesses,"* which is dedicated exclusively to this subject.

Regardless of whether family members are viable candidates for chief executive officer or a supporting management role, there are fundamental requirements for being a manager. These requirements include:

1. Managers must know what they are talking about. They must have technical knowledge and operating experience in the department(s) being managed.

2. Managers must have self discipline. It is unrealistic to believe heirs can manage a business if they cannot manage their own affairs.

3. Managers must set the standard for the control of fundamentals, such as time, money, drugs, alcohol, and emotions. Family members are role models for the non-family employees.

4. Managers must be willing to make personal sacrifices for the welfare of the business. Without self-sacrifice, a family member will never be a management asset.

5. Managers must be fundamentally self-motivated to overcome the relentless parade of challenges that are part of daily business life. There will be good days and bad days. Without the ability to see the glass half full and sufficient enthusiasm to endure frustration, an aspiring manager will be on a short course to failure.

6. Managers must have adequate people skills to establish and maintain relationships with family members, managers and employees. The essence of management is to understand the needs and goals of others and help them satisfy those goals through the business. If managers cannot interact successfully with employees, customers and vendors, they will be ineffective as managers.

The success of any management-development effort depends upon two factors: the quality of the training and the quality of the trainee.

The quality of the trainee is a function of his mental capacity and the developmental environment. When children come to work in a family business, they bring a package of management aptitude skills and attitude mind-sets that impact how well they will do. There is limited potential to influence management aptitude; however, attitudes that are so important to success, to some degree, can be improved.

Parents who are seeking succession are required to deal with the fruit of the seeds that they have sown. To see the rewards of personal sacrifice to hold a marriage together, spend time with children and raise a close family can be very gratifying. It can also be gratifying to see the benefits of struggling to discipline children in a permissive world.

On the other hand, it is frustrating for parents to witness the anger, confusion and poor self-esteem in children who have endured broken families, too much criticism, or too little encouragement. In general, parents who anticipate their children coming into their business should prepare themselves for a profound reality experience. They will have to deal with the fruits of their parenting and commitment...or the lack thereof.

Upbringing plays a major role in the preparation of a young person to be a successor owner/manager. It is unrealistic to expect a family member who has not had the benefit of a positive background to be the ideal successor candidate. Conversely, a child does not have to be the ideal successor to develop into an effective business leader. In fact, I have never met the ideal successor candidate. I strongly doubt if one exists. Everyone has their strengths and weaknesses. That is precisely why a successor manager development program is so important in preparing the average imperfect management candidate who meets the basic criteria for an effective management career.

For the most part, the successor manager development program is dependent upon the conviction of a child to achieve a career in the family business and the conviction of the parent to prepare the successor for the challenge at hand. Preparing successors for their roles can be facilitated by a structured Successor Manager Training Program to provide specific training and positive reinforcement to be a successor owner/manager. It is extremely important that you understand that a program like this can take pressure off the parent-child relationship.

It is unrealistic to expect a family member who has not had the benefit of a positive background to be the ideal successor candidate.

Case History: Frederick and Jack

Reflecting on the talents needed to be a manager in a family business brings to mind an experience with an automobile dealer named Wally who had two sons involved in his business and a daughter who was not. Frederick graduated from college with honors and got his MBA at a recognized school. The other son, Jack, barely made his way out of high school. Both of these young men were in their mid-thirties and ready for their father to retire. They had been working in the business as some form of management job since the day they finished school.

Frederick, the first born, appeared initially to be a dynamo who was highly ambitious and self-driven. He was meticulous and detail-oriented, the model of organization. He was punctual to the minute and was intolerant of anyone who did not act in the same manner. As a result, employees were intimidated to work with him.

Jack, a contrasting personality, was the middle child of the three. His shirt always seemed to need a little more starch and he was not much on organization. However, Jack never forgot a name. Employees approached him to talk about everything from business operations to ball games, children and life's challenges in general. Jack had little concern for time. He would talk to anyone at the cost of being late or even missing a meeting.

To put it mildly, their father, Wally, was perplexed as to how to structure a succession plan for three dealerships with two sons having such contrasting personalities. Wally was the driving personality type, so he related to Frederick better and was not confident that Jack could be a dealer. Frederick, a workaholic, made the situation worse because he resented his brother's easy going approach. Wally, with his father's blessing, asked our company to help develop a plan that would effectively place Jack in the business organization.

Frederick was a "hub and spoke" taskmaster who was respected for his commitment and drive, but was not well liked. A small, highly motivated group of employees expressed a desire to work with him. About 90% of the employees were fans of Jack. If Frederick took over, they said they would have to find work elsewhere. I confirmed that much of the success of the business was due to loyalty of these employees to Jack.

After extended discussions with Frederick, Jack and the employees, I concluded that the personalities of the sons were too polarized for them to work together harmoniously. Frederick showed no interest in changing his management style. Jack confided that he tolerated his brother for harmony's sake but had no intention of working under Frederick's hammer after their father withdrew from the business.

When Wally heard my recommendation to split the dealership between his sons, he told me I was unrealistic. He felt that Jack needed Frederick to survive in business. He told me I was crazy when I responded with, "Actually, it is Frederick who needs Jack." He told me to go home and not to wait by the telephone for his call.

About three years later, Wally called. Frederick and Jack had a big argument about a year and a half after I had visited. Jack quit the family business and went to work with a dealer in another state and was very successful as a sales manager. Nevertheless, Wally wanted Jack and his grandchildren to come home. Jack had said the only way he would come home was if he had his own store and did not work with Frederick. Wally asked me to help him work this out.

It did not take long to work out the logistics of Jack's return. He took over one of Wally's stores, with Frederick, who was assumed to be the more capable, managing the other two. A year later, Wally retired. Two years later, the automobile industry entered a nasty slump. To survive, Frederick and Jack cut their expenses, like everyone else in the business. Leading the way in this cutback was management compensation.

Then, a couple of years later, I got another call from Wally, telling me he was back to work trying to help Frederick, who had over-leveraged himself during the downturn. When Frederick had cut the compensation of his managers, they hit the road looking for better jobs. Without those quality managers, business deteriorated and the banks were threatening to shut him down. Wally had come out of retirement, not only to help Frederick, but also to protect the income stream he had been receiving from the business.

As I studied the situation, I learned Jack had also been forced to cut his staff's compensation. He naturally made lots of mistakes, but learned valuable lessons from each experience. Notably, his managers were loyal and stayed with him to weather the storm. They took pay cuts to help out during the tough times. Jack also never figured he was smart enough to manage the details of the business much less, several stores. So he hired a sharp general manager to watch the details and reinvested profits in his single store.

Where are Wally, Frederick and Jack today? Well, Wally has retired again. Frederick has only one store and is still struggling with debt, part of which is to Jack, who gave him a loan to keep the bankers off of his back. Jack, still humble, owns four profitable stores but spends more time playing *golf than working. He contends that, "If I went to work I would just screw things up." Some of those managers who took pay cuts a few years earlier are now Jack's minority partners and the general managers of his stores. He has a great organization and every one of his managers would die for him. Any day I expect to get a call from Jack (Wally would be too proud to call) asking me to help him bail out Frederick by taking over his store.*

In summary, after a young person assumes a senior management position in a family business, little can be done to enhance his aptitude as a future manager and business owner. In order to have an impact upon his attitude and ability (which make up aptitude), the young manager should be involved in a management development program from the outset of his career.

The Successor Manager Development Program

Assuming there is reasonable management aptitude, success depends upon the quality of the management orientation and training program. Without a doubt, the implementation of a well thought out management training and support program is, in most cases, critical to the succession process. A Successor Management Development Program should include at least the following steps:

- Define candidate's skills, behaviorally and specifically

- Determine candidate's interests

- Identify appropriate sub-management entry level

- Observe and assess performance

- Set goals for improvement

- Evaluate improvements and generally define optimum target management role

- Design successor manager developmental learning curriculum for target manager role

- Monitor performance and refine target management role as circumstances dictate

- Provide accountability, feedback, coaching and training

- Reward development

- Reset new goals for continued improvement and development

To illustrate the value of what we will call the Successor Manager Development Program, consider the similarities of acquiring the skills to be a family business manager to the challenge of acquiring a college degree. As a young person decides whether to pursue a college degree, the prospective student must meet certain basic qualifications, and then someone must evaluate their ability to handle the college program. Similarly, when a child expresses a desire to enter a family business, the parent should see that the child meets certain standards and then make an appraisal of their ability to become a productive member of the business team as a leader or manager.

Consider the similarities of acquiring the skills to be a family business manager to the challenge of acquiring a college degree.

A young person entering college faces a formidable challenge. The college environment is very different from the disciplines of home life and high school. The pace is three times faster, and the young person has the freedom to make their own decisions. Anyone who has ever been to college knows that there are not many freshman who have the conviction or self-discipline to make it past the first semester. In the absence of a work ethic, study habits, and self-discipline, they are overcome by the free time and lack of structure. The college student who survives this significant change in their environment faces at least four years of hard work, priority challenges, frustration, discouragement and confusion. The most impressive aspect of a college degree is that it shows that young people can successfully apply themselves to meet challenges over time.

In order to help college freshmen survive to be upperclassmen and ultimately graduate, an advisor is assigned to give advice, answer questions, build the appropriate curriculum and help the student cope. The advisor does not pamper or baby-sit. If the student is not focused and self-disciplined, he will not succeed.

The requirements for the development of family business managers are similar to the extended challenge of college. The unrefined attitudes and naive assumptions that family members bring with them establish major hazards to the management-development process. Any number of situations can occur that can distract or discourage continued diligence and threaten success. The unfortunate and all too common results of an unorganized, haphazard training program for family members include:

- Disappointment and discouragement of the trainee
- Resentment among family members
- Inadequate training
- Disillusionment with the concept of a family business career

Families can deal with these hazards and challenges in a manner similar to colleges by adopting a Successor Management Development Program, complete with advisors and a curriculum. The objectives of the Successor Manager Development Program are communication, training, support, accountability and monitoring. The success of the program will largely depend upon respect. The candidate must recognize the need for help and the value of advice and guidance being offered.

If the management candidate will not listen to advice, entering the business will usually produce the same results as the know-it-all freshman experience.

A Successor Management Development Program relies heavily upon effective communication. In most cases, a family management candidate comes into the business without a real understanding of what operating a family business involves. Regardless of how closely they have watched their parents, how many summers they have worked in the warehouse or participated on a part-time basis, new employees from the family do not understand the responsibilities of being a manager. The management candidate typically makes incorrect assumptions about responsibilities, how they are going to be treated and what their specific duties will be.

Incorrect assumptions usually pertain to fundamental employment issues, such as work hours, vacation time, relationships with employees, career advancement timetable, pay increases, and the reporting order. And family members frequently have distorted expectations regarding more emotional issues, such as job title, office, secretary, or even a parking place. To further complicate matters, parents typically have preconceived notions regarding how they expect their children to act and perform. Effective communication regarding all of these important subjects usually falls victim to assumptions by both the management candidate and the parent. It is not uncommon for a family member to have more difficulty than a non-family member as a new full-time employee.

The Family Business Employment Policy

To avoid hazardous assumptions, communication with aspiring family managers must begin prior to a family member beginning work. On the informal side, when casually discussing employment, children, siblings, nephews and nieces should be told that, as a family member, employment in the family business is an opportunity, not a right. They should receive the message that managers are exceptional people who distinguish themselves through exceptional attitude and effort. In other words, managers are expected to perform. If they want to be managers, they must be prepared to pay the price of being adequately prepared and effectively trained. Winning the genetic lottery does not make a manager.

Aspiring family managers should be told over and over that there are no elevators to the executive suite. Everyone must use the stairs and hit every step.

Formal communications are also essential for prospective family managers. As the old saying goes, "Do not be so naive as to expect your children to hear what you are saying." A Family Business Employment Policy is the ideal element of formal communication. The following page contains a sample agreement.

Sample Family Member Employment Policy

ACTION BY DIRECTORS IN LIEU OF MEETING

Pursuant to authority contained in [STATE], Statute [#], the undersigned, being all of the directors of [LEGAL BUSINESS NAME, Inc.[, a [STATE] corporation, do hereby take and unanimously adopt the following:

The _____ Family Member Employment Policy

1. Employment of a family member in the [NAME] businesses is not a birthright.

2. A [NAME] family member will be provided an opportunity for employment based upon the following terms:

   a. Confirmed need and affordability of a confirmed staff position or vacancy of a defined job.

b. Favorable employment experience outside of the family business, which has prepared the family member for a role in the business.

c. A favorable record of employment before to applying for employment with the family business.

d. Formal education and/or training that reasonably prepares the family member for the desired job.

e. Compensation and benefits comparable to what would be paid a non-family member in the same position.

f. No higher qualified active candidates.

g. Three year employment monitoring program (probation) to provide on-job training, performance monitoring and accountability for assigned responsibilities.

Acknowledging Directors: Non-Director Family Members:

_____   _____

_____   _____

_____   _____

A Family Business Employment Policy establishes the requirements for family members to obtain employment in the family business. This document is adopted as a corporate resolution and then conveyed to children, siblings and in-laws before they become full-time employees. Children should be exposed to this document as teenagers or as soon as they are capable of understanding what it says. The employment policy should be discussed both informally and formally at Family Business Council meetings to confirm that everyone understands and agrees with the requirements. Having made a deliberate effort to make the employment policy known to all family members, there should be a substantially lower risk of inappropriate assumptions about obtaining employment in the family business.

The advisor teaches the management trainee the realities of what life in a family business is really all about.

The second phase of preparation is also communication intensive -- the actual development as a manager. The management candidate needs guidance, monitoring and counseling to develop into the best possible manager in the least amount of time. A Successor Manager Development Curriculum and an Employment Advisor (or mentors) become the most effective taskmasters for enhancing development. The advisor teaches the management trainee the realities of what life in a family business is really all about. More specifically, the advisor expresses to the management candidate the basic requirements for capitalizing upon this opportunity pertaining to work ethic, attitude, personal hygiene and responsibility. The advisor is there to answer questions and offer encouragement when life in the family business is less than ideal. The advisor monitors the trainee's progress and holds him/her accountable for behaviors that are inconsistent with the family's mission statement and employment policy.

Being an advisor to a family member management candidate is a tough job for a parent or sibling. It is not recommended that parents directly supervise their children because the overall effectiveness of the program will suffer. The management advisor's responsibility of giving honest, objective performance and behavioral reviews creates tension within family relationships. An outside advisor, one who has no relationship history or expectations, is most effective in this role.

The purpose of a written training curriculum is to provide a structure for training. A curriculum relieves any uncertainty for existing managers and the family member trainee about the track to be followed for the next three to five years. This understanding relieves tension and allows the trainee to redirect their mental energy from worrying about the future to learning the job.

The first aspect of this curriculum provides the new family member employee with a written job description and employment policies to communicate exactly what is expected of them and what they can expect from the company regarding compensation, benefits, performance reviews and the opportunity for advancement. This may seem to be unnecessary busy work for an owner's child, but, trust me, it is not. It is just as important, if not more, for family members to fully understand their compensation and benefit package. Ideally, this information is shared in a series of meetings before a family member starts work. A series of meetings works best because it provides the new family member employee time to digest the information and generate questions, which is very important to the smooth integration of the family member into the business. Each time the family member changes jobs it is imperative that this process be repeated.

Every effort must be made to preclude assumptions when an heir enters a family business. The downside risks of a poor start in the business are enormous. The heir may say that he knows everything important about being an employee and you, the parent, may even think the child does know it all. Do not fall for this hazardous assumption. One of the greatest challenges for a family member entering the business is learning the humbling, demanding aspects of being an employee.

A family member can never reach his full potential as a manager unless he fully understands the dynamics of being an employee.

Most family businesses have an informal employee communication environment. There are no employee handbooks written with job descriptions describing employee benefits and responsibilities. The fact is, if employment policies and procedures are not written down, they are subject to being edited by new, aggressive, family member employees to meet their unique feelings, not the needs of the business. The potential hazards of "structuring a job to fit me" is naturally greatly exaggerated with a family member.

The Family Member Development Program

In the absence of a written, well-defined job description, benefit package and training program, parents may assume their children are capable of managing before their children have a grasp of what managing a business is all about.

The Family Manager Development Program endeavors to provide reasonable black and white information to preempt incorrect assumptions by children, parents, siblings and supervisors that complicate the family member's development as a productive manager.

Just as with a college curriculum, a manager development curriculum should describe in detail the specific on-the-job and formal job-related training, including a timetable for the first one to two years. Training procedures beyond two years should be more general to allow for flexibility. During the first phase of this program, the aptitude and aggressiveness of the trainee will be revealed, dictating adjustments for the long-term structure.

This program typically spans a period of three to six years, depending upon the age, experience and skill set development of the aspiring manager, as well as the complexity and maturity of the family business. It must be flexible to address the unique circumstances of the trainee and business. Each individual brings to the business a unique experience, mental capability and practical aptitude. Each business has unique management environment depending upon the size, product line and market. The parent and the advisor should design the preliminary program with solicited input from the management staff. The final refinement includes the trainee, with the curriculum being flexible enough to make adjustments as circumstances change over time. Let's review an actual experience relating the hazards of assumptions.

Case History: The Son and Stepson Dilemma

A few years back, we worked with an auto dealer, named Philip. He needed help with a succession plan for his stepson, Zack, who was the general manager of his store, as well as for his natural son, John, who was still in college. The relationship between father and son, as well as between the stepbrothers, was less than ideal because of a variety of factors, including divorce, blended family and alcohol abuse. Philip and Zack had spent a considerable amount of time contemplating where John was going to fit into the dealership after his graduation.

They had not spent much time with John since he had entered college, so they did not know what his job expectations or performance capabilities were. John was recently married to a previous dealership employee, and he and his wife were concerned about how she would fit into the full scheme of the family and the business, as well. Philip and Zack were quite concerned that the new graduate and his wife would want to jump right into a management slot.

And to put the finishing touches on this challenging situation, Philip was concerned that John might alienate Zack, who was a very capable manager and the son of his second wife, whom he adored.

As we might have expected, Zack was concerned that John would displace his plans to assume the role as CEO and create friction with the various department heads. Apparently those concerns were well founded. As often occurs with divorces, Philip had not done a great job of teaching John responsibility. The young man's reputation preceded him as a spoiled, pushy brat. He was known to get his way most of the time, and this thought put fear into his stepbrother. Both Philip and Zack were facing, in their minds, an impending disaster.

When we first met, it did not take long for them to express all of these concerns. I felt we could avoid their expected disaster. I told them that they may not like the methods and John might not like the results, but I did not see why we could not implement the basic ground rules for his entry into the business program for his development into a productive manager.

Were they relieved! Without asking how I was going to perform this miracle, they seemed confident I was going to solve their problems. I believed they were just relieved that someone else was going to "wrestle with the gorilla." Smiles returned to their faces as though a great burden had been removed from their shoulders. Luckily, they did not know that my staff was just as concerned about the gorilla as they were. We concluded that, unless we discovered that the son/stepbrother was indeed an uncontrollable monster, we would establish straightforward communications and try to prevent emotions from distorting the process.

When I met with John, I was surprised. He was nearly frantic. I was expecting the customary unjustifiable, personal demands for respect, but there were none. When I asked him what he expected when he graduated and started to work, his response was, "I have no idea. Nobody will tell me anything. My wife is asking me questions about how big an apartment we can we afford and I cannot give her a simple legitimate answer. She must think I am stupid. What's the mystery? Are they afraid to talk to me or what? Do I have a job or not? What am I going to be paid? What am I going to be doing? I don't want to seem pushy. I am really grateful to have a job. The last thing I want to do is alienate Zack. But really, I need answers to just a few basic questions."

As I was hearing this sincere young man's plea, I thought to myself, "Isn't this funny? Everybody is scared of everybody." John wasn't a gorilla, he was really a nice kid who was just in the dark. John was not concerned about when he would become the boss, he just wanted to know what he could expect so he could take care of some basic family issues. Our job immediately became easier.

We asked all the parties what they were expecting and determined, much to our surprise, that the expectations were not far apart. We sat with the group and reviewed this information. We then reviewed a Family Member Business Employment Checklist that addressed the important questions about the employment of a family member. Smiles came again. The questions addressed basic issues such as:

- *When will John begin employment?*
- *What will be John's position?*
- *Who will be John's supervisor?*
- *What will be John's compensation?*
- *What employee benefits will John receive?*
- *What type of training program will be provided?*
- *When and how will John's performance and position be reviewed?*

Because this trio had not thought about the intermediate and long-term impact of a new family member in the business, many of the questions could not be answered immediately. Philip and Zack were shocked and embarrassed at the unanswered questions that they had overlooked. John felt relieved that the questions were identified and a commitment was made to develop answers. Within a couple of additional meetings, everyone was happy. We received credit for a significant achievement when all we did was identify a few fundamental questions and facilitate communication between two reluctant parties. We became heroes for just pursuing the basics of communication.

In subsequent meetings with Philip, Zack and John, we developed a five-year Management Development Curriculum that satisfied everyone's expectations regarding training and on-the-job experience. We also established meetings for training progress reviews to provide dad, stepson/stepbrother and John's direct supervisor a forum to review John's business behavior and job performance.

Although each management development curriculum is unique to the circumstances at hand, there are several standard features recommended for each program. The first common feature is that children must initially be encouraged, if not compelled, to work outside the family business. Typically, there are opportunities to work in similar businesses established through industry associations or trade groups. Working under someone other than a parent or sibling provides profound benefits to all concerned. The family member discovers the reality of a workplace relative to salary, schedules, time off, accountability and performance standards. This discovery cannot occur around family members, as reality is distorted under the structure of parent/child relationships. The difficult task of learning how to be an employee is taken care of with a job where your last name does not mean anything. The experience of just being an employee relieves enormous pressure from parents, who would otherwise be required to convey to their child the harsh contrast between being a family member and an employee. More often than not, parents never get this important message communicated because they do not want the pressure or stress of upsetting their children.

Within the family business, a young person is classically considered the owner's child first and a management trainee second. Being an owner's child has the advantage of financial and career opportunities, but the disadvantage of preconditioned attitudes that handicap on-the-job training scenarios. The experience of working for a non-family member provides experiences just like any other employee and is beneficial for building confidence and self-esteem.

By establishing a successful work history outside the family business, a child gains invaluable experience and business maturity, establishing credibility and gaining respect from family and employees. A year or two of seasoning with another business will polish many of the rough edges, which should help quell the natural handicap of employee resentment. With a good work ethic, the child will develop the understanding of an employee's thinking, an appreciation of the value of teamwork and, hopefully, gain respect. This attitude will be converted into better relationships with employees in the family business.

The aspiring family manager will gain the critically needed respect of the employees if he shows an ability to perform well at the lowest end of the business, where getting dirty and sweaty come with the territory.

Fulfilling the value in bringing family members into the business on the ground floor is another important aspect of the Successor Manager Development process. Regardless of the level of their education and experience, the prospective manager will benefit from the requirement that he experience or re-experience the business from the ground floor. The family member may have worked in the back end of the business during school, but that should not preclude going to the back end again upon returning to the business from college and/or employment elsewhere.

The benefits range from a renewed understanding of all aspects of the business to getting to know and gain the respect of the employees. You can be sure that everybody is watching the boss' child as he starts his business career. You can also be sure that the aspiring family manager will gain the critically needed respect of the employees if he shows an ability to perform well at the lowest end of the business, where getting dirty and sweaty come with the territory. The child's education and experience should determine how much time is spent in the various back-end aspects of the business, and specified in the Management Development Curriculum.

Another common feature of a successful curriculum is a regular progress review. Ongoing dialogue and interaction are critical to the development of a manager. On the positive side of discussions, the trainee must hear positive feedback. Equally important, where improvement is needed, they must be given a chance to express their feelings and ask questions. Advisors, supervisors, parents and siblings must also be encouraged to provide counseling advice. However, family member criticism should be constructive or, due to the natural family dynamics, it will not be well received. The dialogue should address training, working experiences, and constructive suggestions, while maintaining a positive outlook.

The final common feature of a successful management curriculum is that the family member trainee must be held accountable for his actions and attitudes. Again, this may appear to be an unnecessary expression of the obvious; however, holding family members accountable in a family business is easier said than done. There is a natural tendency to overlook the shortcomings of loved ones in the hope that they will come around and shape up. Patience and tolerance are important. However, after reasonable counseling, the family member must hear the strong unwavering message that they must move on to a more compatible career if they cannot meet the family's behavioral and performance standards.

Dr. Burroughs emphasizes that accountability should be a positive force in a business environment. He says that most people associate the term accountability with criticism, confrontation and frustration. However, a well-defined, disciplined accountability structure gives managers and employees the comfort of knowing boundaries and expectations.

Regardless of how well family managers develop, they cannot do it all. An important aspect of successor manager development is the supporting staff. No one can run a business without help and it is typically the supporting staff that creates assurance of continuing the operational effectiveness of the business. A parent's step from chief operating officer to chief executive officer dictates a refocusing of efforts from operations to leadership. Leadership involves making sure that the staff is in place and has the understanding of the mission and technology that have been the essence of success over the years preceding this management transition. The supporting staff, as the name implies, provides the foundation, the infrastructure through which the family operates the business.

Recognizing the importance of the supporting staff during the control transition period, parents need to put into place a management support team that will maintain the momentum. There are two tests to evaluate a supporting staff for successor family members. First, can the supporting staff run the business without the son or daughter in a leadership role? If not, there should be serious reflection regarding the motivation and/or quality of supporting staff.

Secondly, does the staff respect the family successor? Are they willing to go the extra mile for his success? If not, I advise caution. If the parent hired all of the support managers, a reasonable lack of confidence towards the successor is natural. However, if the long developed consensus opinion is "no respect," there is a problem. The synergy between future family leadership and existing supporting staff is the infrastructure for success. If neither of these conditions exist, there are serious problems that must be addressed to achieve peace of mind regarding succession.

Leadership involves making sure that the staff is in place and has the understanding of the mission and technology that have been the essence of success over the years preceding this management transition.

There is one major axiom that should dominate the identification and retention of high quality supporting managers. Do not tolerate mediocrity. Talent is the best business investment one can make. Understanding who and what a good supporting manager is will help the family principal work better with them.

Who are the supporting managers? They are the keys to the future of the business. Without supporting managers, dreams of business succession will not become reality. In most cases the family leads, and supporting managers actually operate the business.

What are the supporting managers? They are ambitious, goal oriented, entrepreneurs who may not have the resources, the risk tolerance, creativity or independent-mindedness to own their own businesses. They may not even have the total vision of your business. Just the same, support managers are goal-oriented entrepreneurs who, relatively speaking, have accomplished a great deal and who also intend to accomplish more. The following are some guidelines to easily and effectively develop strong managers:

- Hire above yourself. Identify and recruit managers who are smarter and more aggressive than you.

- Pay a little more and expect a lot more. Quality costs a little more, but outstanding performance can quickly cover that cost.

- Do what you say you will. Be known as a reliable leader. Allow your managers to rely upon the predictability of your behavior as their support structure.

- Show the utmost respect for managers both professionally and personally. Respect, prestige and self-esteem are big parts of their paychecks.

- Immediately replace any manager you do not respect. Your managers are an extension of you.

- Provide your managers with written job descriptions and incentive bonus programs. Do not fail to mention the specific role of each manager in the realm of business succession.

- Empower managers to accomplish their job description. Do not preempt any authority you have delegated.

- Do not change pay plans for any reason other than business welfare or the advancement of a manager.

- Meet regularly with managers and share goals and visions. Ask them to help refine and achieve your goals.

- Take the time to determine the goals of your managers. Help them refine and achieve their personal goals.

- Hold managers accountable for the achievement of your goals as well as their own.

The role of the parent is to assure that an adequate supporting staff is in place, not necessarily to actually pick them. The family successors are going to have to work with these managers, so they should be involved in the recruiting. The parent's role is to use their experience-tempered judgment to make sure a quality support staff is selected to augment the strong and weak suits of each child.

Example

A few years ago, a client illustrated this point as he was describing his son's development in his car dealership. Jim said that during the first two years his son, Steve, was General Sales Manager, he recognized that about every six months the various supporting managers in his department dressed in the same styles, used similar clichés in their conversation, and partied together when they were not working.

Jim would then take his son aside and say, "Look Steve, we are not Sigma Nu (Steve's college fraternity). These guys do not bring any experience or specialized training to this business. Hire managers on their proven capability, not just on their looks and personality. Liking a manager is a luxury. A manager's ability to get the job done is the critical issue, and socializing with them is a liability. If they cannot get the job done, you have to make the decision to replace them. If you have a social relationship, a tough decision only gets tougher."

The key to a supporting staff can be described in two interdependent words: performance and teamwork. As we discussed earlier, team members respect their leader, know their purpose, and do not let their personal agendas get in the way of the objectives of the team. Supporting managers get their job done and leverage their capability through organization, direction, support, correction and encouragement of the team structure. Supporting staff must be recruited with the goals that they can become a member of the family's team. Their ability to become an integral part of the family business unit will depend upon their ability to transition their management perspective from the "me" to the "we." Investing time, money and effort to recruit key managers according to a specific team profile will pay great dividends, because you will rely upon key managers to convey your goals and standards to the other team members.

Building The Family Business Team

The family business is not well regarded as the career choice of unusually talented business phenoms. Family business is not the standard bearer for operating efficiencies or technical development. The family business is, however, known for two very important things: survival and productivity.

A unified, hard-working family does more with less. It will find a way to overcome adversity and thrive where others have failed. But productivity and success are not to be taken for granted. As a matter of fact, countless family businesses end up as miserable, pathetic failures. You just do not hear as much about the businesses that fail as you do about those that rise to great achievement. Indeed, the family business is, pound for pound, the most potentially productive and resilient business unit on the planet; however, the operative word is "potential." The keys are first to survive and second, to reach full potential.

As we have just reviewed, there is no point in burning brain cells considering the challenges of succession until there is confidence that there will be success.

On more than one occasion, classic family business succession candidates, for seemingly unknown reasons, could not make fundamental succession decisions. The owners canceled appointments and lacked motivation to protect and preserve a family heirloom. Later, upon closer examination, the feelings of parents were revealed and it became apparent that they had no confidence that the next generation could successfully continue the business for any one of a variety of reasons, including poor intra-family relationships, lack of commitment and lack of good business judgment. The parents were walking confirmation that business succession is contingent upon success.

It is reasonable to ask how some family businesses achieve succession and others fail. The foundation of success and/or survival is teamwork. Family business succession depends upon synergy, because this is a collaborative business venture that requires personal interaction. Success is dependent upon effective communication of feelings, goals, boundaries, expectations and more.

Having an understanding of the importance of teamwork and learning how to promote it will enable a family business to achieve full potential. After gaining confidence that a business is achieving its full capability, owners can direct resources to other critical but obviously subordinate factors of succession.

To begin our discussion, let's look back a few years at a situation that highlights the basic tenets of teamwork.

There is no point in burning many brain cells considering the challenges of succession until there is confidence that there will be success.

Case History: Teamwork

In 1982, the North Carolina State basketball team was comprised of twelve average to good basketball players, as compared to the typical Atlantic Coast Conference team. This conference is renowned for attracting the best basketball players and coaches in the game. Unlike the 1972 national champions, the 1982 NC State team did not have a superstar, such as David Thompson, or a physical phenomenon such as 7'4" Tommy Burleson. Nonetheless, the 1982 NC State Wolfpack basketball team wrote its name into college basketball history.

The team finished the Atlantic Coast Conference regular season with a mediocre record of fifteen wins and thirteen losses. This record in any given year would not have even earned State an invitation to the post season National Collegiate Athletic Association Tournament. The conference tournament was their only hope for "the big dance." The NCAA awarded the Atlantic Coast Conference tournament champion an automatic berth in the post-season championship tournament; therefore, this group of unheralded young men and their brash young coach, Jim Valvano, approached the conference tournament with a "now or never" attitude. The upbeat, forever optimistic coach convinced this group of average players that they could be a team and, through the power of teamwork, could achieve beyond their realistic expectations.

To the surprise of conference opponents and the national press, this obscure group of players with the streetwise coach from New York City, began the tournament by beating favored Wake Forest with a foul shot made after the buzzer and followed this by beating archival and perennial national contender North Carolina in the semi-finals. The final night of the tournament, they shocked the Las Vegas bookmakers and Tobacco Road by handily beating season champion and number-three ranked Virginia. The ACC tournament title earned them the coveted berth in the NCAA tournament.

Empowered by their amazing accomplishment, the Wolfpack grew in confidence, but stayed loose, laughing at their crazy coach's jokes. Their newfound confidence gained them little respect from the basketball world; they were seeded sixth out of eight teams in the Western region. The seedings showed that the NCAA selection committee believed there were at least forty-eight better teams in the tournament.

To the surprise of everyone, including this loyal fan and alumni, the Wolfpack continued to win. In very close games, and, when necessary, in overtime, they found a way to win against schools that were big favorites. Regardless of the circumstances, they just would not give up. They had made it to the Final Four. Always cast in the underdog role, the team progressed nearly unnoticed by the media, which had all but conceded the tournament to highly touted Houston. Valvano was creating the hype and soaking up the publicity that he and his band of gutsy no-name players had created.

Because of their unexpected rise to fame, the no-name ball players with the cocky, funny young coach were cast into the spotlight at the Final Four. The press looked upon Valvano as a source for comic relief, and he responded by providing great one-liners. The media felt his comedy would be the only worthwhile performance from the overachieving Wolfpack; they could not believe NC State would beat Georgia in the semi-finals. And if a miracle did occur, reporters did not give them a fleeting chance of beating Houston, which had two consensus All-Americans in Akeem "The Dream" Olajuwon and Clyde "The Glide" Drexler. The Houston team, affectionately known as "Phi Slamma Jamma," was an overwhelming favorite.

The game began as predicted, with Houston running up an early lead on spectacular plays by the superstars. But NC State did not go away. The players listened to Valvano's instructions regarding working the clock, waiting for the right shot and giving fouls. Every player had Valvano's vision of what would be required to win. Each team member knew that they could not match up with talent, and that his contribution was critical to the overall performance of the team. Each team member thought only in terms of the team and dedicated himself to following Valvano's instructions. There were no superstars like Olajuwon and Drexler who could be relied upon to pull them out of a hole or carry the team. There was not even an experienced coach who could tell them how to act or what to expect. What they did have were twelve ball players and several coaches who could work together and an understanding of what their individual contribution meant to the *success of the team. The 1982 Wolfpack, in the March Madness tournament converted all thoughts of "me" into "we" and became a team.*

The question is, how did the Wolfpack achieve this miraculous winning streak? How did this group of Tobacco Road no-names rise up to beat teams that had greater talent sitting on the bench? Olajuwon and Drexler were both franchise players. And each of them possessed all the right stuff. They were big. They were fast. They could jump, move, shoot and certainly dunk. Their talent as individuals, however, had little bearing on how good they were as a team. This was not an individual exhibition; this was a group event.

Maybe some of the Houston superstars were second-guessing their coach. After the game, Houston coach Gary Lewis was heard saying that several of his players did not follow his instructions. Possibly Houston did not take NC State seriously. Houston apparently relied more upon their talent than team synergy. The "shake and bake, slamma jamma" would not get the job done against a Wolfpack that was united as a team.

The forte of the family business is over-achievement and doing more with less, capitalizing upon the inherent family assets. NC State's winning streak, winning nine straight games as an underdog, seems even a greater miracle today than it did then. As expected, Drexler and Olajuwon rose to superstar status as perennial All-Stars in the NBA. NC State's players came from obscurity and, after the tournament, quickly faded back into the same position. At the same time, Valvano, and the players received recognition for their achievement. But basketball history recognizes the team. Although there may have been forty-eight better schools in the tournament, there was not a better team.

Similarly, the family business does not commonly have superstars. The forte of the family business is over-achievement and doing more with less, capitalizing upon the inherent family assets.

The better a family understands and implements the dynamics of teamwork, the more successful it will be in its business endeavors. The reciprocal of teamwork is Affiliated Individual Productivity (AIP). AIP describes aggregate individual production that is brought about through common sponsorship (the employer).

Teamwork is like oxygen, the more prevalent it is, the more the <u>*enterprise thrives.*</u>

When teamwork is thin, the enterprise suffers. Teamwork has a geometric impact on the productivity of a group; regardless of talent and drive, without teamwork a group effort will not reach its full potential. In my experience with many sport teams, four years in the military, various charitable associations, several personal businesses, and twenty-five years of business succession consulting, there is no unique perspective to teamwork. Teamwork involves unity of purpose, subordination of personal priorities, leadership and interdependence.

Unity of purpose means that everyone is on the same page and has the same vision of success. The perspective of team members should be "we," not "me." This major undertaking begins with each team member establishing personal goals, and then participating in goal-setting for the team. With a vested interest in the strategic direction of the business, employees can reconcile the priority of the team's goals to their personal agenda. Because of our inherent self-centered nature, regular reinforcement of team goals is needed to maintain priorities.

Effective teamwork depends upon two forms of leadership. First is the ability to lead others; second is personal leadership. A successful team has a strong effective source of direction, discipline and attitude. The source comes from one or more individuals with the gifts of motivation, encouragement and control. However, a strong team is not created by a single strong individual leading weak phlegmatic participants. Strong teams consist totally of leaders.

Teamwork depends upon both a strong individual leader and team members who are also synergistic leaders.

Strong leadership figures are common, even on bad teams. The mark of organizational success is the assembly of a team that consists totally of leaders. What makes a leader? A leader is a risk taker. A leader is willing to express his position, to make a decision, to step out and be definable. A leader is not necessarily outspoken and dogmatic; however, a leader is someone who expresses who he is, where he stands, what he expects, what he believes in and where he is going. By expressing opinions and setting direction and boundaries, a leader is willing to take the risk of failure and criticism. Notably, leaders recognize that the fruit does not grow close to the ground and are willing to take the risk of failure, disappointment and, even worse, embarrassment. Leaders operate out of a belief that failure is sometimes unavoidable, but it is always a temporary condition. Leaders can rationalize an element of success from any set of circumstances, believing that success is not necessarily a consideration of where one is; but equally important, an evaluation of how far a team or individual has come since it started.

Team members may not own the business or the team, but they own the vision and the goals.

A leader also provides order. Teamwork depends upon reasonable expectations that teammates will behave within the boundaries. A team is an unruly gang if the leader is not willing to enforce accountability and order. The magic of a coordinated effort becomes the misery of chaos. A leader is willing to hold himself and his team members accountable for meeting expressed boundaries and expectations. And it is essential to understand that a team's success is dependent upon the leadership ability of each individual member. Regardless of their position in the business, each member of a family business team should carry the attributes of leadership with respect to his role in the business. It is a fundamental mistake for any family member or employee to believe that he is merely an employee working for someone else. A "mere employee" completes assigned tasks without any continuing sense of responsibility for the impact of those tasks upon the goals and mission of the business. Mere employees can never reach their optimum potential for themselves or the team with an independent attitude.

On the other hand, business-team members are "we-oriented." They invest their time in the fulfillment of group goals, not personal goals that they believe will best serve their individual best interest. Team members may not own the business or the team, but they own the vision and the goals. They formulate the goals through interactive communication with colleagues, leaders and the business owner. Supervisors value their opinions and continually solicit their input to improve the team's performance. With feelings of value, they approach their work with diligence, pride and commitment. As team members, they have opinions about their job and have submitted their personal agendas to the agenda of their working unit and the business as a whole. Team members recognize their responsibility in relationship to team goals and continually consider how they can improve their performance and the performance of the organization. The advantage of the family business is that this teamwork structure of interdependency is already in place, needing not to be sold, but needing only to be promoted.

Most family businesses consist of average people who exert above-average effort. The spiritual strength of a family business often draws participants who need support to perform well. The interdependency of teamwork found in a family business not only provides support for less skilled participants, but also creates an environment for those less skilled participants to successfully apply themselves and pursue over-achievement. The greater the presence of lesser skilled and lesser motivated participants, the greater the value of interdependency. The question is, how do you achieve interdependency?

Interdependency is a choice made by independent, capable people. Dependent people do not make decisions; they rely on others to make them. Capable, independent people can be convinced that interdependency is the best way to work. One does not have to be a rocket scientist to recognize the benefits, including lack of pressure, continual support and camaraderie. The first step to achieving interdependency is to recruit independent, capable members who care. Do not recruit mere employees. Recruit only team members who are capable of independent work. You must then sell these independent operators on the value of interdependence. Unfortunately, this means you will have to eliminate overly independent employees and retain only those who can be partners in interdependency. Even those who appear to be the least productive members of your team dramatically impact business performance if they psychologically move from employee to partner.

With personal autonomy, the ability to think and to make decisions, team members can choose to be partners and interdependently strive to achieve common goals. Sell the benefits of mutual support to them. Explain the concept of synergy and describe how every member of your organization will be able to perform better if they empower those around them to work better, and if they can be depended on to meet personal expectations as well as help others. Successful families have the strength of interdependency, because they have decided that the benefits of interdependency are worth the effort. Non-interdependent families stick out like white elephants, because everyone depends on a particular member of the family to make all the decisions; or all the independent parties feel competition is a better system than collaboration.

The key to interdependence is caring. Workers must care about their specific job, their coworkers and the mission of the business. Without caring, there is no hope for interdependency. Caring is an element of character that can only be sold to a limited degree. You can sell the benefits of a workplace where everyone cares, but you cannot make a prospective team member care about the welfare of the work force and the business above his own self interest. The worker must bring the potential to care with him. If you find it, you can nurture it and it will grow. The hard cold facts are that some people are team players, some pretend they are and some simply are not.

Applying and Promoting Teamwork

The science of business management deals specifically with optimizing business productivity. The non-family business must work hard to develop the team environment that is naturally in place in a family unit. The non-family business has to develop its synergistic program from scratch, whereas the ideal family business already has the basic structure of leadership and interdependency in place.

The family's built-in teamwork capability is what gives it an edge in the business environment. Exploiting this advantage is critical to the succession of a family business because there is no neutral ground for teamwork. Depending upon the circumstances, a group either works together as a team or it works against itself as a competitive, contentious group of self-serving brats.

> *Bickering family members in a family business are far more destructive to teamwork than unrelated employees who don't <u>get along.</u>*

The calling of a family business is to recognize the advantage it has to capitalize upon this advantage to the greatest degree possible. The less obvious but equally important calling of a family is to identify and deal with family members who cannot cooperate, cannot subordinate their personal agenda and cannot successfully serve on a team.

Like it or not, the family is a team. How can a family capitalize on its inherent teamwork advantage? Let's review some of the basic principles of family business teamwork.

1. Establish a capable leader and empower him to lead. Unfortunately, in the family business environment, selection of a leader is rarely simple. Considerations, such as the size of the family, the nature of the business, the skill sets of a child or children, quality of supporting managers and the social/emotional package of the child or children usually come into play. The success of the team will, in large part, depend upon the quality of the leader. Under the concept of the Succession Bridge, the leader may not be a family member. Leadership by committee may look fine on paper, but success under a multi-headed leader is indeed rare. Two heads create a confused tail. Any cliche you apply leads to the same conclusion: strong organizations have strong leaders. From a succession perspective, the earlier the successor leader is identified, the smoother the transition of leadership.

2. Collectively establish reasonable performance goals. If you want to run a family business at optimum level, your family business team must consist of people who want and can perform at the desired level. Team members will not make a total commitment to performance goals that they do not take part in formulating. They may be impressed with your goals and even patronize you to express commitment to your goals; however, team members will only truly commit to their goals, not yours.

Optimum teamwork requires each team member to buy into team goals as part of their competitive psyche. Optimally, the achievement of team goals becomes an element of their self-esteem. This can only happen if team members take an active role in the goal-setting process. Goals should be established in relationship to a realistic evaluation of talent and teamwork capability. This means acknowledging that your team has members with varying levels of talent, and everyone has a varying ability to perform in a team environment. Chronically establishing unrealistic goals will ultimately create an environment of futility and defeatism that will undermine team synergy.

3. Promote the team concept. The best way to promote the team concept is to act like a team. Current leadership can sell the team concept by expressing their dependence upon supporting managers and employees. "Hub and spoke" management styles reflect no confidence in managers and employees, and eventually undermine team synergy. Asking for their input and responding to their suggestions will quickly convey the concept of interdependency. Breaking down the vertical management structure into groups of five to 10 employees for goal-setting, problem solving and operational enhancement will initiate team groups and ultimately promote team spirit. The key to promoting teamwork is creating a compatible forum for soliciting employees' opinions and then respecting their opinions through reasonable follow-up.

4. Be enthusiastic. Teamwork feeds off enthusiasm and emotion. Valvano was a master at projecting his enthusiasm and emotion. A positive, optimistic, overcoming attitude is essential for the team environment. Just reflect on the great coaches of sporting teams, business teams, armies and countries. These were enthusiastic leaders who conveyed confidence in their ability and in their team members to achieve the specified goals. Enthusiasm is truly contagious and, in the close confines of a team, the spread of enthusiasm is a major step towards success.

5. Promote coachability. The best way for a leader to promote coachability is to be coachable themselves. As an example of coachability, leaders, managers and family members need only ask knowledgeable employees for advice and, within reasonable boundaries, follow their advice. Successful coaches develop an understanding of the dynamics of interdependence and are easily coached.

The questions to consider in hiring a family member are the same as for non-family members: Are the children, grandchildren or in-laws capable of contributing to the business mission, and are they coachable? History has confirmed that there are many more capable children than there are coachable children. The coachability of a child is an independent consideration from each individual's business aptitude. If family members and employees are not coachable, they become a liability.

You can forget selling the teamwork concept to employees if a family member is the prime example of rebelliousness, contempt, and unwillingness to follow instructions.

6. Establish clear, detailed descriptions of job performance expectations for each employee. In addition to the team knowing its overall direction, it is essential that each member of the team also know specifically what contribution they are expected to make for the team to be successful. Expectations of physical, intellectual and spiritual performance should be specified. In other words, if you want your employee team to exhibit a certain attitude, describe that attitude in detail. It is amazing how well competent people will meet your expectations when they fully understand your expectations.

Any family member or employee who does not clearly understand the mission of the business and their value to the overall achievement of the mission is a liability, not an asset. There are two major causes of substandard performance. The first is that team members do not really know what they are expected to do. They do not understand or care about the total expectations of their specific job. Secondly, they do not understand the importance of their performance to the overall success of the business -- that their good or bad efforts make a difference -- because no one took the time to explain to them the value of their role.

7. Establish compensation and recognition programs that emphasize teamwork. Fair compensation and recognition of an individual's contribution to team success are vital to keeping body, heart and soul devoted to the team concept. Team players are team oriented, but they need personal recognition of the contribution they are making to the team's success. Pay plans and achievement recognition should be on several levels. Of course, individual efforts should be a major portion of a pay plan; however compensation and recognition can also be based upon the performance of work groups and the overall profitability of the business. A well-organized profit sharing bonus plan will generate genuine interest in the overall profitability of the business, which is a major goal of a team effort.

8. Meet regularly to reinforce team thinking and interaction. Regularly allocating quality time for employees to meet in team units to reinforce and discuss the various physical (job execution) and spiritual (attitude) aspects of achieving the collaborative goals of the group will reinforce the teamwork concept. If you expect your family and business to automatically perform like a team, you need a wake up call.

Regularly coming together to reconfirm goals breeds strength, productivity, harmony and teamwork.

Teamwork, like any other challenging and rewarding activity, requires constant practice, encouragement and nurturing. Unlike sports teams, family business teams are made up of members who do not constantly work in close contact with one another. The family business team is a relatively large group consisting of diverse personality profiles aspiring to accomplish various job roles. Team members work in different departments or different locations, creating a handicap to unity. Because of the velocity of business and the physical structure of the workplace, communication between managers is usually in short phone calls, memos and reports. This physical structure does not naturally promote unity and teamwork. Regularly coming together to reconfirm goals breeds strength, productivity, harmony and teamwork.

In summary, it should be no news flash that the success of any family business, regardless of size or industry, is not assured. A family seeking succession must extend itself to the fullest on a daily basis to be successful. In many cases, success can be defined in terms of mere survival. Assumptions by family members about the presence of a team, the essence of leadership and the requirements of teamwork capability will only invite failure.

A passive hope or plea for synergy will return void. An unwillingness to pro-actively work for the team concept will bring the disappointment of mediocrity or failure. Informed, motivated and pro-active families have a natural compatibility with the interdependent dynamics of teamwork. And a family illustrating the interdependent dynamics of teamwork can become an addictive role model to supporting managers, employees and the community at large Succession is important, but succession is predicated upon success; success is in part, dependent upon teamwork.

Family Issues

*W*e are continually faced by
great opportunities brilliantly
disguised as insolvable
problems.

~ Lee Iococca ~

Enhancing Family Communications

Case History: "You've Called the Wrong Man"

Several years ago I received a call from the son of a beer wholesaler who asked if I was interested in doing succession planning for his family. I told him that our firm was always interested in a service opportunity and asked him to describe his family's situation and what he felt were the primary issues.

He proceeded to describe a second generation family business that had been founded by his grandfather in the 1930's, which had become very successful, primarily because of the growth of their community and the emergence of Anheuser-Busch as the dominant player in the beer industry. The man's father had died three years earlier. His mother technically controlled the business, but was retired. She relied on her 35 year-old son, who was calling me, to run the business in cooperation with his older sister and a brother-in-law.

The young man further stated that he was sick and tired of carrying his mother and two sisters. He said that there were "too many horses at the trough." He said his mother had expressed her intention to recognize his contribution to the business' growth and profitability, but was not taking action. He wanted someone to help convince his mother to stop procrastinating and take action regarding estate planning and gifting. He then added it would be my job to convince her to give him future control of the business.

As in many similar circumstances, my response was, "You have called the wrong man." When he said that the size of the fee would not be a problem, I answered, "You do not understand. I am a family business succession planner. In the three minutes you took to describe the primary issues, you did not once mention family. The overpowering subjects of your planning needs are 'I' and 'me.' The critical determinant of a family business are unified goals and purpose. It appears as though you want me to lead the effort to remove family from your business.

I am neither trained nor motivated to be a family business exorcist. I do not work for individuals; I work for families to help them determine what is best for the family. If the issue is money and control, and not family, you've got the wrong guy."

The term "family business" is both a common description and a bizarre contradiction. The word "family" classically describes relationships created by biological (parent, child, sibling) or spiritual (husband-wife, very close friends) connections. The word "business" describes people according to their vocation: what they are doing, how they are doing the particular task, and how well they do it. Family is an organization based upon feelings and emotions. Business is an organization based upon performance.

The implication is that any family member employed in the family's business will do whatever it takes to get the job done and make the business successful.

Both family and non-family businesses depend on relationships to carry out their activity; however, in a non-family business, the primary reliance is upon contractual relationships (expressed or implied) to establish and maintain the productive organization of the business. Non-family businesses usually define job performance expectations in writing, detailing performance expectations and accountability procedures to assure that the employee satisfies the needs of the employer.

In a family business environment, family member employment is not usually as well defined. Job performance expectations of family members are generally unlimited. The implication is that any family member employed in the family's business will do whatever it takes to get the job done and make the business successful. It is this inherent, natural empowerment challenge to family members that can make the family business so phenomenally productive.

In a non-family business, the job comes first; and any relationships that may develop as a result of the job come second. How an individual does his job primarily defines the quantity and the quality of the relationship with the business. Only after having proven they can do their job is there an opportunity to develop the political and spiritual relationships that can have a positive impact upon the productivity of the business.

In the non-family business, accountability is a way of life. Routine performance evaluations put more emphasis on job performance than the spiritual factors, such as being well-liked or being supportive.

As a result, there is a greater inherent uncertainty in a non-family business, because someone may come along who can do a job better. And Father Time inevitably chips away at an employee's primary source of security: their ability to do the job.

History has proven that this combination of strange bedfellows - family and business - is the cause of much excitement in both the family and the business arena. The presence of a business in a family can bond parents, children, siblings, husbands and wives, creating joy and gratification beyond measure. On the dark side, self-centered competition for control, or the rewards of cash from the business can create devastating barriers between family members. The presence of family in a business can create levels of enthusiasm, dedication and productivity that cannot otherwise be achieved. Unfortunately, petty, self-centered family guerrillas can also bring a good business to utter destruction.

Strong intra-family relationships are critical to the succession of a family business. If family members cannot work together in harmony, it will not matter how sophisticated the financial plans are or how productive the business is, succession will only be a fleeting dream. If your family is dominated by strife and dissension, then forget succession; because, regardless of outward expression, the inner hearts and souls of family members will flee from this environment. If relationships prevent parents from communicating the vital knowledge about running the business to their children, forget succession. If siblings, cousins, and other family members do not unite as a family business team with common goals, forget succession. Relationships may not appear to be too important to the success of a family business until you witness the unraveling of a great organization because of family bickering, back-biting or outright conflict.

Anyone who has ever been a witness to these pitiful consequences of a family turning on itself will verify that it is ugly. With heirs having the expected burdens of management transition, estate taxes and banking pressures, they can rarely bear the additional emotional burden of intra-family conflict. Relationship friction in a family business is a spiritual handicap that can zap away both the profitability and the ability to carry the business to the next generation.

Ideally, a candid awareness of the importance of relationships to succession sets into action practices that build relationships, and increases the strength of the organization and the probability of succession.

In cases where the dye is already cast, this same awareness can potentially identify problems and highlight methods through which problems can be resolved. PQ

If the family members can successfully carry on the business and work together, their feelings about each other are not the foremost concern. The pivotal issue is whether the family members can work together for a common goal. Personal feelings become important when these feelings overpower the intention of working together.

Case History: The Rebellious Son

An auto dealer asked me to help with succession planning for two of his three sons who were active in his three dealerships. Later I learned about his third and oldest son, who had come to work in the family business on the ground floor as a used car salesman after serving in the Vietnam War. This dealer was notably a very dedicated Catholic. On more than one occasion, he had personal conferences with the Pope.

While working nights, his oldest son developed a relationship with a young woman who was providing custodial services for the dealership. The son soon fell in love with the young lady, who had a child by a previous marriage. The son went to his father to tell him of the relationship and his intention of marrying her. The father told his son it was wrong to marry a divorced woman, and he would not recognize the marriage. The son thought long and hard about his feelings for his fiancee and the demands of his father. The son had very strong ties to his family, but also was head over heels in love.

After several gut-wrenching weeks of indecision, the son told his dad to shove it, quit his job and married this very nice, attractive, hard-working woman. He then took a job across town with a competitive dealer. And the rebellious son had grown in his career, buying three dealerships in a nearby community. More importantly, the spouse of the rebellious son had never been in the dealer's home and, as would be expected, his grandchildren seldom visited.

And so, Dad hit me with the big question, "How do I get my son and grandchildren back?" I asked, "What are you accomplishing by not recognizing your son's marriage?" He explained that he was abiding by his Catholic beliefs. I further asked, "Are you abiding by your beliefs or are you trying to force your beliefs on your son?" He did not like that question and discontinued the discussion regarding his son. I did not press the issue, continuing to work on succession dynamics for his other two sons.

About a month later, I received a call from Dad, and to my shock, he said that our prior conversation about his estranged son had been weighing heavily on his mind. He admitted that he had been trying to force his beliefs on his son. But as much as Dad wanted his son back, he just could not accept this previously married young lady as his daughter-in-law.

A choice can establish the foundation upon which great relationship developments can occur. However, after establishing the foundation, there must be more than just a choice to support the ongoing bond of a relationship between two individuals. There must be mutually gratifying communication that holds the relationship together. Unlike choice, communication is a two-party event.

Communication is the medium through which individuals and families positively create or negatively destroy the bonds of a relationship. Relationships build on positive, reinforcing communication that demonstrates respect, affection, understanding and/or empathy. Effective communication allows families to avoid problem relationships, as well as to facilitate positive rationalization of negative historical events.

Communication makes the family unit strong and resilient to the many disruptive forces encountered in a business environment. It is the medium through which trust is gained, plans are made, action is coordinated and problems are solved. Most importantly, communication is the medium through which children are prepared to be the successor managers of a family business. Without relationships that provide effective communication, children cannot learn values; and junior managers cannot effectively be prepared to own and operate the family's business.

Unlike choice, communication is a two-party event which influences the attitudes and conclusions of both participants in a relationship.

Accordingly, ineffective communication constantly undermines family bonding. Dysfunctional communication is common in the family business. Family members can bring to the business the emotional baggage that creates a dysfunctional family. Some families have bigger problems than others; and some problems are so big that they inhibit family interaction and the succession of the business. This is usually created by individuals becoming engrossed with their own priorities and feelings, and failing to listen to and understand the feelings of others.

Subsequently, mindsets of resentment are cultivated which then block interaction, fellowship and communication. Less expressive family members become overpowered by louder or more zealous family members. More sensitive family members become afraid of criticism, judgment or embarrassment, so they fail to express their opinions; and some are not willing to endure the uncomfortable environments that are associated with improving communications and dealing with important issues.

How do you go about choosing to communicate? The only way I know is to truthfully evaluate your motives, your options for achieving your goals and the collateral ramifications of each option. The potentially positive results of communication will then provide motivation for choosing to communicate. If there is sufficient motivation, barriers will be overcome, personal priorities will be subordinated, and dialogue will be established that will satisfy your goals.

For the purpose of succession planning, I recommend using a relatively simple five step Communication Improvement Program. I have repeatedly witnessed substantial improvements brought about by this program in the exchange of feelings and the enhancement of harmony and productivity of the family business.

The Communication Improvement Program

Although basic, my suggestions can improve communication among those who want help and are willing to accept coaching.

- Commit to improve.
- Create a forum for airing out feelings.
- Select a mutually agreeable third-party facilitator.
- Discuss and practice listening techniques.
- Develop a discussion agenda.

1. Make a commitment to improve your communications. A commitment to communicate is more than just a willingness to meet and talk things out. A commitment to communicate is recognition that your family can not survive without effective communication. It is an agreement of the family members, partners or management team to communicate, irrespective of the problems at hand. This is not necessarily a solution to individual problems and hang-ups. This is either a self-improvement commitment or a commitment to survival in the face of negative circumstances. Communication problems can be traced to many sources, such as busy schedules, personality conflicts and past misunderstandings.

Making a commitment to communicate recognizes that the succession of the business is a higher priority than personal convenience, ego, pride or the scheduling demands of family and business.

Communication involves both a commitment to listen and express truthful feelings. Listening allows one to understand the attitudes and opinions of others that must be addressed when expressing feelings. When immersed in long-standing family issues, a commitment to express your truthful feelings and listen to criticism or ridicule is substantial. A commitment to communicate also means that an individual will continue the interaction, and history has shown that when there is a commitment to communicate, issues can be effectively addressed.

2. Create a forum for communication. Regardless of commitment, environmental circumstances have a significant impact on the ability to communicate and the quality of that communication. In most situations, this involves simply finding a compatible time and place to meet, and making a commitment to talk.

Example: The "Good" Listener

A classic example of the need for a communication forum includes a highly successful, strong-willed, dynamic father who has concluded he is a good communicator, and believes that he and his sons and daughters "freely exchange feelings and information." In reality, however, the father's confident, positive attitude miscalculates his ability to communicate with his children. The father is so preoccupied with running the business "right" and teaching his children the right things about business and life, that he never gives them a chance to express themselves. The father thinks they communicate well, but he loses sight of the fact that he does 90% of the talking on the important issues.

The father thinks he's a good listener, but never listens to his children's serious talk about the business because nobody knows as much as he does. He has done this for so long that his children are frustrated and accept his overbearing nature and have just given up endeavoring to be heard. The father then, without resistance, continues his ignorance, thinking that his children's lack of rebellion (apathy) is confirmation of a strong family that never fights. He never recognizes the need to allow his children to express themselves and develop the confidence that their opinions and thoughts are important and valued.

Communication becomes a joke to the children, who just go through the motions of their jobs without any feelings of value or self-worth. The eventual result is a conclusion of, "Since dad does not care enough to listen to me, I am going to stop listening to him." Feelings never get aired out, and, like Florida thunderstorms, resentment builds until it cannot be contained. Depending on the circumstances, the results are, at best, an extreme strain to the family. Certainly the succession of the business is put in great jeopardy.

In the absence of a spontaneous forum for communication, schedule meetings for the sole purpose of communication. In other words, never assume that your family communicates effectively. Establish a time, place and an agenda to exchange thoughts and feelings. In some cases, improving communication may mean that you begin meeting daily for fifteen to thirty minutes. In other cases, weekly or monthly meetings may be adequate. The frequency of the meetings depends on the severity of the circumstances and the emotional tenacity of the parties. Classically, when a Communication Development Program is initiated, meetings are required more frequently. Time may be needed to warm up relationships, especially when there has been long-standing tension or animosity. After a regular forum for meetings has been established, communication will become easier and more productive, allowing for the frequency of meetings to be reevaluated.

It is predictable that some parties will not look upon these meetings warmly. Admittedly, improving communication can be very emotionally demanding.

Do not become discouraged if the communication meetings are not immediately productive. It takes time for a freeze to thaw.

As emphasized in step one, communication improvement requires a personal commitment: to make scheduled meetings a priority and to be willing to put aside other activities that may appear equally important. Otherwise, the effort required to make the meetings happen will overpower the desired goal of the meeting.

An ideal forum for family communication is a Family Business Council (FBC). A Family Business Council is a group of family members and special non-family managers who are active in business operation who meet on a regular basis, such as monthly or quarterly, to discuss and hopefully work out circumstances, problems and opportunities. The FBC serves as a developmental board of directors to make decisions on the three P's: Policy, Procedure and Politics. At the appropriate time, the FBC changes from a communication body to an actual board of directors that substantially impacts the direction of the company.

3. The next step in the Communication Improvement Program is to select a mutually agreeable third party facilitator for the meetings. The facilitator can make good circumstances even better. In more severe communication problem environments, creating a regular time and a specific place to meet and share feelings is a major step forward to communication improvement, but a facilitator will probably be needed. The facilitator provides leadership for initiating discussions, managing dialogue and overcoming obstacles. As we all know, there are formidable communication obstacles that can create an impasse and bring communication to a halt. Family members may not have the capability to overcome communication obstacles without help. This third party communication facilitator initiates discussions, maintains order, holds the parties accountable and keeps records of conclusions, agreements and assignments. After communication begins to flow on its own momentum, the third party facilitator may be needed less frequently.

The participants must agree in advance on the third party, as well as agree that the third party has authority over communication sessions. There must also be a willingness to allow the third party to arbitrate any deadlock situations. The issue is progress. With a standing agreement to allow a third party to resolve deadlocks, continued progress towards the goal of communication is assured.

4. The fourth facet of a Communication Improvement Program is to discuss and practice listening techniques. Knowing someone closely, as in family, promotes stereo-typing and prejudicial thinking that blocks effective listening. And to further complicate the environment, listening skills are rare commodities among the aggressive, competitive personalities who commonly populate the family business. Struggling family members are either too busy to take the time or too confident to seriously consider another person's ideas, especially the ideas of an old-fashioned parent, a hard-headed child, a dumb sibling, or a deadbeat in-law.

Being a good listener is the premier family business communication skill. Understanding the circumstances, facts and situations brings knowledge and leads to understanding. Understanding is power, as effective listening facilitates the development of the appropriate response for effectively communicating information, resolving problems and building relationships. Understanding another person's thoughts, feelings and perspectives greatly reduces the risks of relationship friction. A natural by-product of listening is empathy. It is through listening that one can learn to better appreciate what it is like to walk in a brother's moccasins.

The first step to listening effectively is to place a higher priority on understanding what the other party is saying than on expressing your own thoughts. Without a priority to listen, the information, feelings, and ideas of others will blow right by us.

Relationships in a family business are based upon the respect one family member has for another. A parent can tell children what a great business people they are until they are blue in the face, but the words might as well be barks at the moon if the parent does not respect their children enough to sincerely listen to what they have to say. The message of approval and encouragement sent by listening is many times greater than any message with words. This theory can be summarized in the cliché utilized frequently by Warren Deakins, a truly great communicator and my first employer:

> *"People don't care how much you know until they know how much you care." Warren Deakins*

How much one cares is a direct reflection of their willingness to listen.

5. The fifth facet of a Communication Improvement Program is to follow a discussion agenda. Most of the time, communication problems are the result of arguing, stonewalling, resentment, overpowering personalities or poor listening habits. These handicaps are substantially reduced if the discussions follow a predetermined agenda. The structure of an agenda directs attention specifically to the critical points on which there needs to be an exchange of information.

The disadvantage of an agenda is that it inhibits the personal spontaneity that is needed for two people to develop a relationship. If this spontaneity exists and critical points are being addressed, an agenda is obviously not needed; however, communication problems and natural spontaneity are usually mutually exclusive. The assumption is that if problems are significant, the awkwardness of a discussion agenda will be overshadowed by improvements.

In its most simple application, a discussion agenda keeps excited, emotional and impulsive parties on the same subject.

If the parties can begin exchanging information on the specific subjects that are giving them problems, then they will take a major step toward resolving conflict and hopefully, building a better personal relationship.

Needless to say, two family members who are having problems communicating cannot be relied upon to develop a worthwhile discussion agenda. This is when a third party communication facilitator comes to the rescue. The facilitator should know enough about the family business to understand the pertinent issues for an effective agenda. As a product of this understanding, the facilitator's role is to propose the agenda and solicit input from the parties for refinement. The agenda should address anything important to the parties involved, including business operations, their families, and personality peculiarities. The agenda determines the direction and boundaries of the discussions. As communication improves or deteriorates, it is the facilitator's responsibility to make the necessary adjustments.

Relationship history, choice and communication collectively impact family business succession by enhancing intra-family relationships. To illustrate the impact of intra-family relationships on succession planning, join me as I attempt to reconstruct an experience from several years ago with a third-generation construction business.

Case History: The Relick Family
The grandfather had started the business 45 years earlier. Grandpa Relick had three sons, all of whom took jobs in the business. Two of Grandpa's sons had one son each. The third son had two sons. All four grandsons came into the business. Grandpa ran the business with an iron hand; his three sons did not communicate very well with him because "he was a man of few words who accepted no excuses." In fact, the sons were afraid of their dad and did everything they could to stay out of his way. To avoid conflict with him, the sons immersed themselves in little corners of the business and their individual families. Dad never promoted family unity and interaction, so the sons rarely spoke to each other about their private lives or business.

Grandpa died relatively young, in his mid-fifties, and his sons found themselves in the uncomfortable position of being pulled together to jointly address business decisions. They had never learned to communicate, and because of their dad, they had learned to avoid confrontation. So after

Grandpa Relick's death, they continued to mind their own segments of the business and to avoid interaction on business issues. For better or worse, the business proceeded on auto pilot. By default, Harry, the oldest brother with two sons in the business, took over the administrative duties of the company.

When the second-generation brothers were ready to retire, they were not equipped to discuss the sticky issue of how to distribute stock to their sons or how to fill the various leadership roles in what had become a significant company. The only plan came from the family's banker who agreed to loan the four third-generation cousins and brothers the money to buy out their fathers. As a result of his creditor position, the banker dictated that the cousins each own twenty-five percent of the company and have an equal voice in control.

I was retained by Gordon Relick, the oldest of Harry's two sons, to help his family of two cousins, his brother and himself develop a successor management structure and a stockholder's agreement. I quickly discovered that there was a long and difficult history. The boys had bought the company five years earlier from their fathers. During this period, friction had developed between the cousins. Their fathers had been great role models for dysfunctional relationships. Concerns regarding control prevented them from agreeing on who would be president or the terms of a corporate buy/sell agreement.

In my initial interview, Gordon told me I would earn my keep if I could establish agreement of all parties. He said his brother Lewis was very down on his cousin, Simon, and emotions were fever pitched. It soon became apparent that Gordon was speaking only a half-truth. Gordon was also at odds with Simon because he blocked his plans to succeed his father as the recognized leader of the business. Gordon was in fact, using his impressionable brother to challenge Simon's competency, hoping the buffeting and frustration would move Simon out of his way.

I interviewed each of the cousins and their wives to achieve an understanding of the circumstances and developed a full appreciation of the negative history of the three families that generated these four cousins. Inasmuch as their dads were not close, the cousins did not develop a sense of family as they grew up. When they came into the business, they had no bond with their cousins. When their dads were ready to retire, an immediate struggle for control began with major bickering over pay plans. The banker had dictated that, until they paid off the loans, their compensation would be equal. Evidently, this was a very ugly environment that carried over to their divisional subordinates within the business, as well as family and friends outside the business.

After determining that guerrilla warfare was not going to provide a business control winner, they apparently chose to try to improve their situation by bringing me in to facilitate planning. Based upon what I had understood from Gordon, overwhelming frustration motivated them. On Gordon's initia-

tive, they rationalized their overpowering negative history and agreed to cooperate to find solutions to their problems through my involvement.

I had several data-gathering meetings to learn about the facts of their business and their history, and then I called a meeting to talk about the buy/sell agreement. It was profoundly apparent from the way these guys avoided small talk and eye contact, that they did not effectively communicate. They were paralyzed by a history of no dialogue and much resentment. Most communication was through body language, expressions or the unwillingness to talk. No one was talking except the brothers, Gordon and Lewis, with an occasional comment by the attorney and comptroller. Simon and the other cousin, Steve, did not even look each other, or anyone else, in the eye.

From my private discussions with each of the cousins prior to our meeting,, they rarely, if ever, met to discuss business. Aside from me, only their banker could get them all in the same room. Simon had assumed the role of president when the buyout of their fathers was completed because he was the oldest cousin and had the most experience. He liked this executive white-collar role because he was comfortable with banking and administration.

However, apparently because of his own ambition, Lewis had taken exception to Simon's role as president. A deadlock of corporate control had developed because Steve had chosen to side with Simon. He had concluded that -- if Lewis and Gordon disposed of Simon -- they would have control of the company and would undoubtedly unload him next. The struggle for leadership control was well-known by employees, vendors and customers. As a result, the company was floundering in a very competitive market. Profits had been marginal, requiring additional operating debt on top of the debt used to buy out their fathers. Without the cooperation of the banks, they would have gone into the tank. Although Gordon felt he had the banking situation in hand, it was clearly just a matter of time before their lenders pulled the plug. The unfortunate state of affairs illustrates the vulnerability of intrafamily relationships to history, choice and communication.

"Let's get on with this. I have got things to do that will earn this company money," smirked Lewis. He was an outspoken hothead, and it was well-known that he had despised Simon from childhood because his older cousin had delighted in putting him down.

"It certainly is apparent that you would be more comfortable elsewhere," returned Simon who continued to glare at Lewis' blue collar attire while pulling his french cuffs from his coat sleeve, revealing his engraved gold cufflinks.

I felt compelled to pull the control rods on this reactor to avoid critical mass. "Okay, guys, lighten up and relax a minute. We have a big day ahead of us. Let's not have all the fun at once."

Behind my calm, I was wondering what I was going to do if these guys started to tangle. I had heard that they had resorted to blows the year before at the company picnic.

Henry, the comptroller, rolled his eyes to the ceiling and raised his hands in disgust saying, "Ah, let them have at it. I frankly think we ought to move the chairs back and let them duke it out and finish what they started last year. My money is on Simon. Anybody want some action?"

Gordon tried to disguise his self-serving agenda by acting as a diplomat. "Come on, put your emotions aside for once and let's discuss how we can structure a buy/sell agreement that will give our families peace of mind about our investment in the business. Surely you realize the mess we would be in if one of us died. There is no written agreement on the valuation of our interests or the terms for the purchase of our stock."

"Yeah, can't we get along, guys?" pleaded Steve, who rarely said anything unless he perceived that Lewis and Gordon were getting the best of Simon. "Can't we have some dignity? Can't we quit picking on each other for a change?"

"There is plenty of support for Simon," responded Lewis. "We're supporting him 100%, and he is doing nothing in return. He hasn't done anything productive around here to support himself since I walked in the door five years ago. He is probably the highest paid racquetball player in the country."

Simon put both hands on the table while staring at me and started to rise. Things were starting to unravel. "Sit down, Simon," I shouted. "And stop talking, Lewis. Please cool it long enough for us to have a discussion."

Obviously the idea that I was going to help these guys develop a stockholder's agreement was a five-star laugher. Since they had bought out their parents, they had not been able to agree on the day of the week. I realized that I had been hired by Gordon to further his agenda of removing Simon. There was no hope for me to get them to do anything but have another fistfight unless I could first get them to bury the hatchet on the past and choose to get along.

Simon looked as if he was about to go ballistic as he responded. "Lewis, you and your brother amaze me. I have at least ten years seniority on you ingrates. Lewis, I ran your department in my spare time for five years prior to your coming to work here. I have paid my dues. My dad groomed me to take over leadership of the company because I had both the experience and the education. Back when we purchased this business none of you guys had any concept of what running it involved. Now, five years later, you are suddenly experts and jealous of my achievements."

As Simon finished, Lewis stood up and looked Simon in the eye. You don't really think we believe that bull do you? Your dad did not groom you to become president. You just grabbed the job so you could mooch off of us for the rest of your racquetball career. We do not cooperate because we don't like what you do or how you do it. The only fair thing in this business is for everyone to carry his own weight. I can replace you with a secretary."

Lewis then turned to Steve. "Steve, you don't buy his crap do you? We need to find this guy a job, preferably away from here. How can you stand him making equal money to you and doing nothing productive to justify it?"

Steve crossed his arms and responded in his typical reluctant manner, "Lewis, I think you are overreacting and are being a little harsh." The attention in the room had now shifted to Steve, and he was noticeably nervous. "Your dad assumed the job because he was the oldest. We don't have any more departments that Simon could manage. Someone has to manage the overall business, why not Simon?"

"Very simple," Lewis responded as he stood up straight, pushing his chair back, "Because he is an arrogant oaf. Do any of you guys feel comfortable with him representing us?"

I tapped Lewis on the shoulder and asked, "Will you please sit down? The purpose of this meeting is to work out a stockholder's agreement and a compensation plan, not to indict Simon."

"Save your breath, Loyd," blurted Simon as he stood. He was starting to step out and come around the end of the table after Lewis. The family attorney jumped up and grabbed both of Simon's shoulders to restrain him. Gordon had stood and was reaching to restrain Lewis. I was the only thing between them; and just as I began to see my life flash before me, I heard at the doorway behind me a strong voice: "Boys, what's going on in here? I'm standing out here trying to carry on a civil conversation, and I hear all this commotion."

Lewis' demeanor instantly changed. Turning to his father standing in the doorway, he struggled briefly for words. Then, a well practiced smile came to his face as he raised his hand to greet the gentleman. "Hi, Dad. Sorry we disturbed you. We are just having a little family interaction like you suggested."

"Hi, Uncle Harry," offered Simon, who had abruptly gathered himself and also turned to direct his attention to his uncle standing in the doorway. "Yes, we are just having one of those management meetings that you and I discussed. Not to worry," he continued with an especially phony smile, "We will hold it down. Everything is going fine."

"Hi, Dad," added Gordon from behind Lewis. He had changed his death grip on Lewis' neck to a brotherly, across-the-shoulder arm hug.

Everyone in the room acknowledged Mr. Relick. The sixty-eight year old, grey haired, six foot two inch gentleman looked lean, fit and quite capable of ending any squabble. He was Gordon and Lewis' dad, as well as the oldest of the three second-generation brothers who, by default, had assumed the presidency twenty-five years earlier. "Should I join you?" he asked with a sheepish smile, indicating he knew what was transpiring. "Can I help with anything?"

"Oh no!" blurted Simon authoritatively, as if speaking for the group. "We've got it under control. Go ahead. We are about finished." Mr. Relick looked around the room at everyone as if he were checking their opinions. Receiving no contrary opinions, he said, "Okay, call me if you need me. But don't stop. I know you guys need to work out some rough spots, so stay at it." Then, keeping his eyes on the group as long as possible, he slowly turned and stepped away from the doorway.

Everyone but Simon started to get resettled in their seats; however, Simon stood behind his chair, pushed it under the table and, avoiding Lewis' stare, looked to Steve and said, "Meeting adjourned." As he stepped to the door, he sarcastically shot, "Lots of fun, Loyd. Please don't forget to invite me to your next party."

As he faded through the door, the others began to stand. Lewis, obviously delighted at what he had done to Simon, yelled, "I hope you're not late to your racquetball game, Simon. Work hard. Make us lots of money."

This visit with the Relick family provides insight into the impact history and choice play in intra-family relationships. Simon and Lewis had bad chemistry dating back to adolescence, providing further proof to the Brother/Cousin Relationship Axiom: Brothers generally tolerate each other because of family influence, but cousins will stick the knife in and break it off.

Apparently, as a result of the intra-family rivalry of the past, Lewis and Gordon chose to accept the state of their relationship and the impact the acrimony was having on the business to further undermine Simon. I concluded that there was no hope for these relationships or their planning goals, because Lewis and Gordon did not want to communicate; they wanted to get rid of Simon. I advised them I was unimpressed with their "decision to cooperate," and unless they changed the nature and motives of their choices and decisions, there was nothing I could do for them. If what I had experienced was cooperation, I certainly did not want to be around when they might have a disagreement. They did not need a facilitator; they needed a referee.

The real culprit of the Relick's problem was that their fathers had survived without communicating, and they passed on the curse to their sons. The only thing their fathers thought they had to do to provide for the succession of their business was to arrange for their sons to buy them out. The dads defaulted to the ultimate cop-out, "They'll work it out." Unfortunately, I was not with the dads twenty years prior to share my Brother/Cousins Relationship Axiom and motivate them to address the leadership and deadlock vote issue.

The dads neither recognized nor addressed their stewardship responsibility of choosing a successor leader. They provided no successor leadership structure and no example of how to communicate and work together. When the cousins considered buying the company from their dads, the rush of excitement surrounding the purchase of the company overpowered the fact that they did not like their prospective partners. The prospect of future frustration and acrimony was no major problem because they had witnessed their fathers living in this environment all of their business careers.

History and negative choices were dragging this business into the pit of self-destruction. A few weeks after the meeting I just described, the company's banker called and asked if I would become involved again. He apparently was obtaining information about the state of affairs from someone inside the business. We had a frank discussion about the relationships, chaos and petty power struggles between the cousins. I expressed my unwillingness to get involved in situations when family unity was not the priority. The banker said he was going to get involved and asked my opinion as to how to improve the situation. I told him that the only hope for harmony or unity was a decision by these guys to communicate and work together for the good of the group. I continued to say that communication required a sincere, dedicated decision to cooperate; and I did not see Gordon and Lewis making this choice. The banker's response was that he was going to make a decision that he felt would generate some cooperation.

A few days later he called back with assurances that the attitudes of the cousins had changed. He even said he was paying my fee, so I should have no concern about being fired for being honest and aggressive. It takes a little imagination to appreciate what the banker said to the squabbling cousins who were apparently running the banker's credit into the ground. With their credit line at risk, he convinced them that a choice to communicate was appropriate.

Not long after the banker called, Gordon called and asked me to meet with them again. He felt his brother and cousins were now motivated to make progress. What an understatement. In our next meeting, without so much as a single sour word from Lewis, we outlined pay plans and a stockholder's agreement. After two more meetings, the agreements were signed and sealed. It is amazing what a decision to communicate can do for productivity.

With a signed agreement, I thought my work with these guys was completed; however, the banker recognized that a signed stockholder's agreement was no solution to the real problem. He called me again and asked if I would work with the cousins, specifically to improve their communication and deal with the simmering leadership problem that was sure to resurface. I agreed, with the condition that he again compel the cousins to participate. The banker heartily agreed, and we initiated a Communication Improvement Program focused on Simon and Gordon. The banker had given them motivation, so I scheduled a series of eight meetings. The banker attended our first meeting to ensure that every Monday afternoon at 3:00 p.m., the three of us would meet. Everyone also agreed that I would be in control. Moreover, they realized that I was not going to babysit; if they did not cooperate, I was "out of there" and they were in deep trouble with their banker.

The rules for these meetings were very simple, as they generally are for sessions of this nature:

- *I could designate who was to speak.*
- *I could interrupt and determine when an individual should cut off an expression.*
- *Neither of them could interrupt the other.*
- *We would talk for 50 minutes, take a 20 minute break and talk again for 50 minutes, ending at 5:00 p.m.*
- *They would keep substantive notes in a ring-binder, exchanging binders at the end of each meeting.*
- *If I stipulated that a statement or conclusion was note-worthy, they would both make an entry in their notebooks.*

We began with several awkward sessions of intense verbal sparring. After Simon and Gordon realized the insults were not going to make the meetings any easier, the discussion became more substantive. At the beginning of the third meeting, Simon returned Gordon's note pad, making reference to a note he had made two weeks prior. He said Gordon totally misunderstood what he had said. Gordon acted confused so they both opened up their notebooks, found the point which related to how Simon initially became president, and clarified the point to the agreement of both. That was the point at which posturing ended and they began to communicate. The notes made them listen to each other to prevent being embarrassed.

In the next meeting, Simon revealed he was in the business because his father made him feel it was his responsibility as the eldest cousin to manage the business. Simon stated that he had wanted to be a stock broker. Gordon was shocked, as he felt Simon wanted to be president for the pride, prestige and easy duty. Simon added his father felt that, after Gordon's had father served as president, it was only fair for his side of the family to have a turn at president.

Amazingly, Gordon began commiserating with Simon and counseling him to live his own life. He assured Simon that, although they had their differences, he would not renege on payments to Simon's dad any more than he could renege on payments to his own father. After the fifth meeting, the environment between cousins changed from conflict and rivalry to collaboration.

After two or three more meetings, we brought in Lewis and Steven. The awkwardness between Lewis and Simon only lasted a couple of weeks. With Gordon not feeding Lewis' emotions, he also settled down. Ultimately, Simon and Lewis relived their juvenile playground experience and exchanged apologies. After a few more meetings, the subject of career choices came up and, with the encouragement of his partners, Simon took a leave of absence to explore a career in the securities business and Gordon took over the presidency. A year or so later, Gordon, Lewis and Steven bought Simon's stock and he pursued his first choice of careers, the stock market. The business prospered and grew dramatically, primarily because of the harmony and unity between Gordon, Lewis and Steven.

This experience illustrates that it is simply amazing what happens when people communicate; and communication is not difficult when it becomes a priority.

> *The economy can be bad; the competition can be unmerciful; but, strong, bonding relationships within the business can overcome these obstacles.*

The contrary argument also holds: If the economy is great and the business has a lock on the market, family dissension and rivalry can take a business down.

It is the responsibility of those in control of a family business to communicate and to teach communication to their family by example. It is further the responsibility of family business owners to ensure that communication, unity and harmony are achieved. No guts, no glory. With the intestinal fortitude to demand communication and address issues, parents can have peace of mind that the business succession goals will not fall victim to pettiness and self-serving agendas.

Building relationships is not rocket science or brain surgery. A commitment of time, energy and emotions to family communication does require a sacrifice, but the results will build the best support structure for success and happiness. The primary requirement to achieving strong relationships and setting a strong foundation for future achievements is to decide that communication is essential to business productivity. Relationships are a natural by-product of people who choose to communicate. Spend your most valuable asset -- time -- on your most important opportunity, building productive relationships.

Thoughts for the Successor Children

Children of parents who own a family business are in a unique position. As a group, they face an environment replete with contrasting advantages and disadvantages. The resulting challenges merit both caution and encouragement. The issues are incredibly important and they are hugely influential on you and everyone around you. And so it's essential that you take a long, frank look at them.

The following comments are directed specifically to the prospective heirs and successor owners/managers of a family business. However, everyone involved in the business, especially parents, can hopefully gain productive insights through consideration of these thoughts and suggestions.

The consensus of employees, in-laws, advisors and the citizens on the street is that an heir to the owner of a prosperous business is very fortunate. You are referred to as the "Owner's Kid, the fortunate winner of the procreation lottery." Those on the outside looking in believe you, heir apparent to the business, are in a can't lose situation. You have a built-in, guaranteed successful career. If you just come to work everyday, do what is asked and show a little initiative, you will have more financial opportunity than 99.99% of the world ever considered. If you work hard you can be your own boss and control your destiny. Moreover, if your good fortune holds, you could receive an inheritance that can provide luxuries and opportunities that are experienced by few. Under the worst circumstances, you will sell the business, harvest those golden seeds of your parents and enjoy a life on easy street.

These same experts typically will not give you credit for anything. "The kid struggled to get out of school, bought his college degree and Daddy's influence was the only way Junior ever achieved anything." As an owner's kid, the world considers that you have never really earned anything through your independent effort. If you are good at what you do, it is luck or circumstances. If you are successful, someone under you is responsible. If you are early to work, it is because you are going to slip out early. If you are late to work, you are irresponsible. If you make any mistakes, it is a sign of your impending failure because you are lazy. Any learning miscues are amplified beyond reason. The citizen on the street does not recognize your accomplishments, acknowledging only that you are the luckiest person on the planet, and is unappreciative of your good fortune. Proving yourself as worthy of respect is a continually frustrating uphill battle.

There is no doubt that being a successor to a family business has some advantages. On the other hand, there are also some disadvantages. Few fully understand the ramifications of growing up under the tutelage, judgment and refinement of a highly successful, typically demanding and usually compulsive parent, and then trying to work with them as an adult. Being a family business successor is no cake walk. The near futile challenge of proving yourself to friends and employees rates in comparison to meeting your parents' typically distorted expectations. This can be an overwhelming challenge, because parents' stereotypical memories of "how they did it" pollutes their reaction to any effort that you project. Furthermore, their mind-set of you as a teenager, college student and young adult similarly distorts their attitudes and your opportunities. It certainly would not be considered a privilege to live under a microscope of both jealous employees and predisposed parents.

Twenty-four hours a day, seven days a week, they watch you, seeking validation of their dream of your super performance or their predisposition of your future.

A job can really become a drag when anything you do or say, on or off the job, has a bearing on how successful you will be. By and large, the world does not understand that there is a formidable price to pay for the opportunity of working within and possibly carrying on a family business.

Each situation is unique. With regard to your specific situation, you may be in a very enviable position. As a bright, aggressive and responsible young adult, you may have a lock on the good life with guaranteed ownership in a successful business with longstanding, highly competent managers who make your job a snap. You may understand the business and have confidence that working in your family's business is the career for you and you can run it, top to bottom. As long as we are speaking hypothetically, you also may have mastered the role of business leader; and you are just waiting for your parent to retire so you and your siblings can step in and take over.

You may have understanding, sensitive parents who accept and respect your individuality and have unreserved confidence in your capability. You may have perfect harmony with your parents, your brothers and sisters, in-laws and each of the employees of your business. Your family may cherish and honor your spouse, and your spouse may dearly love their position in your family environment. You may be satisfied with the responsibilities you have been given, the opportunities in your future and the accomplishments in your past.

If your situation reflects the above example of gratification and harmony, thank God for your good fortune. Actually, you may even want to pinch yourself to determine if you are dreaming. The facts of life are that everyone has problems. Very few families are living, breathing examples of continuous harmony. Even fewer families who are in exceptionally close contact, as in a family business, are examples of perfect ongoing harmony. There are just too many points of vulnerability. It is rare indeed that all aspects of family and business are acceptable and gratifying to all family members and in-laws. The combination of extended parental control, career aspirations, economic ambition, sibling tension, in-laws and emotions make for a very volatile situation. If life in the family and business is good and has always been that way, you should quickly write a book and tell the world how you did it. Write it quickly, because, before the ink is dry, your good fortune could pass just like a dream.

The environment you are enjoying or hating is of your choosing.

On the other hand, your situation could be the pits. You may not feel fortunate to be the child of a business owner for any number of reasons. You may not enjoy the business or the lifestyle that the business creates. You may feel you are being railroaded into a career that you really do not want. You may resent the business for occupying too much of your dad's time when you were young. Your "nit picky" parents may be continuing to try to whip you into the perfect person that they were in their fantasy. You may have an obnoxious brother or sister who is making your life miserable. You may not be able to please them or your parents with anything short of working 80 hours a week with a willingness to do more. You may be in a position where you do not believe you can please anyone, including your parents, your spouse, your supervisor or even your dog.

You may have come into the business only to prove your "worthiness" and, having made your point, cannot find a way out. You may despise the business, your parents, your siblings, your job and the very essence of your family's business. You may feel your parents love the business more than anything, including you. It may be apparent that you feel they do not respect who you are, what you can do or what you have to offer. They may have made up their minds about what you are, what they think you should be and are not interested in your opinion. You may be in the business only because of profound guilt or a lack of nerve to be yourself or try something new. The amber light could be blinking, the alarm could be sounding that the Chernobyl Syndrome (meltdown) of your life could be imminent.

You have been dealt your unique circumstances for better or for worse. You did not apply for your position as your parents' child. You did not win this opportunity for a great career through long hours and effective hard work. By God's sovereign choice, you are the child of your parents, a member of your family, raised a certain way, in a certain community, an heir to an estate and a possible successor to the family business. Those are appointments beyond your control or choice.

On the other hand, if you are an adult employee in the family business, this is a choice you have made. The environment you are enjoying or hating is of your choosing. If you are part of the real world, your family business has challenges and opportunities. You are experiencing the typical enjoyment, gratification, frustration, disappointment and stress of the family business. It just comes with the territory. Business can be fun, and it can be tough. Parents can irritate children and children can disappoint parents. Siblings struggle and compete to prove themselves and achieve control. Such is life in the family business. Every day is a new adventure with inevitable disappointments and victories.

Regardless of your circumstances, you are in control. There is no denying the hard cold fact that for better or for worse, you are where you chose to be. "But, but, but" does not apply. Regardless of the extenuating, physical, economic, social or family circumstances, you are the captain of your ship. As you address decisions about your attitude, behavior, career and happiness, remember that you are at the helm. Although it may sometimes be difficult to recognize, you make the-long term decisions about where you work, whom you work with, your attitude towards others and your attitude about work. Sure, you are under the authority of others. And there may be a great deal of economic and social opportunity at risk. However, no one can make you stay in a situation against your will.

When considering how to deal with your situation, your life will become much simpler when you recognize you are a responsible adult and are in control. No one makes you have a bad attitude. You have the ability to change where you work and whom you work with. You are in a position to make a difference in your personal circumstances and in the business. A profound truth in life and the family business is that there is no such thing as a free lunch. In some form or fashion, there is a price for performance, position and power. Your major question should be: "Is the price I am paying worth the benefits I will receive?"

You cannot change your mother, father, aunts, uncles, brothers, sisters, cousins or in- laws, but you can, look in the mirror. Here are some suggestions you may want to consider to help you deal with your circumstances:

1. Accept responsibility for where you are and what you are doing.

2. Accept your parents, brother, sisters, and other family members for what they are and do not use them as an excuse for who you are, how you feel or how you behave.

3. Do not embarrass your parents in front of their clients, associates or business-related community.

4. Do not use anyone or any circumstance as an excuse for your unwillingness to be responsible and take charge of your life.

5. Do not waste your productive energy complaining about what you cannot change.

6. Do not act irresponsibly and then call for the sympathy of the world.

7. Maintain a rudiment of faith that your parents have some grasp of what they are doing.

8. Accept that some criticism and some less favorable decisions may be justified and that, in time, you will be able to work through difficult circumstances.

9. Work extremely hard to listen.

10. Acknowledge that this opportunity may be worth hanging in there.

It is best that some owners' children do not participate in the family's business. To assume otherwise is an invitation to disaster. The temperament, ambition, intelligence, compatibility, character, drive, maturity and common sense of each child is a function of Divine Design and environmental influence. The makeup of some children is such that they are not compatible with the family business environment.

It is the joint responsibility of parent and child to determine if the business is right for each child.

Addressing this responsibility is one of the keys to success in the family business. We will address the parents' part of this responsibility in the next chapter. As for you, the lineal descendent, to thine own self be true. Sure, you could be walking away from a great opportunity. However, the future is dismal for you if the family business is not the right career. If the business does not excite you, if the business is too demanding or if the environment is too much of a grind, a family business career could be a terrible mistake.

It is frustrating and demeaning to be a financial captive in a family business. In the long term, money is not a reasonable trade-off for a life of day-to-day aggravation and frustration. Maybe you do not like the business or the business does not like you. The reasons can cover all angles of aptitude and attitude. Some kids don't have the physical, emotional or mental makeup that the business requires. But inevitably, some career decisions are an agonizing struggle between economics, and other preferred careers. Do not consider your future in the family business casually. No doubt, money and social standing are very important. However, money and social standing are not worthy compensation for a miserable life, a broken marriage or family friction.

Having said that, let me go on record to express that entering your family's business and playing a role in the succession of that business into the next generation is a tremendously unique opportunity. Yes, you must be true to yourself and determine if the family business is the proper career for you. If the answer is a resounding "No," press on in your chosen career without guilt or reservation. If there is no clear decision or significant doubt, give the family business a chance and you may find unparalleled freedom, independence and opportunity. And you do not have to risk falling off the edge of the world. Your only risk will be a little time. You can always pack it up and seek new surroundings to pursue your dream. Your particular circumstances aside, carrying forward a family business is a great opportunity. Generally speaking, you will be hard pressed to duplicate the career challenges and exceptional opportunities.

Before making your career decision, give your circumstances and goals time to crystallize. Do not make a hasty decision. If you work elsewhere, keep your mind open to the possibility of returning. If you are confused, seek counsel from those you respect and who know you well. Listen to your parents. They may appear to be "boneheads," but they do have a unique perspective of both you and the business; however, because you are their child, some of their advice is biased. If you are married, listen to your spouse. Your spouse is part of you and should have a strong influence on your decisions. The important issue is your happiness and gratification and, if you are married, the happiness of your spouse.

If you intend to be successful, you must be satisfied both with how you are spending your working hours and who you are spending them with.

Recognize that a successful family business is not necessarily a golden goose, but it may very well be a golden opportunity. A golden goose is a family business that is prepared in all respects to endure the challenges of inter-generation transfer. As we have previously discussed, there are innumerable specific challenges, any one of which can rain on your parade. Indeed. many highly successful family businesses are not aware of these challenges or are adequately prepared to deal with them. Do not misread your circumstances. In spite of the fact that your family's business may be fabulously successful in today's terms, your family's business is not bullet proof and not necessarily prepared for succession. In order for your family business to achieve succession, you must be willing to work hard and sacrifice for that goal.

Business succession is not a ride that you can plan to take. In order for your family's business to survive into the next generation, you must get out of the wagon and push, pull or do whatever it takes to maintain progressive movement. The business will not be given to you. You are going to have to take it. You will need a passion for the business, not an affection. You may simply be enamored with the prospective freedom, prestige and the financial fruits of the business like most red-blooded capitalists would be in your circumstances; however, this will not be enough where you are going. In order to cross the mountains ahead, you will need a hunger for the essence of the business and a definition of success that includes the continuity of the business.

If you are committed to succession, avoid self sabotage. Be aware of what you say and do and try to direct your thoughts, words and actions toward the achievement of your goals. Humility is essential, but so is confidence in your ability to learn and ultimately shoulder the responsibility of leadership. As we have already addressed, there is no future in expressing to managers and employees doubt about your ability to succeed. As we have already addressed, there are plenty of "naysayers" out there who will project doubt and even lay a few land mines. They will take any doubt you express in your ability and blow it totally out of proportion. Do your very best to make good impressions on family managers and key employees. Their opinions count, and they can have a positive or negative impact on your career achievements. If you are not yet serious about a career, while making up your mind, do not take a position that requires more commitment than you are willing to make. If you cannot have pride and enthusiasm in what you are doing, get out before you create negative mindsets that will irreparably damage your future career opportunity.

Business succession is not a ride that you can plan to take. In order for your business to survive into the next generation, you must get out of the wagon and push, pull or do whatever it takes to maintain progressive movement.

For those of you who are willing and able to make a career commitment to your family's business, beware of over-responsibility. I frequently speak with young and even middle-aged managers who feel trapped in the business. They have bought into the concept that parents or siblings are depending upon them to run the business. They accept sacrificing their happiness for the actual or perceived well-being of family. In spite of success and prosperity, they resent the business and dependency of family members. This is an unfortunate predicament that is not in the best interest of all concerned.

There are instances, because of unforeseen, extraordinary circumstances, when family members are reasonably relied upon to step forward and assume responsibility for running the business for the security and welfare of all concerned. Supporting and helping one another is what family is all about. If this is your situation, thank God you are able to help your family in time of need. You should feel good that you are able to make a difference. Hang in there and help get family members or the business out of the unfortunate circumstances that can be caused by an unexpected death or business downturn; however, this is an opportunity for you to help, not become the victim of indentured service. You have no responsibility to stay in the business long-term to support your family.

After a reasonable period of time, which can only be determined by the circumstances, your family support role has been satisfied. You have your life to live, your mountains to climb If the family business is not your career calling, establish a reasonable time frame to help out as best you can and then move on to your chosen career. You are not indispensable or irreplaceable. A non-family manager can be hired or the business can be sold with the proceeds utilized to satisfy your family's security needs. It will not be healthy for you or the business if you continue in the business against your wishes for the long-term.

Any motivation for being in your family's business other than your own self-generated desire will eventually lead to feelings that are damaging to you, the business and the family unit. You will resent yourself for not having the will to take action. You will resent your family's dependency that has smothered your life. And you will resent the business. The heart of the business, which is formed by the enthusiasm, synergy, and drive of the family, will experience a slow, cruel death. The daily frustration and aggravation of being in the wrong business will reduce your ability to cope with stress. Your effectiveness as a leader, manager and team member will ultimately decline.

Make the right career choice for you, and you will also be making the right choice for the family and the business, even if your decisions are contradictory to what other self-centered members of the family think.

Sibling rivalry can be a beast in the family business. I wish I could tell you that real families genuinely support and encourage each other; however, my experience confirms that real families have competitive environments. The fact that the familiar face across the table is that of your sibling does not change the fact that you have ambitious goals, and she or he may be between you and your goals. Competition can motivate you to new heights that could not be achieved without the definition of outperforming or surpassing a sibling. Competing with family members for recognition, achievement or position is a positive motivation to achievement as long as there is reasonable restraint and respect for family members. Historically, the inherent motivation of sibling competition has enabled families to achieve the reputation of hyper-productive business units. Unfortunately, family members commonly conclude that their gain or growth can only come at a cost to siblings. The resulting pitiful lows in family interaction undermine business effectiveness and success.

Sibling Rivalry

Some key issues in sibling rivalry are: How important is your success? How far will you go to achieve your success? Will you abuse family members and your own overall well-being to achieve your personal goals? Are you compelled to further your cause by undermining your sibling(s) with sinister innuendo, subversion or outright attacks on their motives and efforts? An unrestrained ambition for personal success can overwhelm the sense of family, unity and decency. Sibling rivalry raises its ugly head by rationalizing that self-serving, disrespectful behavior is an appropriate response to a sibling's perceived position or tactics.

Sibling rivalry is a product of self-centered rationalization of a sibling's unfair circumstances. Initially, one sibling concedes that he cannot express his genuine feelings and compete straight up. He believes that the natural development of circumstances is unacceptable; therefore, the sibling retreats to emotional guerrilla warfare and surreptitiously protects turf or attempts to obtain what he feels he is "entitled to." As we observed with the Relick family in Chapter 12 on family communication, the ugly jungle warfare reaches crescendo as both siblings conclude that they are unfairly disadvantaged and that a family commando attitude is the only way they can achieve their rightful status.

> *Sibling rivalry raises its ugly head by rationalizing that self-serving, disrespectful behavior is an appropriate response to a <u>siblings perceived position or tactics.</u>*

The equally immature, insecure sibling recognizes the attacks and returns what he or she feels is an appropriate protective or retaliatory response. A crossfire ensues that wreaks havoc on the family and business environment. The casualties are widespread. The siblings suffer from the waste of emotional and mental energy on self-centered strategy and retaliation. Other family members suffer because they must emotionally struggle to remain impartial and unaffected. Notably, the business suffers because productive energy of team members is wasted on petty, self-centered causes. Also, the attitudes of employees, vendors, creditors and advisors are affected. These important players evaluate how current or future family owners treat each other and recognize their relative vulnerability. In other words, employees, key managers and supporting vendors acquire a sobering understanding that if their current or future boss will do unscrupulous things to "blood," they are certainly capable of doing the same or worse to them.

The First Family Business Golden Rule

If you are struggling with sibling rivalry, stop! Take a step back and count the cost. Sibling rivalry will dissolve, obliterate and utterly destroy the synergistic advantage of a family business; the spirit of unity will be unraveled. Sibling rivalry will serve as an example to the employees who witness this childish behavior, providing them motivation to also serve their selfish needs at the cost of other employees and the company. No attack goes unnoticed by those whom you are dependent upon to run the business and who will depend upon you for their welfare in the future. No one remains neutral. Lines are drawn between family and among the employees. The cost is a total disintegration of the team attitude.

Practicing the first Family Business Golden Rule will effectively eliminate sibling rivalry. Do unto your brother or sister as you would have them do unto you and give them the <u>benefit of the doubt.</u>

Sibling rivalry will cease when you stop rationalizing that you are the victim and have a right to further your personal interests at the cost of a family member. You and no one else are in control of your life, so, from a family perspective, you cannot be a victim to anything other than your own self-pity.

Looks, words, attitudes and actions can be lethal weapons in a family jungle. If you really feel that you can justify your gain at the cost of another family member, you are not really family. You may be "blood kin," but family indicates a spirit of mutual support and interdependency. Any effort to undermine a family member is drawing spiritual blood and breaking spiritual bones of the family body. Too much damage and the family unit cannot survive. From a personal perspective, you should be aware that as a family member, some of the spiritual blood and bones are your own. Stop the self-centered rationalization and the behind-the-back cowardly shots. Have the character and respect to create dialogue to address problems and work out solutions.

Exercise the maturity to directly express your grievances to a sibling.

Trust me, I understand the difficulty of dialogue with an obnoxious, insensitive sibling. However, you do not understand the destructive nature of sibling warfare, or you would have never gotten involved. If you are a participant in a petty struggle with a sibling, stop. Confront your struggling sibling and ask him to do the same thing. Compel him/her to sit down with you and reconcile your differences. I know it will not be easy, but the benefits are worth the effort. If need be, include an arbitrator or even a counselor to help you both talk it through. Unity and harmony and even investment into professional help are critically important. A little humility and a few apologies can create a healing salve for the relationship and the family.

Be prepared for your sibling to reject any offer to reconcile differences and bury the sword. Unfortunately, their feelings and reactions are beyond your control. It takes at least two for sibling rivalry. You are in control of your actions. Take control by ceasing fire, even if it is unilateral. If you elect not to participate, the war is called off. Step back and examine the insecurities that would lead to the extremes of tearing down a family member. If you need help, get it. Count the cost of what can happen if your business and your family come unraveled. If you are unwilling to deal with a sibling about attitudes and actions, you must assume a portion of the responsibility for the negative circumstances that develop.

A third-party mediator may be essential to resolving sibling rivalry. I assure you that those around you will recognize your restraint and strength of your character and come to your support. Unfortunately, there can be circumstances when your refusal to lower yourself to attacking family will cost you what you may want the most. Trust me; sibling rivalry is the premier example of the reality that there are some things that are not worth fighting for.

The Second Family Business Golden Rule

Another common issue of business succession is guilt. If you have taken advantage of a business succession opportunity to achieve fortune and success, there is no reason for guilt.

> ## The Second Family Business Golden Rule: Succession of a family business is a golden opportunity.

If you are the child selected to be the next leader of the business, there is no reason to feel guilty that you are the "chosen one." An attitude of gratitude to your parents and God Almighty is fine, but guilt is both useless and self-destructive. Assuming you did not rob a bank or "assassinate" a sibling to get where you are, cast off the lie that you are unworthy and celebrate your good fortune by living up to the expectations of those who chose you. Respect the "procreation lottery" and avoid showing the shallowness of arrogance. Your circumstances are, to a significant degree, a result of the miracle of birth. Where you were born has had a substantial impact upon your success. There is no justification for guilt, but you should be humble, because the real difference between you and the group that is working for you is really very small. Be humbly confident in your ability and quietly proud of your accomplishments.

Continue to do your job to the best of your capability and make the best of your situation. Keep in mind there is no such thing as a free lunch. You indeed may be fortunate, but as a business owner and/or family leader, there will be sacrifices and trade-offs. There is no assurance that you are the lucky one. Dealing with obnoxious or insensitive family members who do not share your values may be your fate. But times change and so do circumstances and attitudes. There are many variables affecting our personal lives and the business. What may seem terrible today may be okay or even great tomorrow. What may appear great today could go into the tank tomorrow. However, the one thing you can control is your patience, your attitude and the effort you put out to achieve harmony and unity. The most important issue is for you to believe in your heart that you are doing the best you can to take advantage of your opportunities and promote harmony and unity within your family.

Let's review an experience with a family who owned a substantial residential construction business:

Case History: Jake and Donna

Everyone in this family was strong willed and vocal, including the son and daughter. The father and mother were in their mid-sixties, looking to retire and move to Florida. They contacted me to help them make important decisions about transferring the business to their children. They were struggling with the decision of how to split up the business between their children. The son, Jake, was in his mid-forties and had devoted his career to building the business. The daughter, Donna, was employed in the business, but at thirty-five and divorced with three children, she was primarily a homemaker and only capable of support positions. However, Donna had made it clear to Mom and Dad that she wanted to pursue a more active leadership career in the business after her kids were a little older.

Upon hearing this, Jake took the offensive to convince his parents that Donna did not deserve owning any more of the business than her current 10%. Mom and Dad did not agree with Jake. They believed the business was a family asset and had asked me to help them deal with this dilemma. They wanted the business to be operated by Jake but felt Donna should also have a career opportunity. The business was a long standing, second generation, highly profitable institution. They were concerned about Donna's security and her feelings if she did not receive a significant portion of the stock through gifts or the estate.

Jake was a straight-up guy during my interview. He did not come across as greedy or pushy. He said that he was responsible for the company's outstanding growth over the last 10 years and he expected the business to continue growing. He did not consider it fair for his sister to receive a substantial benefit from the growth with no meaningful contribution. He said she was trying to influence his parents to give her other significant non-business assets of equal value.

He expected that Donna would not come to work for at least another five years and, at over 40 with no experience, she probably would never make a significant contribution. He also stated that he needed to bring some of his key managers into the ownership ranks or risk losing them to competition. The ownership of key managers combined with a distribution to his sister would leave him with barely 51%, and that was not sufficient incentive to work sixty-five hours a week .

I spoke to Donna, asking her how she felt about a career in the business. Mom and Dad had been unwilling to discuss the stock issue with her because they did not want to catch any emotional flack. Donna was indeed a demonstrative, strong-willed lady who could take care of herself in any argument, debate or wrestling match. Actually, after speaking to her just a short time, I thought to myself, "I think she could run the company better than Jake. She is attractive, very bright and assertive. Wow, is he missing the boat by not having her working in the business."

My jaw literally dropped when, in response to my inquiry about her goals and the business, she responded matter-of-factly, "I don't want any more stock. The stock should rightfully go to Jake." I was preparing to do the "asset distribution two-step" with an argumentative, strong-willed woman; and she just rolled over. She said that she had changed her mind about a career in the family business because she could see that this was becoming an issue of contention. She had no desire to put pressure on her parents about how they should divide their estate.

Donna continued to say without emotion that Jake deserved to control the business and, if her involvement would threaten him, she would bow out. I supported her rationale, stating that it was very apparent that the distribution of the business was an issue Jake was willing to wrestle over at the cost of parental anguish.

To say Jake was pleased with the outcome of our discussions would be a gross understatement. Almost overnight he changed his demeanor with both Donna and his parents. Apparently owning all of the company was a much bigger deal to him than we had estimated. With the agreement and support of everyone, I then started the wheels moving to have stock purchase agreements and estate documents drafted that allocated the business to Jake and other property to Donna.

We made gifts of stock to Jake and gifts of real estate to Donna. Jake entered into a stock purchase agreement with Mom and Dad. We amended Mom and Dad's revocable family trust to state that Donna would receive the real estate and cash from Jake's buyout of the remainder of their parents' stock. A life insurance policy funded the stock purchase and estate taxes. Four years later, eager beaver Jake was doing so well with the business that he personally purchased his parents' voting stock and adopted an ESOP to purchase the balance of their non-voting stock and Donna's stock.

All appeared to be going very well for both the business and the family. Both Mom and Dad passed away during the next five-year period. Their estates were probated without any unusual complications, as the life insurance was adequate to cover estate taxes. Jake was happy that he owned or controlled all the stock. Donna appeared to be happy as a homemaker, part-time employee and owner of significant cash and real estate including the building occupied by Jake's business. She did not make any outward contentions of ill feelings towards Jake. And hopefully, Mom and Dad were resting in peace, because their son and daughter were well provided for and apparently working in harmony. Then circumstances began to change.

After his parents' estate was settled, Jake became a magnet for problems. Unbeknownst to the world, Jake had been engaged in an extramarital affair. Evidently, he was involved with a young lady in her mid-twenties, who could be described as "high maintenance." As we learned later, Jake was taking money out of the company to support his dual life and notably to keep this "hot number" happy. Jake's wife found out about his mistress and sued him for divorce. Jake found himself confronting big problems. Needless to say, if Donna had been a stockholder, these problems would have been hers as well.

Unfortunately, the company's chief financial officer was impressed with Jake's example. He had instigated his own "profit sharing plan," and distorted the books to cover his crime. An audit precipitated by the divorce revealed that the CFO had stolen in excess of $500,000 from the business. In order to pay off "the curse" of his divorce, which was about $1,500,000, Jake had to take more cash out of the business and take on more debt.

Just when he did not think life could get worse, it did. He lost his concentration on business fundamentals and his competition took him to the woodshed.

When the cash dried up, his young girlfriend also stepped out in search of greener pastures. Jake came under pressure from banks and the Teamsters, whom the employees asked to represent them because of their concern about the declining business value in the ESOP. The business was in free fall.

Fortunately, Jake was able to sell the company; however, he was the target of litigation from the employees. They asserted and ultimately proved that, in allowing the business to decline dramatically in value, he had violated his fiduciary responsibility as trustee of the ESOP. After the smoke cleared, Jake was broke.

Donna, on the other hand, was sitting on the sidelines of this demolition derby doing quite well. She owned the real estate, which she was able to lease to the new owner. The rental income combined with her cash made her financially strong. She proves my theory that being the anointed successor is not a guarantee to success and prosperity.

In the aftermath, Donna and I reflected on what had happened and on her feelings. She said that, years earlier, she had been very disappointed that she was not encouraged to seek a career in the family business. She said that, before I arrived on the scene, she recognized her brother's drive to obtain control and ownership of the company. She said she felt the pressure Jake was putting on her parents and personally experienced a "stiff arm" in response to her desire to get more involved. She chose her non-participatory attitude to avoid making a bad situation even worse. Her parents did not deserve the frustration and agony of two adults arguing as children trying to control toys. She attributed her ultimate good fortune to luck *because, given her preference, she would have gladly taken 49% of the business and Jake would have taken her down the tube with him.*

Reflecting upon this experience, I encourage you to express your business career ownership objectives, but neither celebrate nor mourn the ultimate business disposition decisions. Business is a marathon, not a sprint. What may appear to be good fortune may turn out to be a disaster. What may appear to be disrespectful and unfair may turn out to be a blessing.

You should be committed to the achievement of your business involvement and leadership goals. However, you should also be sensitive to the total picture. Seek an understanding of the many factors, such as the perspective of parents, siblings and vendors, that come into play in determining the future owners and operators of a family business. Assess which of those factors you want to influence for the achievement of your personal goals. Keep Donna's attitude in mind: that the integrity and harmony of the family is at least as important as your goals.

If your choice is to be an owner/operator of your family's business, dedicate yourself towards taking it to a higher level. Prepare yourself to be in the spotlight. Recognize that everything you do will be an example for all the employees you are endeavoring to motivate. Every word and deed will be cast either as a positive or a negative influence on employees, customers, bankers, and vendors.

Unfortunately, as fate has it, you may not be on a track to assume an ownership or leadership position. You may be destined to be a co-owner, co-manager, support manager, employee or bystander. You may even be the victim of a misunderstanding, bad luck, birth order, learning disability, personality conflict, or, worst of all, favoritism. Admittedly, the pain and frustration of any of these circumstances can be overpowering. I offer my regrets and sympathy. Having witnessed the agony of these unfortunate circumstances on many occasions, I appreciate the burden of your frustration and the pain of what ultimately is rationalized to be rejection.

Beyond this empathy I offer important advice. First, regardless of perceived equity or luck, work hard and diligently at your assigned duties or chosen profession. Let your walk be your talk. Do not plead your case over a sibling or challenge the choice and capability of the person chosen ahead of you. If you start griping, your bitterness will undermine family harmony and business productivity. Let your outstanding performance, not idle words, plead your case.

There is no greater advocate for your ability than consistent, dedicated, high-quality effort directed at your assigned duties. Your performance will impact minds faster and better than presumptive words.

Dedicate yourself to learning the business. The level of your effort and commitment will set the standards for the respect you receive. You will reap what you sow in a family business environment. Family and advisors begin evaluating you even before you start work. Your attitudes, actions and statements determine how people will deal with you.

The Third Family Business Golden Rule

Being ambitious, aggressive, and, to some degree, impatient are good attributes of a future owner and leader. However, none of these character traits are an excuse for taking shortcuts in learning the various jobs and skills that will be required to operate your business.

> ### There are no elevators to the leadership position of a family business. You must take the stairs.

Taking steps to learn each phase of your business requires patience and submission to the guidance and judgment of supervisors and parents. In most cases, submission is a greater challenge for a family member than learning the trade. Take heed to the third family business golden rule: A family member can never learn to be a good manager until he or she learns how to be a good employee. Being held accountable as a rank and file employee is a fundamental step to learning how to be a family business manager. Your parents, older sibling and employees have been where you are going and deserve your respect. If you are not prepared to maintain or improve your family standards of attitude, effort and humility, choose another career.

The key to the transition of ownership and control is to avoid the problems your parents incurred and take advantage of the opportunities they see. If you are compelled to "take the elevator" or do things your way, trust me, you are going to make very expensive mistakes and feel the pain of nasty falls. You may find yourself at the top of your business confronted with problems you are unprepared to resolve. Even worse, you could find yourself ready to take over leadership only to be rejected by the lending institutions or franchisers who enable your business to operate. You only get one chance to go through training. Be humble and grateful that others are taking the time and effort to give you their greatest resource, knowledge. Your parents and/or the experienced key people you depend upon are not going to be around forever. They represent a resource that you must harvest or suffer the consequences later.

I personally thought my mother and father were "double dumb" when I was in high school, college, through four years in the military and up until I was about 30 years old. I loved them and tolerated what I thought was their ignorance because they did not have formal education; and they really had not seen what was happening outside of our home in a small North Carolina community. They would infuriate me by suggesting that I slow down and stop looking for short cuts. My Dad sounded silly to me saying that what employers and customers valued the most was dependability and character. Amazingly, as I grew older, Dad seemed smarter. When I was about 30, married and with children, I started feeling the embarrassment of some of the costly screw-ups I had perpetrated. It is obvious that I was the dumb one and I thank God that my Mom and Dad maintained patience with me during what was certainly a discouraging time for them.

As you progress up the steps to learn your family's business, you may come under unreasonable pressure from your parents to make you first a model employee and then a perfect manager. They may expect you to be "Super Successor." All they may want you to do is work 70 hours per week, be everywhere on time, read their minds, perform perfectly and be the perfect citizen. And when you do not act like "Super Successor" they may pick, pick, pick. If you think you can never live up to your parent's expectations, consider yourself a typical owner's kid. If you feel that you are perfect in the eyes of your parents, you had best be careful, because you may be grabbed and put in a museum as a one of a kind. In varying degrees, all parents feel their children never live up to their potential.

Although they mean well, a parent's desire for children to be the best they can be usually comes forth as unreasonable criticism.

The fact is that very few parents ever lived up to their potential, either.

There is only one reasonable solution to being the object of your parents' overzealous, critical desire for you to succeed: communication. You must show your parents you are doing your best and then convince them that you have heeded their advice and they no longer need to pick at you constantly. Unfortunately, this is usually easier said than done. If your father or mother has made a second career out of finding fault with what you are doing, then they may not respect you enough to engage in communication. This situation does not mean that they do not respect you as their child. It simply means they do not respect you as someone trying to accomplish their dream of what you should be. Consequently, you will probably need someone else to argue your case, such as a succession planner or a family advisor. Someone they respect and who respects you can possibly convey that you are trying and their criticism is not helping you get better. However, if you keep making the same mistakes over and over, do not expect anyone to extend their credibility on your behalf.

Do not hesitate to ask your parents to bring someone in to help. Find a third party who can empathize with your predicament as well as your parents' feelings. Don't take the lead in selecting this third party. If your parents are not the leaders in the selection, they likely will not respect the advice. An uninvolved third party's perspective can help you adjust your opinion of yourself or defend your opinion. You should also prepare yourself for hearing news that agrees with your parents concerning your attitude, effort or commitment.

If you bring in a third party to facilitate communications with parents, you must positively respond to recommendations regarding changes in your behavior and attitudes.

An effective facilitator will make specific behavior modification recommendations to both you and your parents. If you drop the ball, your parents are going to fall back into the behavior that you found so detestable, with even greater conviction.

It is wise to give your parents the benefit of the doubt. Being a parent is a tough job. Being a parent and a boss goes beyond tough and over the horizon. Trust me, they are also feeling the frustration and pain of their inability to communicate and coach. More often than not, parents feel greater pain from ineffective communication.

Your first job in the family business is to come under operational authority, physically and spiritually. This means not only doing what you are told, but also accepting the instruction as the proper organizational methodology. As I recently told a young man who was struggling in a subordinate role to his brother, "If he tells you to do cartwheels in the parking lot, get to it, because he is the boss." You do not have to accept the instructions as being right. Being right is the burden of your parent, sibling or supervisor. You can talk about right or wrong in family strategy discussion if you are asked. But on the job, your burden is to bea team player and role model. If you show rebellion, defiance, and/or insubordination to a senior family member, you will be planting the highly predictable seeds for some employees to react the same way. And the other employees will conclude you are a jerk.

Unfortunately, your best efforts to show or tell your parents you are doing your best may not stop them from perpetually expecting you to do more or do better. Do not overlook the possibility that you can do better. Remember, your parents are members of the small group who really know you. Actually, the highest likelihood is that you can be more attentive, be a better listener, clean up your act or pick up the pace.

There are, however, circumstances when you are giving your job all you have and your parents just cannot be satisfied. This is indeed a frustrating and demoralizing situation. There is no encouragement for what you may be doing right. There is limited reinforcement of who you are and what you can be. This being the case, remember that you are in control. Your only hope for happiness and gratification is to assume total responsibility for where you are and exercise your control. If you have developed a resilience to their cutting remarks, press on. If you have reached your limit, examine your options and take the course of action that is dictated by your emotions, family and personal goals.

Case History: The Perfectionist Father

To illustrate an example of taking control, let me share the story of an auto dealer client who was at odds with his son. Junior was general manager of the family business and doing a great job. The father was an impulsive stickler for minute detail. Junior was a natural salesman who focused on the goal line, not the yard markers. Junior could sell cars but, otherwise, do nothing right in the perfectionist eye of his father. After several years of this frustration, Junior told his father, with as much respect as possible, to keep his job and the dealership to himself.

The frustrated, impulsive father wished Junior good luck as he took a similar job in another community. Junior maintained an amicable relationship with his father as he prospered in his independent career. They compared notes regularly and grew in mutual respect as both businesses did well. Four years and five sales managers later, Dad recognized that, although Junior was not perfect, he was better than anything he had seen.

His "hub and spoke" micro management style had created constant turnover among Junior's successors.

Having reached critical frustration, to my amazement, Dad ate humble pie and asked Junior to return to the family dealership. Junior called me and asked what he should do. He said he would like to operate and someday own the family dealership, but he was happy with the job he had. Moreover, he said he could not handle his father standing over him and second guessing his management decisions. If everything disintegrated a second time, he was afraid their relationship would suffer irreparable damage.

I told him that having his last name on the sign out front was not a fair tradeoff for being miserable and creating family division. I further pointed out that he showed his character when he withdrew a few years earlier. He had proven his capability. This was not the time to compromise. I urged him to spec out the "deal" he would like to have from his dad and hang tough until his dad met his terms. I told him that, if he came back under terms that were not genuinely acceptable to him, it would be a matter of time until Dad would run him off again. I told him to be prepared for his Dad to laugh at what he would probably see as ridiculous demands, but regardless, to hold his ground.

A few days later Dad called me, flabbergasted with Junior's response. He explained what his "brash, ungrateful son" had said and asked what I thought he should do. I responded that it was clearly evident that Junior had the necessary skills to be successful in the family business or working for someone else. I further pointed out that Junior appeared to like his current job, so I would not waste my time calling him names, such as brash or ungrateful. Dad responded with a frantic cry of "He said he will not come back unless I move my office out of the dealership." He continued by asking if I would call his son and tell him to be reasonable.

I responded, "No," and pleaded for him to examine his priorities. I did not feel that I could call his son and try to convince him to do something that I would not do. I would have no credibility. I further explained that I felt life was too short to spend the better part of a career under the thumb of micro-manager parents. Dad was 65 years old. No doubt he was enjoying running the dealership, and no doubt he was good at it. However, Junior was "a chip off the ol' block," and at 42 was not about to be second-guessed.

I explained that I believed Junior was demanding that Dad move his office out of the dealership because there could only be one dealer, and that was the job Junior wanted.

Junior was doing everyone a favor by facing the reality of his priorities. It was simply time for Dad to do the same.

Dad did not like what he heard from me, so, without any small talk, he said goodbye. I did not receive follow up calls from Junior or Dad for about three weeks. I figured Dad had told Junior to "forget it" and had written me *off because I would not lobby his son. But then Dad called saying, "Loyd, I need you to come up here and work out a buy/sell agreement with Junior. Incidentally, I have a new phone number."*

I subsequently asked, "Does that new number mean you moved your office?" He responded sheepishly with, "Yes, Junior moved his old man out into the street and is taking over the dealership."

"Hold on Dad," I followed. "He is not taking anything. No one has ever taken anything from you, so stop feeding me the sympathy routine. But let me offer my congratulations. You have just made probably the toughest decision of your life. It was the right thing to do and you should not lament giving Junior the opportunity to do what you have always dreamed would happen."

He chuckled, "Yes, I suppose you may have something there. I may have had to give up control of my Baby (the business), but I can always find other things to do." And Dad did just that. While Junior was taking the family's Chevrolet dealership to new levels of profitability, Dad opened a chain of used car lots that became fabulously successful. As a learning experience for all of us, the family business successor assumed responsibility of his career and made tough decisions. These decisions showcased his capability. With an undeniable track record of independent success under his belt, the successor/heir gained confidence, respect and power over his destiny.

If you are in a similar position, hang tough. Be tolerant, forgiving and, like Junior, be strong. Try to understand the difficulty of simultaneously being a parent, an employer and a trainer. Try to understand the relationship your father and mother may have with the business.

Without your help, your parents may fail at the toughest job in family business ownership: letting go.

The Fourth Family Business Rule

It will help you as a junior family member aspiring either to take over or take part in the family's business if you can see things through your parents' eyes. They have the inevitable calling to nurture you as a successor while tolerating your shortcomings. Even though you are a product of your parents, the DNA lottery has made you a unique person, in all likelihood, quite different from your parents' dream child. That does mean that they may have just as tough a time tolerating you as you have tolerating them. They not only have to tolerate your shortcomings; they have to live with the responsibility that they created them. This grind creates understandable frustration and anxiety that can manifest itself in bizarre forms of behavior. In other words, your parents may act crazy and have every right to do so.

You may also be able to better reconcile your circumstances by recognizing that your parents have developed and/or maintained an impressive business based upon the fourth and certainly the most famous family business Golden Rule: "He who has the gold sets the rules."

This philosophy has enabled them to get where they are; and, unless they have lost their faculties, they are not going to give up the rule until they feel totally comfortable about their gold. This means that your parents are going to keep control until they are comfortable about their bank accounts, your maturity, your management capability and your ability to work in harmony with family. As a result, your parents have reasonable expectations about your actions and attitudes that include:

- Being honest and above reproach in all business affairs.

- Respecting their responsibility to prepare you for ownership and leadership.

- Respecting their experience, know-how and proven capabilities.

- Respecting your siblings as team members and giving them the benefit of the doubt.

- Preparing yourself through education and experience to fill a productive role in the business.

- Respecting employees and serving them.

- Submitting to authority and accountability.

- Being on time for work.

- Dressing according to your position.

- Giving your best effort.

- Recognizing that you are a role model for other employees.

- Living within your financial means.

- Providing them salary and benefit continuation after retirement.

- Respecting their decisions regarding disposition of their assets and the treatment of long-term employees.

I suggest that you reflect on this list and determine if you agree that these are reasonable expectations. You may feel that some are unreasonable. That is okay, depending upon the circumstances. Your parents may also have additional expectations that are not on the list. The point is that there is a list of reasonable parental expectations for your situation. Ideally, expectations will be discussed with your parents and confirmed. With a confirmed list or the above list, I challenge you to evaluate yourself to determine if you are holding up your end of the partnership that is required for succession. No one is perfect. It is acceptable for you to have shortcomings, but it is not acceptable that you do not endeavor to achieve your parents' reasonable expectations.

Reflection can bring recommitment to achieve balance in the parent/heir succession partnership. Incidentally, do not feel neglected. You also have reasonable expectations, which will be pointed out to your parents in the next chapter. If you feel unable or unwilling to meet your parents' reasonable expectations, honor your family by seeking a career elsewhere. Working in a non-family environment, you would be forced to come to grips with a similar set of written and unwritten Golden Rules under the heading of Rules of Employment.

Your role as the successor is to learn and become self-sufficient and independent. Unfortunately, just like your parents, you can get carried away with your title or position and not the job you are performing. It is easy to become sensitive about employees, vendors and customers who do not respect your position, knowledge or ability. Keep a grip on reality. As long as your parents are involved in the business, regardless of your position, longstanding associates may look first to them for support or decisions. Even worse, they will take confrontations to your parents in lieu of accepting your word. Refer those who do not accept your authority directly to your parents. Optimally, your parents will not tolerate this and give you the full authority that is due your management position.

Your Role in Succession Planning

It is your responsibility to take an active role in the succession planning process. An insecure or ignorant parent may want to keep you on the outside of the planning circle and in the dark. It is inappropriate and profoundly unwise for you to be passive and wait for your parents to thrust the business into your lap. Succession, as we have previously described, is like a relay race. In other words, you the successor(s), must take the baton (business) and run with it. Do not make the assumption that dad, mom or the family attorney will take care of succession planning. The reality is that mom and dad may not be concerned about succession planning. Left to their own resources, mom and dad may never address succession planning.

Unfortunately, because of the inevitability of the grim reaper, a passive attitude could be very costly to you and to the business.

Do not expect the family attorney or accountant to push the subject or represent your best interests. They are not fools and will not risk a client relationship by pushing an unreasonable issue or, in some cases, an unpopular subject. Don't lose sight of the fact that attorneys get paid more for resolving problems than avoiding them.

Show an interest in succession planning and encourage your parents to do the same. Take advantage of every opportunity to discuss the subject with parents or family advisors. Advise your parents that addressing succession planning is admittedly difficult, but not addressing succession planning is unmercifully disastrous. You must get involved whether you are an active member of the planning team or simply a cheerleader on the sidelines.

Your first effort should be to evaluate how your parents make decisions. Parents make decisions for a variety of reasons. On one extreme, a small category of parents will be bold, aggressive planners and make decisions prior to problems surfacing. You don't hear much about this group because they proactively address planning needs and rarely encounter problems that are not resolved before they make the newspapers or the cafe gossip circuit. If your parents are in this stellar category, count yourself fortunate. By the time you learn to spell succession, the process will be under way.

On the other extreme there is a larger category. These parents make decisions only when they have no other evasive course of action. Regardless of the circumstances, they will find ways to change the subject or get sidetracked onto more productive subjects. Retrospectively, this group is identified because they don't like to discuss succession; and when they die, their succession planning is typically a mess. If your parents fall into this category, fate has done you no favors. An unfair amount of succession planning responsibility will fall upon you.

If you are mature enough to recognize succession planning problems, and your parents are unwilling to discuss or address the problems, recognize that your parents are your biggest problem. Focus first on your parents' fears or insecurities. Maybe it's you, a sibling or an in-law. It could be concern about control or income security. Or it could be a fear of death.

Whatever the cause, the result is potentially catastrophic to you, so throw yourself into the job of relieving your parents of the burden that is preventing them from addressing succession planning. Ask them why they are not ready to address succession planning.

If your parents will not give you a straight answer, you can assume one of two possible situations. Either you are the problem or they are embarrassed to admit the problems.

Regardless, stop generally asking why and go fishing. Over a period of time, ask specific questions as to the "cause of their planning reluctance." It may take them a while to reveal their true feelings. However, if you are sensitive to the circumstances and gently persistent, they will ultimately tell you what they are thinking.

Be prepared to make the needed changes. Do not argue with your parents about their feelings. They may respond by closing down and excluding you from the planning process. Show respect for their feelings while asking them to consider yours. You will reap what you sow. Express your feelings to the advisor team and have faith that good judgment will prevail. Then think about your parents' feelings, the feelings of other family members and the general situation before you act. This is tricky terrain. You do not want to alienate anyone, and you do not want to embarrass your parents.

With solid forethought, you can usually figure out ways to make your points and deal with an issue that your parents are afraid to address. If and when your parents confess, do not try to force them to deal with their concerns. They do not necessarily want your solutions. But they do want your understanding and respect of their feelings and concerns. Simply ask how you can help. If they give you an opportunity to work on one of their concerns, do it! Respond promptly in hopes that planning momentum can be achieved.

Do not volunteer or assume responsibility for any task or project that you are not fully prepared to handle with all your might and resources. You are far better off being known as cautious or reluctant than being known as someone who will not follow through with a project. Your parents and colleagues, above all, want to be able to count on you. If they give no feedback, do not stop. Think about how you can make something happen in the succession planning process. You can do a lot behind the scenes. However, when dealing with fears and/or concerns of your parents, proceed delicately.

On the other hand, if after great patience, deliberation and offers to help nothing happens, doing something wrong can be better than doing nothing at all.

Consider the motto of a friend and highly successful client. Mason is a genuine "go getter" who will find a way to succeed regardless of the obstacles. He does business by the philosophy that has made him an acclaimed leader in the marine industry: "It is better to apologize than ask permission."

If you get checked for taking the initiative or making an assumption, you can always apologize; however, an opportunity to promote succession planning that is passed is an opportunity lost.

Furthermore, you can be confident that, among the various characteristics that are tagged on prospective successors, being aggressive will speak well for you.

The majority of parents make decisions based upon the evaluation of circumstances within a reasonable time frame. They are generally conservative and more concerned about not making the wrong decision than with making the right decision. The average parents could be a little late or a little early, but they generally are sensitive to succession planning issues and take care of business at the right time. You will know if your parents are in this larger group because they will not avoid business succession or estate continuity issues. If they postpone action, there will be a logical reason from their perspective. You may think it is silly; but they may believe you aren't old enough, business is bad or partners are preoccupied. When these issues are resolved, the door will open for more significant action.

While they meditate, you can make progress on other fronts, such as identifying the planning issues. It is your future, so you should take the effort to understand the issues and, equally important, the options available.

You may need to do your own research to get good information. It will do you good to improve your knowledge of estate and business structuring issues. You can also make sure that you and your brothers, sisters and/or cousins have discussed intra-family succession issues. If you work out resolutions to those tricky questions that frustrate parents,you will have promoted the succession process. You can discuss and even decide such questions as career path, management structure, pay plans and stock transfer restrictions.

Being prepared with well-thought out questions when your parents do become involved will speed up the succession process. It is important that you prepare yourself to react when your parents say the magic words and give you an opportunity to take major steps in the succession process. When you hear the magic words, "Let's get going with this succession planning," have an action plan ready, and, with their subsequent blessing, get the job done before they get cold feet, become preoccupied or ,even worse, die. As the one who has the most to gain, take the responsibility; be willing and prepared to take the initiative.

On a similar front, if your family has done some succession planning, do not assume that the plans remain up-to-date. Complacency can become very costly. It should be no news that you are living in an ever-changing tax and financial environment. Parents have a tendency to throw themselves at estate and succession planning and then close the book, assuming that they have finally addressed an uncomfortable subject. They look at the project like emotional surgery and feel greatly relieved when their mortality is not the primary planning topic.

The truth is that you must continually update your plans or run the risk that you have not adapted to a changing environment.

Feelings, finances, federal tax law and family circumstances are constantly changing. It will be very costly if you, the successor, do not remain sensitive to the need for constant review.

Your Attitude

The most important aspect of being an owner's child is attitude. Your attitude will set the stage for how you interact with your parents, siblings, in-laws, key personnel, customers and competitors. Your attitude will speak for you when you are not around or when no one is willing to defend you.

Keep in mind that forgiveness is very common in a family business, but forgetfulness is not. Everything you say and do impacts the attitudes of those around you. Your actions have a lasting impact. When you don't understand why people treat you in strange ways, recollect your attitude in those years and you may gain insight into why you are being treated in a particular manner. The people you work with on the bottom end of the business may one day be the people you are going to depend upon to help you run the business; so, remember that everything you do, or don't do, counts. Everyone you deal with is important. Build bridges and never think that you have the luxury to burn one.

With the right attitude, employees will rally behind you, giving your parents more confidence in you. Employees will never miss a chance to reflect your behavior in their work. Unfortunately, you will get credit for more of the negative than the positive. Consequently, it is essential that you create a high volume of good things that can be said about you. You can be sure that a good word about you offered by an employee is more valuable than any pearl of wisdom that you can personally display.

As you grow and mature, consider these important points. If you have one or more brothers or sisters working in the business, you will be facing the reality of economic dilution. You and your brothers and/or sisters are not going to be able to duplicate your parents' lifestyle unless your business becomes substantially more profitable or more efficient. The division of the profits your parents realized between two or more second generation families will create stress on lifestyles, or the business, or both. Do not cry over this reality or try to project a guilt trip on your parents that the business owes you a lifestyle equal to theirs. In order to maintain the lifestyle of your parents, simple math will confirm that you must become more productive and more efficient.

You will need patience regarding compensation. Your parents probably did not achieve economic success until late in their business careers. A new business is an endless pit for working capital (cash). Rather than enjoying the good life, your parents reinvested profits in the business to minimize the risks of a volatile economy, and so you could come into a business with a strong capital base. Your parents now want to enjoy their prosperity. They also want to assure their financial security before they start dividing assets between their children and giving up control.

It is very important that you understand that the greatest fear of a parent is that, in their old age, they may become dependent <u>upon you.</u>

Therefore, your parents will be deliberate and dedicated in their efforts to build retirement security. Do not expect to equal their lifestyle unless you also sacrifice to grow the business. Do not expect any significant transfers of assets or control until you convince them that they are secure and/or you are responsible. Your parents may also feel that, if they were 50before they began to prosper, at 25 or 30you should pay your dues for a few more years.

You must be patient.

In conclusion, recognize that the president's office has only one desk and chair. Leadership and input are expected of everyone, but one person must operate as the business leader. If it's you, give it all you've got! By all means, get all the help you can from your brothers, sisters, parents and key personnel by always having the attitude of the servant. If you are not the designated leader, respect that your parents created and built the business and they have the right to make succession decisions.

Moreover, you have the right and the responsibility to make your own career decisions. If you have a problem because you are not the designated leader, don't let resentment spoil your attitude. Try to achieve peace. If you cannot, protect your family relationships. Move on to another career where you can achieve gratification. You will always be well served to remember another family business golden rule: the family business is not a golden spoon; it is a golden opportunity.

Thoughts for In-Laws & Distant Relatives

In-laws and distant relatives have special places in the family business environment. In-laws are individuals who have the distinction of being married to a member of a family who owns a business. In-laws fall into one of two categories: actively employed or passively involved. There is no such category as "passively uninvolved," because a family business impacts everyone in the family in some fashion. Distant relatives are individuals employed in the business who are related to the business owners as cousins, uncles, aunts or step-relatives. Active in-laws, passive in-laws and distant relatives are subject to unique circumstances, so we will address each category individually.

The Active In-laws

Prior to offering any comments, I heartily acknowledge that active in-laws categorically should be provided "hazardous duty pay." Being an in-law in a family business is a tough job that is only appropriate for tough people. When an in-law shows up for the first day of employment, the nomination for a Purple Heart should be submitted; the only question is how many oak clusters will ultimately be attached.

This is not an experience for the thin-skinned, timid, impulsive or uncommitted.

If you are hypersensitive, you are going to feel like your skin is being peeled. If you are unwilling to take the initiative and become unmercifully vulnerable, you are going to be ridiculed as an incompetent leech. If you speak or act without thinking, you are going to be categorized as a buffoon.

Active in-laws are traditionally subject to becoming the "in-la" sandwich." They become the meat between the stereotyped expectations of the spouse's family and the ever changing expectations of the spouse for the in-law to effectively represent his or her position in the family business. Needless to say, as the meat of the "in-law sandwich," one can be smothered. The spouse's parents, brothers and/or sisters typically give an in-law credit for brains or initiative, and the family member expects the spouse to act just like one of the family. Before submitting to the recruitment of your father-in-law or the financial pressure of your spouse to take a job in the family business, count the cost.

The success of an in-law will, in large part, be dependent upon the right motives and commitment. Motives reflect why you chose to work for your spouse's parents and/or siblings. Categorically, it should come as no surprise that the success of a family business in-law is dependent upon being motivated to make a mark in the business irrespective of whether your spouse's family has ownership.

Successful in-laws see the opportunity to pursue a career working with their spouse's family as just one of several options. Having several options at their disposal, they conclude that, overall, the family business is their best option, but by no means their only option.

The key to an in-law's success is to truly believe that this job represents the best of several options and, if it does not work out, for any one of a variety of reasons, they will move on to the <u>next best option.</u>

From another perspective, the successful in-law does not need a job in their spouse's business to fulfill their personal needs or self-interests. If an in-law is capable of making an unreserved commitment to the mission of the business and the existing leadership, he or she will have the highest probability of success. And it is admittedly difficult to work for someone who's only claim to a job or position is the good fortune of the "procreation lottery." From the reciprocal perspective, if the in-law's job is an attempt to protect his or her spouse's perceived share of the "golden goose," the odds for success are poor.

Bringing it down to a personal level, if your job with your spouse's parents is merely their way of paying your spouse a fair share of the family business booty, you will be caught on the rotisserie and, eventually, your spouse's siblings are going to turn up the heat. If you do not have any heart for the business and are seeking the easiest way through life, what may currently appear to be heaven will ultimately turn into hell.

If you have defined your personal career success only in terms of protecting your spouse's spot on "easy street," hang on tight.

An in-law's success in a family business is dependent upon two factors: the emotional makeup divinely bestowed and the chosen attitudes that are reflected in motives and commitment. The strongest advice I can offer is "to thine own self be true." No one can effectively evaluate your internal makeup as effectively as you. I have seen in-laws in one of two extreme categories: pathetically miserable or ridiculously happy. The determinant as to which category they occupied was whether they followed their instincts regarding the compatibility of their emotions, motives and commitment to their spouse's family business environment.

Under the presumption that you are already employed in your spouse's family business, I offer these thoughts for your consideration. If you are happy, congratulations. You are very fortunate to have found gratification in such a vulnerable position. You are also a special person to be able to confidently deal with your in-laws and do a good job. No doubt you have had your challenges, but your willingness to be personally responsible for your actions and to communicate openly with your in-laws have been the keys to your success. You are filling an important, special role in the business. Your commitment is gratifying and hopefully, productive.

Long-term success as an in-law in a family business will be enhanced if you limit your expectations to those of any other non-family employee. The instant that you begin to expect favoritism or compensation based upon your in-law status, you begin to decline. There is no middle ground on the perception of your integrity. You are going to be viewed as either a hard-working team asset with character and integrity or as a gold-digging, self-centered, compromising opportunist. If you expect nothing more than the opportunities afforded every aggressive and capable employee, and you apply all of your conviction and resources to being successful, you will be considered a member of the positive category. Make no mistake; you are being watched very carefully, and you are not being given the benefit of the doubt by those around you. Everyone is expecting you to be a gold-digging opportunist and the burden of proving them wrong falls solely upon your shoulders. If you are viewed as a gold digging opportunist, you are going to experience a wide range of emotional ups and downs with little to no long term gratification.

Just for the sake of academic theory, let's assume you are a gold-digging opportunist, you are very comfortable in your environment and have no problem being considered the frog that married the princess. You are not hung up on proving your worth. Furthermore, you are most interested in achieving the good life with the least effort. If you can play this game, good for you. However, it should be no surprise that this attitude is not good for the business.

My advice is stay out of the way of anyone who is trying to grow the business, and do not have unrealistic expectations about achieving the respect of coworkers and family members.

I assure you that your feelings and motives are no secret. Everyone hears loudly and clearly what you are not saying. Over the infallible test of time, the true nature of your motives will surface. Do yourself, the business and your in-laws a favor by not pursuing job positions that require more effort and commitment than you are willing to make. If, for the sake of your ego you get in over your head, admit your shortcomings and get help before you create frustration and grief for everyone.

The in-law who genuinely wants to make a contribution to a family business should push for his supervisor to define expectations. In order to be successful, you must clearly understand the desired end result target that defines success. Regardless of whether you are working for a father-in-law, brother-in-law or non-family member, you should step through the traditional informality surrounding family members and press to be treated as any other employee. Clearly expressed performance expectations allow you to have security in your achievement. As a result of your in-law status, many around you will be insecure and envious. These personalities are very common in family businesses, and are renowned for moving the bar of expectations to frustrate an in-law's efforts to be successful and gain respect. They would also love to use you as the excuse for their shortcomings. To protect your vulnerable position as an in-law, seek as much written definition as possible regarding what is expected of you.

The most valuable resource for an in-law in a family business is respect. The respect you receive is both a product of your effort and the perception of family members and key employees around you. Unfortunately, for reasons beyond your control, the expectations of those around you may be hopelessly poisoned just because you married the boss' son or daughter. The rationale of small minds can be amazing. The only thing you can do about this situation is to press on, give the business the best you've got and do not take it personally. Trust me, no one wants to hear you griping about being the frog that married the princess. Fortunately, these circumstances are not predominant. Normally, the respect you receive will be dependent upon your commitment to the family and the business.

As an active in-law, you should realize that, with few exceptions, you will never be considered an equal alongside your spouse and his or her siblings.

Regardless of the level of your success, you may never own an interest in the business. The ultimate challenge is that the business ownership you earn may be given to your spouse. Further, in the event your spouse predeceases you, the assets that your deceased spouse would have received from your in-laws will go not to you, but to your children. You may someday be managing assets for your children that your spouse would have received. A fact of life is that your father and mother-in-law are concerned that, if you obtain direct control over family assets, you may direct those assets outside of the family through a subsequent marriage. Do not take this natural reaction personally. You would probably feel the same way. Regardless of your dedication and sincerity, you will probably never overcome the reality that "blood is thicker than water."

As an actively employed in-law, restrain yourself during business discussions. Avoid discussions that may be interpreted as critical of any family member. Unlike the family members around you, your rights do not include the ability to indirectly criticize family members. You can criticize family members directly to their face, but you cannot freely join in the national family pasttime of complaining about other family members. Those around you will not hear any truth in your statements anyway. They will only hear envy and/or resentment. Take comfort in the fact that the truth about your in-laws is self-evident and does not require your support or amplification.

Also, be very careful about the nature of your business pillow-talk with your spouse. As a member of the business family, he or she has perceptions of you, parents, siblings and key personnel that are tainted by emotional relationships and historical experiences that you cannot duplicate. A little casual criticism or self-pity can inflame your spouse's preconceived opinions and initiate otherwise avoidable friction within the family. As an in-law involved in the day-to-day operations of the business, there are significant elements of business to which your spouse does not need to become involved. Wherever possible, leave the business at the office so that you can go home to a peaceful household.

The Passive In-law

The passive in-law in a family business can be described in one word: frustrated. As an employed non-family member, you have the advantage of seeing things as they really are and the disadvantage of not being able to do much with this enlightened body of knowledge. You likely have the rare combination of purpose, zeal, knowledge and energy; however, for the most part, with respect to family or business issues, no one in the family respects your opinion or the reasons you adopted your opinion. Therefore, regardless of how right you may be, publicly expressing your feelings on business matters usually creates more problems than they are worth. On the other hand, your loving spouse is indeed interested in your opinion; however, his or her opinions and concepts of proper behavior are strongly influenced by the many years of family involvement. Even though your spouse may love you beyond the realm of imagination, he or she is still going to follow the family instincts ingrained in them prior to ever meeting you. Forcing your pillow-talk opinions on your spouse will create unmerited frustration and may cause marital discord.

Unfortunately, your spouse may be less assertive and less aggressive than you feel he should be. You may be frustrated because you perceive that your spouse is being edged out in the inevitable races for the most desirable business position, job title, office, or perks. There is nothing you can do about this other than to privately encourage your spouse to assert himself more. Trying to force a square peg in a round hole is only going to cause problems. To be sure, if you want to alienate your spouse's family and be awarded the title "Pushy, Greedy In-law," just let anybody related to family business know that you are unhappy with the way your spouse is being treated.

Keep your feelings about your spouse's treatment in the family business or the fairness of gifts and estate bequests behind <u>closed doors.</u>

Insecurity is by far the greatest handicap of passive in-laws. You are essentially along for the ride, exposed to the emotions and frequent inequities common to family businesses. I counsel you to find strength and reassurance from within yourself, the love of your spouse and the confines of your immediate family. The fact of life is that you are never going to be treated as an equal to your husband's sister or your wife's brother, because their parents own the business. Do yourself and everyone else a great favor and avoid comparing your prosperity, welfare and security to others. Life can be great for you, but it will not be the same as it is for direct offspring.

Do not be so naive as to believe that secrets are kept in a family business. Everything you say to family members, fellow passive in-laws, friends or employees will find its way home. If anyone can interpret your expressions negatively, they will, and you will lose respect. The only way for you to avoid criticism is to mind your own business, understanding that how your spouse's family business is operated is not your concern.

In summary, as a passive in-law you are in a position to promote or undermine family harmony. Your attitude, remarks and innuendoes are very important to the team unity of the family business Your contributions are indirect, but none-the-less important.

Case History: The In-Law Children

About 20 years ago, I was engaged in what would later become a very interesting in-law environment. Mom and Dad owned a marginally successful chain of fast food franchises. They had a son and daughter, good kids, in their sophomore and junior years of college. The family generally had a blue collar attitude and did things right. Mom and Dad worked hard at business and parenting. Son and Daughter stayed out of major trouble and applied themselves to school.

Time and circumstances were generally good to this family. They aggressively purchased and built new stores. Their community grew and the fast food business fully matured. Mom and Dad recognized their limitations and hired a dynamic general manager. Over the next 15 years, their marginal success blossomed into a fabulously profitable holding company of more than 50 restaurants. And, as would be expected, both Son and Daughter fell in love and got married within a few years of each other. And that is when the excitement began.

Daughter was first to marry. She fell in love with a struggling golf pro. After they married he continued his dream for three or four years until their first child was born. Then Daughter talked Son-in-law (SIL) into taking a job in the family business. As we might expect, the pay was more than he had ever earned playing golf. He started as a management trainee and did reasonably well, when he wasn't out playing golf in company sponsored outings.

Son married a couple years later after living with his girlfriend for almost five years, in spite of his parents' objections. Mom and Dad were dedicated Christians and, because of their beliefs, did not embrace Son's "live-in" as one of the family. Needless to say, when Son married, Mom and Dad were forced to do the "let's be friends two-step." Although visibly awkward, the wedding ceremonies were completed without a major incident.

For the next 10 years, life was pretty good. The business continued to grow and prosper under the iron hand of the General Manager, who did so well there was no pressure on Son or SIL to assume a responsible role in management. Son's response was to pursue the path of least resistance. Being the anointed "prince" and having no higher status to pursue and no necessity to perform, he simply floated through the company as a perpetual assistant to the General Manager. Actually, his specialty was representing the family business on the perk trips the family was awarded by vendors. On my advice, the family had established production-based pay plans.

Daughter-in-law (DIL) was more of a driving personality. She put pressure on him to earn more, but, to her frustration, he was not motivated by money. Even with children, she was working as a sales rep in order to keep up.

The son-in-law matured over these years. The General Manager effectively communicated to him that he was not going to be highly paid to play golf and party. To my surprise, SIL became obsessed with proving he was not the frog that married the princess. Within a couple years, he realigned his priorities and approached business with the same competitive intensity as he had golf. He would do any job that would maximize his earnings and enhance his comparison to Son. Methodically, he worked his way up the ladder to Operations Manager. And it was apparent that SIL had his eye on the General Manager's job.

About five years ago, life in the realm of in-laws began to heat up. I had initiated an update in estate planning. Various technical issues needed to be addressed and Mom and Dad wanted to refine asset distribution provisions. I had advised them many years earlier that a 50/50 deadlock business control might seem fair, but decisive leadership would be the continuing key to long-term success. Long thought and debate had led them to the conclusion that, although SIL was more aggressive, they wanted Son to have control of the business. Dad was very concerned about how SIL was going to deal with this news. As we discussed the estate planning update, Mom also mentioned to me that DIL and Daughter recently had an ugly exchange at a family dinner.

As they saw it, DIL was upset because Mom and Dad had given Daughter a much nicer Christmas gift. Mom and Dad asked me to run point on communicating the potentially volatile estate planning changes with *both sides of the family and, while doing so, attempt to cool down DIL. I said they should be prepared for a challenge from Daughter and SIL on the business contract issue, but I had no idea what to expect from Son and DIL.*

I felt it was appropriate to first meet privately with both Son and Daughter. The meeting with Son was first, at his request. It was immediately evident that he was looking for help. Before I even started discussing estate planning, he said his wife (DIL) was an emotional mess. She was, in fact, threatening to leave him because "no one in the family or the business liked her." He begged me to talk to her and convince her that this was not the case. With respect to the business control issue, he said he didn't care whether he received 50% or 51% of the stock.

The meeting with Daughter was equally exciting. Before I could get through the opening small talk, she said that her Mom had mentioned their plans and she had a big problem with them. She had shared the news with her husband (SIL), who was preparing to resign and move their family to another community where he could work with another fast food operation. He would already have resigned but wanted to hear what I had to say first. Daughter also was unhappy at the thought of working for her under-motivated brother and the possibility of working for his big-mouth, jealous wife if he were to be killed on one of the crazy trips he frequented.

She went on to say that, unbeknownst to either of them, she and DIL used the same hairdresser. Recently the hairdresser had said that DIL told her that Mom and Dad did not like her and were showing their feelings in how much they paid their son and the difference in the quantity of Christmas gifts. Daughter justified the ugly scene at dinner saying it was high time someone put DIL in her proper place.

"Okay, let's all take a deep breath!" Obviously more meetings were needed Assuming business welfare was a priority, I met first with Daughter and SIL. As I walked into their living room, SIL gave me the body language of an offended 13-year-old. After several unsuccessful attempts to get him to share his feelings, I said that I understood he was planning to resign and he unloaded. "Mom and Dad are crazy," he said. "Son is a nice guy but he is not in the game. He is content with being an assistant for the GM and taking trips. He is not capable of leading this company and I am not going to stand by and watch him run this company into the ground. And DIL would put us out in the street if Son died and she inherited the stock. No way am I going to run the risk of having our family disrupted by that."

I offered support with affirming nods and regularly reflected, "I understand how you would feel that way." After about 10 minutes, he closed out his verbal assault and looked to his wife for support. She offered an "it's not fair" and an "I can't believe it" and then the three of us sat there in silence. After just a few moments, which seemed like an hour, SIL asked what I was thinking.

I responded that I was confused. On one hand, he was thinking about quitting because he could not stand by and watch his brother-in-law run the company into the ground. But, by leaving the company, he would be putting his wife's largest asset at risk. And if the company ran aground, it likely would be more a result of his abandoning ship than from his brother-in-law's mismanagement. As he well knew, his brother-in-law was not a control freak and would be inclined to empower others to run the company while he played. While he was grasping for words, his wife jumped in and again said she could not believe her parents did not give her an equal vote with her brother.

My response was that there was nothing personal in her parent's decision. Son was not as aggressive as they would like, but he was active and a sound conservative thinker. On the other hand, she had chosen to stay at home with her children. Although SIL was a fabulous son-in-law, they wanted an active child to have the ability to control a deadlock. As an off-setting balance, Mom and Dad were planning to designate Daughter as the controlling partner of the company that owned the business real estate.

Moreover, there would be stock transfer restriction agreements that would prevent DIL from ever controlling the business. They were confident Son would rely upon managers such as SIL to run the company. I concluded my remarks with, "Can you appreciate Mom and Dad's rationale? It may not be perfect, but it is well thought out."

"So, I'll be in control of the real estate and he'll be in control of operations." Daughter looked over at her husband and said, "You know, Son does not want to be General Manager." It was downhill from there with Daughter and SIL. I said that the family hoped SIL would be the next General Manager and I encouraged SIL to discuss his career path with Dad.

Dad did finally say the magic words to SIL in a later conversation, "We appreciate what you have done and need you to stay with the business." That sealed the deal for SIL.

The next challenge was DIL (daughter-in-law). I asked Son to arrange a meeting for her and me. I had no more than asked how she was doing when she started to cry. "Nobody likes me. Mom will not come over to our house and Daughter just flaunts her pretty things that Mom buys for her. And my husband just doesn't care. He does not understand me and makes no effort to listen to my side of the issue. We would both be better off divorced."

It was apparent that this young lady was carrying some major baggage. Although the woman appeared to be strong and hard driving, she was amazingly immature and desperate for acceptance as a member of the family. I was in over my head, but I could see she was very fragile and would not be able to deal with a harsh introduction to reality.

My response to DIL was that she was dealing with several complex issues, but there was no need to panic. I felt her biggest problem was her perspective. The fact was that her husband loved her dearly and his family cared for her and wanted her to be happy and secure as a member of the family.

Unfortunately, that caught a nerve and she started in on me again, "What do you mean they care for me? Mom embarrasses me with a cheap bracelet and Daughter makes a scene at dinner in front of the entire family. They hate me! They want me to leave and I am going to give them their wish. Who needs their money? They are just self-centered, back-biting snobs." "My guess," I said carefully, "is that you have not shared these feelings with anyone other than your husband and you feel better for having gotten it off your chest."

What a relief, when I noticed a thin smile as she took a deep breath and replied, "Well yes, I do feel better. All my husband does is tell me what I should be thinking. He never really listens to my feelings. I apologize for being such a mess, but being accepted as a member of this family is really important to me. I am an only child, and my parents divorced when I was 13."

I responded by saying, "Oh, I have a clearer picture. Your hypersensitivity stems from the fact that you would like to achieve relationships through your husband's family that you were never able to achieve in your own family." Somewhat startled by my candid statement, she hesitated and sheepishly replied, "Well, I guess maybe you are right. This family has everything I always wanted. Can't they just accept me for who I am?"

"Well they can," I replied, "but I am afraid you have lost sight of who you are. You are indeed a lovely, caring, sensitive woman who is surrounded by a great family that wants you to feel loved and appreciated. However, marrying Son did not make you an equal member of the family. They will honor and respect you as Son's wife, but you are going to have to build intimate relationships with your in-laws on your own, just like you have built other close relationships in the past, including your marriage.

"All valued relationships have a price. None can be viewed as a marital property right, even true intimacy with your husband. You must also be aware of two profound facts. The first is that you came into this family with baggage. As you are aware, Mom, Dad and Daughter did not agree with you and Son living together before you were married. Just because you got married, you cannot expect those preconditioned opinions to just go away. Second, having married the Son, you are part of the royal family, but you are not the princess. No matter how strong you build your relationship with Mom and Dad, you will never be their daughter. The feelings for a daughter-in-law can become very strong and gratifying, but they will never be the same as feelings for a daughter. Surely, you can put yourself in their position and recognize this basic truth.

"The best advice I can give you is try to accept your current circumstances, determine what you want and dedicate yourself to a course of action that will get you there. I appreciate that, with your background, accepting your circumstances is a tall task. You may find it better to cut and run. However, I know your husband loves you and nothing would make Mom and Dad any happier than for you to become a close member of the family and raise their grandchildren right here. You may even need help from a counselor who can enhance your ability to improve relationships with your husband, mother and sister-in-law. But irrespective of what you decide to do, for everyone's welfare, you must understand that in a family business environment, with the exception of a professional counselor, there are no secrets hidden from an in-law. Anything you say to someone, like your hairdresser, you must be prepared to have repeated all over town. To assume otherwise is equivalent to playing soccer on a minefield. DIL cracked a smile and confirmed that she had learned that lesson the hard way." She subsequently thanked me for listening to her and offering tough but good advice. A few days later, Son also called to thank me and to ask for referrals to a counselor.

I am happy to reflect that DIL hung tough and learned to adapt to being a duchess in lieu of a princess. SIL also stayed with the business and now, seven years later, he is the General Manager. All this did not occur without a few scrapes and bumps. The family has not only survived, but is also much stronger, having grown through two in-laws who determined that the challenges of adapting to a new family environment were clearly worth the time and effort.

Distant Relatives

Distant relatives in a family business are another special class meriting recognition, encouragement and coaching. Cousins, uncles, aunts, nephews and nieces frequently play an important role in the operation and succession of the family business. Distant relatives have the distinct advantage of being part of the family. The existing relationship as a member of the greater family provides a foundation of trust and familiarity that can facilitate employment and career advancement. Opportunities are usually accelerated. However, distant relatives usually are not a part of the close family culture that exemplifies a typical family business.

Unless an unusual opportunity enables a distant relative to become a substantial owner in the business, they will not be consulted on strategic decisions and will not be on the track for the top leadership position, irrespective of talent. Sooner or later, the distant relative earns everything they get.

These circumstances can be frustrating and even disheartening There is the profound possibility that, through a common last name, you may even carry the frustration of being known as a member of the ownership family without the benefits. Unfortunately, you are going to have to pursue your career on your own merits.

If you project an attitude of jealousy, resentment or self-pity in the workplace, your job will suffer. Nevertheless, you potentially have some advantages, particularly if you are a role model for work ethic and positive attitude. No one made you take the job, and no one is making you stay. Get over the inter-family issue and strive to be the best contributor you can be. On many occasions I have witnessed business owners show their appreciation for the unrelenting efforts of distant relatives by accelerating their careers and even providing them opportunities to own stock or to start their own business.

If you have been on board for a while, you know your way around. Being a veteran of family business minefields, you have learned your place and, most importantly, you have learned what places, discussions, and situations to avoid. This can help you avoid abrasions and scrapes from playing on the wrong team. If you have not been on board, keep your wits about you and heed these words of advice:

- You are a magnet for controversy within the family.

- You are disposable, so you cannot afford to take sides.

- If you become a close associate of a particular member of the core family, you will be identified with the good or bad of that family member.

- Any criticism of a core family member must be based upon supportable facts or you are history.

- You do not have the luxury of taking shortcuts in your career development.

- You must earn everything you get or you will lose it.

- You will lose part of what you have earned anyway.

Make sure that you are receiving adequate preparation for the career role you are seeking. If you rise to the level of your incompetency, you may feel lucky for a season, but you will ultimately experience stress and frustration. Regrettably, only core family members have the potential luxury of surviving as an incompetent. You are going to have to prove yourself to advance and protect yourself to stay there.

Distant relatives can also be equity owners. There are many examples of nephews, nieces and cousins being rewarded for hard work with a piece of the action. If you are the benefactor, congratulations. However, it would not be prudent for any distant relative to expect to be part of the ownership succession.

Any evidence of an entitlement attitude could quickly turn you into a "persona non grata" and you could be looking for a job. It is not uncommon for family dynamics to dictate that distant relatives (cousins) will be partners in a family business. These are generally very delicate situations. You might recall from a prior chapter on family relationships the situation with the Relick family, wherein business ownership evolved from grandfather through sons, and ultimately to four cousins. The unfortunate self-centered agendas of the four cousins created a pathetic example of how family in a business can be transformed from an asset into a liability.

Hopefully you have learned that equity-owning, distant relatives in a family business have options. They can strive for the fruits of team synergy or play "look out for number one." The choice is yours and you will surely harvest the fruits (good or bad) of your efforts, as the environment can vary from the brutal chaos of the Relicks to a highly gratifying family synergy. However, it bears mentioning that the best-case scenario for distant relative stockholders is typically less rosy than it is for close relatives. A more vivid way of describing the circumstance is embodied in the Laws of the Business Jungle: Partners tolerate each other to the limit of self-interest. Parents support children beyond imagination. Siblings give each other the benefit of the doubt and cousins rarely forgive.

There is a special place for in-laws and distant relatives in the family business. In most cases, the businesses cannot be successful without your collaboration and cooperation. In many cases, the businesses cannot achieve succession without you. The flexing of your ability and emotions have an immediate positive or negative impact upon the business environment. Your marital relationship or your distant family ties give you the responsibility of amazing leverage over the harmony and prosperity of the business environment. Depending upon circumstances, your position may be perceived (by you and others) as a curse or blessing. Irrespective of the circumstances, I encourage you to commit yourself to being a positive influence in every situation you encounter.

Thoughts for Parents

As a family business leader, you have the stewardship responsibility to consider the succession of your business. You have been the longstanding captain at the helm and family leader. Therefore, you are the only one who has both an understanding of what your business requires and what your children have to offer.

But you do not simply have a responsibility to pass your business onto your children.

Your responsibility in considering succession is to determine if passing your business to your children is the best course of action for you, your children and your employees.

This decision is further complicated by the reality that successor children rarely match up perfectly with the management succession challenge. As young adults, they did not struggle to survive and were not challenged to the fiber of their being as you were. Consequently, your children probably do not have the fully developed ownership instincts that are critical to building a strong business. Environmental selection has not had the impact upon them that it had upon you. You were successful because you were the best, the most determined or the most creative. Your children will be successful for reasons other than survival, which may not give you the depth of confidence that you would like to have.

Your feelings are very important to the succession process. If you are a typical long-term owner, you have strong feelings about your business. In some cases, you may even hold stronger feelings for your business than for your children. The fact is, you have conceived and/or raised your business just like a child. You have spent more of your quality time with your business than with any member of your family, including your spouse.

Your business honors you, does not challenge your authority and does not embarrass you. The lifetime of constant challenge and excitement has created a tremendously strong bond between you and your business. The history of business relationships and business achievements provides you with gratification, pride, encouragement and a profound sense of identity. Consequently, there are strong emotions at the thought of business succession or termination.

There could be anger with children and/or partners for not sharing your passion about the continuity of the business as a legacy, or your willingness to sacrifice. You may be frustrated with your spouse, children and employees who take the business for granted as the source of their security, prosperity and social standing. These feelings are very common. These feelings have been a part of the foundation for the commitment required for success and succession. No one looks upon the business as you do. They never will feel exactly as you do, because they have not and cannot walk those miles in your shoes.

And so, succession planning is not a simple endeavor. You realize that, if you are going to reap the benefits, you must pay your dues. And if your children have not paid in the past, they will surely pay in the future. You have worked hard and sacrificed a great deal with very reasonable expectations of passing your business to your children and what you get back is often a lack of genuine appreciation for what you have done to build your business, and what they are going to have to do to achieve succession.

Having withstood the challenges of building a business, it may not seem fair that you should now have to deal with the challenges of succession. However, fairness is not a parental issue. The personal cost of succession is real. If you get stuck too long on the issue of what is fair, the opportunity for succession will pass you by and the product of your efforts will be washed down the drain. If you dwell too much on this fairness issue, or just lay back and hope everything will work out for the best, remember that Murphy had families in mind when he developed his famous law. Regardless of how frustrating, costly or depressing business succession may be, you must get the ball rolling if you want your children to have the opportunity to carry on your business.

If you just assume everything will work out for the best, remember that Murphy had families in mind when he developed his famous law. If action has to be taken, if changes must be made, you must be prepared to do it. In 99 out of 100 cases, it is the parent leading the way when important strategic action is taken in succession planning Every family member in a succession planning environment is part of the problem or the solution. If you are taking the initiative to deal with the problems, you are virtually eliminating the prospect that you are part of the problem. As General George Patton said, "Lead, follow, or get out of the way." Typically, leaders are called to make tough decisions.

When you show a willingness to seek advice and make decisions, those around you will show a similar willingness to make changes including, of course, where they are working.

As a parent, you are expected to carry the weight of several challenging and even conflicting roles. You are depended upon to manage the business, train your children, be a sensitive parent and a model spouse. The pressure from these multiple roles can be overpowering. If you are like most mortals and have difficulty with your position, you may be looking at yourself in the mirror each morning wondering why you are putting yourself through the agony of trying to train your children to deal with the business succession challenges that you know are on the horizon. You may have concluded that, if circumstances do not change, you are going to need therapy because your children are driving you crazy.

Rest assured, it is a normal experience if you feel you need help dealing with your children. As a result of these circumstances, you probably have not been able to achieve the decisiveness and conviction for succession that you would like to have. Your heart longs for your children to take interest in your business and continue a family legacy. But you question whether they can do it.

Regardless of the nature of your emotions, your financial and family circumstances dictate that you do not put your personal security or the security of a surviving spouse at risk by placing your business under the management of children you cannot rely upon. If your security is dependent upon the business, you do not have the luxury to hope your children will master the skills, catch the vision or grow up before the business takes a downturn. Personal security is a first priority to succession. If you have security independent of the business however, you can take a riskier position.

Furthermore, there is nothing to be gained and potentially much to be lost in setting a child up for a fall. You know what it takes. The leadership of a complex, vibrant business requires exceptional motivation and talent.

Your children may be wonderfully average. They may be good employees and great kids who aren't cut out for management or leadership.

Unfortunately, a successor's aptitude is rarely a black and white issue. Your children could be meeting or exceeding your expectations and prayers. You could be facing frustrations from your children as a result of the quality of their work, the attitude of their spouse, their relationship with you, or their personal behavior. You could feel that you are beating your head against the wall as you deal with greed, apathy, drugs, irresponsibility or even worse. It may appear that your children are always breaking new ground with their imaginative ways to frustrate you, and your succession dream is not worth the seemingly endless parade of disappointments. It is also disheartening to recognize that, regardless of your desires, your children must have the motivation to take the business from you.

If they are not motivated, capable and mature enough to operate the business, you cannot in good conscience give it to them. So now, amidst everything else, you have this burdensome decision to make about their ability to carry your business through the next generation.

You are very fortunate if you are not dealing with at least one challenging, emotion-sapping issue involving your children's roles in your business and your succession plans. Frustration is an inevitable by-product of combining business and family. Fate has dictated your circumstances. If you are pleased with your situation, be thankful. If your situation is bad, take comfort in the reality that at least one person (me) recognizes your challenge and offers encouragement. I have witnessed miraculous changes. Even a 45 year-old child can find responsibility. If you have concluded that your situation is hopeless, I offer my sympathy. There is no equal to the depth of frustration when your dreams are confronted with the reality that your children cannot or will not continue your legacy.

To those who are confidently proceeding down the road of succession or precariously hobbling along a trail of doubt, let me acknowledge the obvious: Succession has its price. There are inevitable potholes of disappointment and there are regular crossroads from which you can be distracted, lose direction and become frustrated. Unfortunately, there are no guarantees that, even under the best of circumstances, your prayers and efforts will bring good fortune.

Assuming your family business has a good chance for succession, you may be disillusioned over recent developments. Years ago, as you struggled to start your business and keep your head above water, you dreamed of it growing into something worth passing on to your children. As your children were young, helping out during the summer and weekends, you envisioned them growing in character and wisdom. This motivated you to sacrifice to grow your business and now, as you're in a position to make your succession dreams happen, you have come to grips with sobering realities.

Notably, you cannot simply give your business to your children. You now realize that there are totally ridiculous tax regulations that limit your disposition control over an entity that you created with your own hands and mind.

These unfair laws discriminate against you for taking risks and converting a dream into a valuable business.

It is going to require extra cash to pay estate taxes and a team of lawyers to establish equitable estate distribution.

Mentoring children is one of the most frustrating and demanding exercises that a parent can undertake. If at all possible, avoid personally managing and training your children or in-laws. Sleeping on a bed of nails or walking on hot coals is usually more gratifying. If your organization is large enough, identify a strong employee/manager to supervise your children. Give them the authority to hold your children accountable. Limit your involvement. Maintain a sense of what is happening through regular progress reports. Avoid entertaining your children's job gripes during family fellowship. Meet individually with each child and the supervisor regularly to hear the feedback and always support the authority of the supervisor.

Keep in mind that you must teach your children how to be employees in order for them to ever learn how to be good managers. Promote the chain of accountability and do not allow them to take shortcuts by packing your ear with emotional pleas. If your business is not large enough to provide an in-house supervisor/mentor, identify someone outside your business, whom your children respect, to serve in a mentor role. This person does not have to be a business wizard, but he must be mature and willing to speak forthrightly regarding issues common to young people in the workplace.

You may have recognized that your children have everything figured out. You may have even concluded that a training program is a waste for a child who has all the answers. In far too many cases, children have made up their minds and do not want to be confused by the facts. They may be impatient and downright pushy. But the fact is that your children did not originate the business. They did not grow the business. They have not done without or even sacrificed to perpetuate the business. Regardless of their confidence, they do not know the business as you do. Furthermore, they are not in control, you are. Be patient with their inexperience and be strong with your convictions.

The most important steps for business successors are the first ones. Do not move a child up the management/responsibility ladder until he or she has mastered the responsibilities of each assigned job. Compel them to join the business on your terms or encourage them to seek gainful employment elsewhere. The foremost family business golden rule is that you have the gold, so you set the rules.

Do whatever it takes to teach your successors that only after they successfully work for the business can the business successfully work for them.

The good news is that succession is not totally a sacrificial effort for ungrateful children. There is also a practical financial motivation for succession planning. The highest economic return on your business investment of time, money and effort can be realized through succession. Selling your business may look very lucrative on the surface; however, costs associated with selling dramatically affect the net return. Capital gain tax, income tax, legal fees, accounting fees, and brokerage commissions can convert an outstanding sales price into a replacement asset that cannot come close to duplicating the net return of the business. It is rare, indeed, that the reinvested net proceeds from the sale of a business can even approach the total financial benefits received from the business.

Furthermore, life after the sale is not as simple as it may appear. A business owner understands the opportunities and hazards involved in the operation of a business. However, unless the business owner has an exceptional financial mind, he or she does not have the same familiarity with the vehicles into which they will reinvest the net sale proceeds derived from the business. It is easy for a business owner to invest excess cash into the stock market and real estate ventures. If money is lost, the income-generating capability of the business will replace the loss. On the other hand, the lack of familiarity with other investment vehicles makes it difficult for an ex-business owner to risk financial security built up over a lifetime with anything other than secure investments.

The typical business person who has developed and sold a business will worry more about the reinvested proceeds than they did about the business. They will quickly discover the hazards of stocks, bonds and T-bills and the insecurity created by being dependent upon securities brokers, portfolio managers and trust departments for information to support decisions that now impact long-term financial security. If you are able to develop capable family members to take over your business, the comfort of your surroundings, the avoidance of taxation and the continuation of salary and benefits will more than likely give you a greater return with less worry than selling.

In addition to economics, there are several other good reasons to pursue succession. Your business may be irreplaceable because of franchise developments, tax laws and/or competitive forces. Succession may offer your children unique career opportunities.

The money that you could receive from the sale after it is discounted by estate tax could not duplicate the recognition, prestige and power that your children would experience by carrying on the business.

You may also have longstanding loyal employees who could be impacted by the consequences of succession. New owners typically put these people out to pasture as soon as possible to reduce overhead and to initiate their new work culture.

You may be thinking, "I really want my children to come into the business, but I am not going to try to overly influence their opinion. I want them to do their own thing and make their own decision." You may be planning to stand back and watch your children try other careers, even though you know in your own mind that the best place for them would be the family business. I have, on numerous occasions, seen parents passively watch while their children turn away from the family business and take jobs in corporate America.

If you want your children to come into your family's business, you are going to have to sell the business to them. Sure, young adults should make up their own minds. Otherwise, both you and your children will regret making the wrong decision. You should even encourage them to look around and work in another business first. However, if you want the children in the business and/or if the business needs them, forget this passive "Que sera', sera'" approach. Become a wise, resourceful recruiter.

If you feel a child is suited for the business, extend yourself on the benefits of a career in the business just as though you were trying to recruit a <u>talented third party.</u>

Begin this sales job as early as possible. Do not give up your advantage of being a family member and the owner of the business unless you are prepared for your children to seek adventure and fortune with corporate America. There are many very attractive alternatives out there that are competing for your children's interest. If it is fundamentally important that your children come into the business, recognize that you are involved in a formidable recruiting competition.

When considering your children's willingness to pursue a career in the family business, recognize that you have programmed their receptiveness based on your past attitudes, reactions and circumstances. If you expressed more love to the business then you did to your children, expect your children to resent the business. If your business was the cause of the break up of your marriage with their mother, don't be surprised if they hate it. If you continually complained and moaned about the problems of business, expect them to be afraid of it. If you were a compulsive workaholic, expect them to value free time over business opportunity. If you used the business just to satisfy your personal lust for power and things, do not expect your children to respect it.

Your children's attitudes and actions regarding your family business are fruits of the seeds you have planted. Children listen much better to actions, habits and character than they do to words. Your children hear amazingly little of what you say to them but hear almost everything you say to partners, managers and employees. They draw phenomenally correct, instinctive conclusions based upon your lead. If your children are still young, be aware of how impressionable they are with respect to your relationship to the business. If, as adults, your children are not interested in a career in the family business, take the time to discuss the source of their feelings. Possibly you can clarify misconceptions or even reconcile legitimate concerns.

If your adult children have poor attitudes, dispel the concept of whipping them into shape. They are not going to change very much. The clay on the model has dried, and you have had a substantial role in the molding process. You can refine young adults, but do not kid yourself by thinking you can cause a major change in their attitudes or actions. You may develop better ways to interact with each other, but there will not be any personality makeovers.

Your most formidable challenge is dealing with a dual identity. You are obviously a parent, but you are also an employer. As a parent, your motivation is to spare no effort or cost to provide for the welfare and ultimate success of your children, your flesh and blood. In the fighting competitive spirit of a little league parent, you believe your children deserve the best and you will do whatever is reasonable to provide them the opportunity to have the best. These are natural feelings for a parent with the resources of a successful private business that maintains an impressive standard of living. It feels good to use whatever resources you have to help your children achieve and have the best.

Opposing these parental instincts is your other identity -- the ambitious, industrious and demanding employer whose children commonly do not meet your standards. In spite of your continual coaching, advice and constructive criticism, your children may not seem to make the commitment to successfully follow in your footsteps. You are regularly frustrated by their apparent lack of commitment and unwillingness to sacrifice for the welfare of the business. You continually find yourself in a quandary between trying to maintain performance standards in the business and maintaining your children's self-esteem and living standards.

All too commonly, the predominant employer mentality pollutes the father or mother role, or the predominant parent mentality pollutes the employer role.

The pressure and grind of the family business environment is largely a product of that continual struggle to find the balance between the roles of parent and employer.

Case History: Catch 22

In a recent succession planning situation, my client was at his wit's end trying to manage his son's growth in his business. Unfortunately, his son had been irresponsible and unmotivated for many years. Having had previous problems with drugs, the son was frustrating my client to the limit with predictable immaturity and a lack of dependability.

In talking with the son it became apparent that the prospective roles of both the son and his father overlapped, creating an emotional turmoil. The son could not differentiate between his role as employee and his role as a child of a business owner. He expected his father to make him a partner in the business, irrespective of his attitude and lack of dependability.

The father was profoundly angry with his son for embarrassing the family and being a poor employee role model. This anger caused the father to give his son the cold shoulder and prevented the critically needed fatherly communication and interaction. In a pathetically circuitous Catch 22, the son's rehabilitation and growth were profoundly affected by his father's rejection. He apparently achieved revenge by embarrassing and disappointing his father. He made the reasonable assumption that his father's love was conditioned upon him becoming the role model employee.

My advice to this client was the same as what I offer you. Do everything you can to differentiate your roles as parent and employer. Put the highest importance upon your role as a parent. The business is subordinate to the family. The maintenance of a family and the development of a successful business are directly dependent upon you fulfilling your role as a quality parent. If you do not gain the respect of your children as a parent, you will have no hope in obtaining their respect as a supervisor and employer. As a parent, convey to your children love, value and esteem with no strings attached.

The best way to show parental love is to verbally express and physically show your feelings. Those of you who are too tight to tell your children that you love them or give them hugs are at a tremendous disadvantage. The best way to show esteem and value is to genuinely ask for your children's help and opinions. Being all capable and all knowing generally provides little room or incentive for their development. Do not criticize your adult children, but critique what they do. You have little or no chance of changing who they are, but you may be able to impact how they behave. Accept them and celebrate what they are. Any changes that you institute in your adult children will come from coaching, not criticizing. A common trait of successful parents of adult children is the unwavering ability to notice and affirm the good things their children are doing.

Unfortunately, reality may occasionally require your children to get a good chewing out. Their supervisor (not you) should render the thrashing. Stay out of the fray. In the unfortunate circumstance when your children report to you, work hard to speak only as an employer. Reinforce your parental position by expressing your love and understanding. This is admittedly difficult, especially in emotional circumstances. However, this reaffirmation of the parental bond is critically important. It is not unreasonable for you to expect your children to respect you and your business. If a chewing out is required on a regular basis (more than the average employee) you should reevaluate your attitude toward the child and your child's compatibility to the family business.

It bears mentioning that employment of an in-law or other relative also introduces the possibility of double identity frustration. If you hire your son-in-law, you will face some sticky situations. The obvious solution is to be very careful in hiring. Do not for a minute believe that you would be doing a good deed for your daughter by employing her husband in a position for which he is unqualified or overpaid. The brutal truth surfaces sooner or later at substantial cost in dollars and relationships. You do not know in-laws and other relatives as well as you know your children and you will have a more difficult time expressing your true feelings regarding the job performance of an in-law without fear of causing an uprising with the in-law, married child or relatives.

Recognizing that you will generally have more awkward relationships with in-laws and relatives, spend extra time in the pre-employment phase explaining employment expectations. The smart move is to talk with your son-in-law and daughter at the same time, and establish a written record of employment expectations and accountability practices.

As an employer/parent, one of your more important responsibilities is to establish consistent, reasonable employment expectations. You must work diligently to effectively communicate these expectations to family members, because the natural reaction is, "I'm a family member, these rules do not apply to me." If family members do not respect the rules, how can you expect any other employee to? Family members will be role models in both their good and their bad behavior. If you tolerate irresponsibility from your children, you had better be prepared to tolerate the same from other employees or spend substantial portions of your time finding replacements. Hold everyone, starting with yourself, accountable to the same expressed standards. Accountability does not require criticism, it requires unwavering conviction to maintain and enforce reasonable employment standards.

Accountability supports the independent roles of friend, parent, in-law and employer by expressing through action that, "if you are working in this business, I respect you enough to hold you to the same standard as non-family employees."

This is not a difficult policy to initiate from the outset of your involvement with family employees.

However, it is difficult to implement after family employees have become accustomed to a double standard in accountability.

If you have never held your children accountable (school, manners, money, dress, household chores), introducing them to accountability in business will be nearly impossible. The order and respect that comes from accountability is essential to business operation, management and succession. Regardless of how difficult the task may be, if you are dedicated to succession, trying to initiate accountability is worth your best effort.

Depending upon the maturity of your son, daughter or in-law, initiating accountability can be an emotional issue. It may be difficult for everyone to understand that "no" is indeed a good word that has many favorable implications to family and business order. When dealing with family members it makes sense for you to communicate to them that you feel it's essential to separate the roles. It may seem juvenile to keep repeating, "As you know, I am responsible for both the business and the family, and I am committed to do my best in each role." However, it might relieve you of at least some of the double jeopardy of your double identity.

The quality of your relationship with your family successor will have a direct impact on the process of succession. You do not have to be a management consultant or a family therapist to recognize that the characteristics of your relationship with your child will be transposed to your business environment.

Before establishing ambitious training and development goals for your children, make a realistic evaluation of your relationships. Your conclusion may be "damn the torpedoes, full speed ahead." You may conclude that you have a few problems, like every parent and child, but you can handle the challenge. Or you may break out in a cold sweat at the thought of trying to teach your children anything.

Your conclusion may lead you to seek creative methods of improving communication. It is never too late to begin trying to improve communication. You may decide to look at other business disposition alternatives. But do not throw in the towel before you think through your challenges.

It is important that you are honest with your children regarding their current and future position in your business. It is easy to tell them what they want to hear about future advancement, compensation, and job titles. It is easy to move them up the management ladder into a vacated position, even though they have not mastered their current position. It is easier to give them a pay raise than it is to endure their remarks about not being able to afford a house on the right side of town.

Family members are supposed to have impressive titles and nice offices, aren't they? Who wants confrontation when you can avoid it? Can't someone else explain the concept of sacrifice? Why can't you just be the bearer of good news regarding gifts of stock, job titles, and compensation?

The temptation to grease the pathway for children is even greater if relationships have been strained by divorce, alcohol, drugs or other personal difficulties. Guilt about parental shortcomings can lead you down a perilous track. Any time you are not honest with your child, you plant the seeds of unrealistic expectations that inevitably grow into problems. The hard cold fact of life is that your children will have to deal with the reality of their aptitudes, attitudes and convictions.

Either you address your children's circumstances straight up and honestly or the free market and real life will make them family business casualties.

If, after your retirement or death, they are squashed by a competitive marketplace, there will be a lot more pain and frustration than if they had heard the truth from the beginning.

On innumerable occasions I have been asked to help reconcile team management problems that focus on a specific family member. In almost all of the cases, Junior is at odds with the management program because he is not given respect. Invariably, after snooping around the situation, I find that, to avoid family conflict, the family member had been artificially supported as a manager and was serving in a figurehead position.

Managers and employees know the facts of life and attribute the operational inconvenience to family baggage as they work around the incompetent family member. This management bypass program can work until the issue of respect raises its ugly head. Junior realizes that, although he has the title, no one respects him. He recognizes that being a good guy does not gain him any respect, so he sees no downside risk in being a real pain in the rear. Efficiencies and harmony suffer. Frustration builds as profitability declines. Then someone is called upon to work out a plan to build business teamwork and give Junior the respect he thinks he deserves.

At best, the resolution of this problem is a distraction to the operation and succession of a family business. The worst case scenario is ugly family trauma and concessions to performance mediocrity that threaten business viability.

Give your children and/or in-laws the respect they deserve by being honest about their capability and longer term management potential.

You do not have to be crass, brutal or insensitive. However, unless you are prepared to constantly referee squabbles and compromise business expectations, you do have to be honest. A family business is a very expensive nursery for children who have not been prepared to deal with reality. Your child's success will be dependent upon four factors:

- Opportunity
- Aptitude
- Attitude
- Commitment

Generally, there is a strong suit and a weaker suit. Success requires a solid position in all four areas. A parent cannot use opportunity to overcome a significant deficiency in aptitude, attitude or commitment. In the interest of family harmony, financial security and the integrity of the business, parents must maintain balance with the opportunities they provide. A child who, over an extended period of time, has been given unreasonable opportunities can become a volcano of resentment and anger. Who can fault children for being angry if you allow them to make reasonable assumptions and subsequently broadside them with the reality that they cannot handle the challenge of succession? And who can fault other family members or employees for resenting your indulgence in your children's success?

The relationships between siblings also are important succession considerations. If there is existing animosity, distrust or disabling resentment, your retirement will only further inflame the situation. Brothers, sisters and cousins usually tolerate each other in your presence under threat of your recrimination. If they are quarreling in front of you, you can bet it will get really exciting in your absence. Siblings usually give each other the benefit of the doubt, whereas competitive cousins are usually less cooperative. You are the control rod. Around you, quarreling siblings or cousins are going to be on their best behavior. In your absence, critical mass can happen quickly. Face reality. Sit down with the problem parties and tell them to get along or get lost. Emphasize that they are either part of the problem or part of the solution and your business cannot afford problems.

Do not get involved as an arbitrator or relationship advisor between family members. This is a lose-lose formula. If they genuinely need a third party to help figure out their problems, hire a non-family member who is expendable. Eventually force them to work on joint projects to determine if they can work together. If this does not work out, eliminate one or both of the problems. Do not be coy and assume that after you retire, relationships will work out.

You should be aware that you have a significant impact upon how your children deal with each other. As an example, in order to motivate your children to higher performance in school, athletics or behavior, you may have created competition between them. The apparently wholesome exhortation of "don't let your brother beat you" may have worked well to keep your children's grades up. However, that form of competitive encouragement may become a handicap in business. Successful families have something to prove: that they are capable of keeping ahead in a competitive world while maintaining a cooperative and even mutually submissive attitude within the family business.

Thinking through the past may reveal that you are the creator of sibling rivalry. If this is the case, you had better prepare yourself for one of two courses of action. First, sit the rivaling children down (ideally with the help of a counselor) and explain what has happened, apologize and search for ways to deal with the friction. If this does not work, prepare yourself to select who will run the business and who will seek a career elsewhere. Realize that family business succession involving all or most of your children is, in most cases, an idealistic dream. Rarely do all, or even most of the children, achieve sufficient harmony and unity to run a business together. Usually, after soul searching by both parents and children, one of the children carries on the succession effort and the other children pursue other careers with balancing estate-asset division benefits.

You must respect your children as adults who are trying to make their way in life. When a child comes into a business, you have the responsibility of disassociating yourself from preconceived opinions. Indeed, you should do everything possible to meet the "Reasonable Expectations of Heirs" which include:

- Do not try to control my life; I am an adult, just like you.

- Make no assumption that I know how to act as a family member employee.

- Describe to me in writing the fundamentals of employment such as hours of employment, dress, parking, breaks, vacations, drug policy, sexual harassment policy, etc.

- Give me a detailed job description and the expected employment attitude.

- Share with me your vision of my progression through the business with a general timetable.

- Keep me informed of my job performance.

- Value my opinion.

- Listen to me.

- Respect my spouse.

- Don't embarrass me in front of my peers, advisors or business community.

- Pay me fairly.

- Challenge me.

- Do not expect me to be like you.

Hopefully, you'll agree that these expectations are reasonable and that they are not overly complex, costly or demanding. This list reflects the fundamental expectations of any employee. The point is not to make the assumption that your children can read your mind or tune into your dreams.

If you want your children to meet your succession expectations, you must satisfy their reasonable expectations for guidance, boundaries, communication and accountability.

One of the most common succession planning mistakes of parents is undertaking succession planning without involving their children. When this occurs, decisions are usually challenged after the parents' death. The children jump to conclusions about fairness, feelings, intentions, and motives. The interpretation of circumstances varies dramatically between individuals. When money, control and pride are involved, these differences can be astounding. Resentment and animosity can result, bringing irreparable damage to family relationships.

Don't jeopardize family harmony or a favorable legacy because you do not want to deal with any challenges to your decisions. There may be a better way to accomplish your goal that can only be identified with your children's input. The right way is the way that achieves your goals and promotes family harmony. Your children may or may not make productive contributions to your decision making process; however, history has proven that their involvement will minimize the risk that your good intentions will create bad circumstances.

Case History: Good Intentions

Not long ago a charitably inclined client, Jack, informed me that he was going to amend his estate documents to add a charitable beneficiary. I encouraged him to think charitably and referred him to his attorney without discussing his detailed intentions, assuming that they could handle it. I asked that they just send me a copy of the executed amendments for my files. About a week later Jack called me and said that his wife wanted to talk to me about estate planning and asked that I make arrangements to visit with her the next time I was in town. I agreed, but advised him that I currently had no trip planned. About a week later, he called again. He said that his relationship with his wife was strained and his children were making life uncomfortable for him as well. I responded, saying that I would schedule a trip immediately and asked why everyone was in such an uproar. He said he would explain when I arrived in a couple days. I made an appointment to meet with him before meeting with his wife.

Upon my arrival, Jack said he had made a terrible mistake by telling his wife and children what was in his will. Having already done so much for his children, he said he had decided to give a national Christian organization half of his estate. He continued to lament that, for the first time in their marriage, his wife was challenging his judgment. Over the years, I had helped this gentleman transfer millions of dollars in assets to his children. His wife had no concerns about security. His dream was to endow Christian charities. He was really out of sorts about his wife's reaction to what he considered reasonable in light of what he had already done for his family.

I responded with a reminder that, regardless of what he had done previously, we were talking about a charitable gift of more than $5 million. I said that I thought a decision diverting that amount of money from the wife and children should merit input from them. Even though he may have made the right decision, he should consider discussing, even arguing, the virtues of a decision of this magnitude with his family.

To my surprise, my comments did not convince him. It was very apparent from his uninspired responses that he was not convinced to change his attitude. In an all-out effort to persuade him, I stepped into my family-involvement monologue. If you think this situation is uncomfortable, just imagine the shock and emotional trauma that would have occurred if you had adopted this plan, never advised your family and then died. This would not have been a pretty scene as your children tried to figure out the reasons that you had rejected them in favor of a charity. You do not have to be a brain surgeon to avoid this unfortunate circumstance. Bringing your spouse and children into the estate planning decision-making process will prevent them from misinterpreting your good intentions.

I said family can add valuable balance and insight into difficult decisions. Yes, there may be contradicting opinions, but this is not necessarily bad.

Jack's children did not disagree with the Christian endowment. They just wanted to be part of the decision-making process. Unfortunately, a self-centered family member could have reacted negatively. A negative reaction to a parent's intentions may create moments of awkwardness, but this awkwardness is well worth the knowledge gained about the children's motives and feelings, even if one has to reverse the current position to maintain civil decorum. Understanding a child's character can provide direction on how to deal with future decisions of a similar nature. This understanding can also give motivation for coaching to help children build attitudes that are less self-centered.

Surprise is clearly the nemesis of good estate or succession planning. Surprise leaves the interpretation of intentions to random chance. Nevertheless, estate planning intentions should not be shared unless you are prepared to listen to the ideas, suggestions, grievances or disagreements that may be offered. You will be offending your children to the core if you do not at least show them the respect of acknowledging their feelings.

If you are in a second marriage, and your current spouse is not your children's parent, the above advice merits even greater emphasis. Make sure that you personally deal with both your second spouse and your children on the "fairness of asset distribution" issue. By all means, do everything possible to insulate your wife and children from negotiating property divisions or joint administrative decisions after your death. A blended family is a very delicate business succession situation. As a spouse, parent and/or stepparent, you should personally attend to loose ends that affect the future of both sets of loved ones. This means openly communicating and letting everyone know what to expect from your estate and, more specifically, from the business.

This also means tightening down the provisions of buy/sell agreements.

With a blended family, think twice about utilizing an estate-tax deferral trust, which totally subordinates your children's access to the business or other assets until the death of your second spouse.

The result could be that your children could resent you and your spouse, if they are required to stand by until a non-relative dies before they can participate in any benefits from your estate. Tensions are tight enough between second spouses and children. Restricting your children's access to assets will only make matters worse. When a step-parent is involved, consider a direct distribution to your children to relieve tension. Even though this distribution will be subject to estate tax, you will have loosened the knot between your surviving second spouse and your children.

Case History: The Second Wife

I recently had a client who resisted my efforts to tighten up his business and estate planning between his second wife and his children. He was in his early 60sand his second wife was 50. His oldest son, who was the designated successor of his automobile dealership, was in his mid-40s, just a few years younger than his stepmother. My client's net worth was in excess of $20 million, and he wanted an estate plan providing total deferral of estate tax through his second wife. He also was reluctant to give his oldest son an airtight contract to complete the purchase of the dealership, in which the son already owned 40%. His rationale was that he did not want to restrict his second spouse's options, in spite of the fact that she had never worked a minute in any aspect of the business. Is love strange, or what?

My counsel to this headstrong gentleman fell on deaf ears. In frustration I wrote him a detailed letter asking him, "What is wrong with this picture? Your wife will be the sole beneficiary of a $20 million estate that will continue rapid growth. She will not spend 25% of the annual income. She will naturally want to withdraw this income from the trust so she can provide benefits from your estate to her own grown children, whom you do not particularly like. Your children, who are all less than 10 years her junior, will stand by coveting the income she does not spend, realizing that, only after their stepmother dies -- when they are approximately 75 years old -- will they receive any portion of the principal or income.

Further, when your son sits down with his stepmother to negotiate the details of purchasing the business that he operates (won't that be fun), your daughters (his sisters) will be watching very closely. If stepmother sells cheap, she will be showing preferential treatment to their brother. If she pushes for a fair market value, she will be deemed a greedy witch. This estate and business succession structure is a no win dilemma for her.

Regardless of how well your new wife gets along with your children today, your estate trust should authorize providing her with a bodyguard."

Prenuptial or antenuptial agreements between you and a second spouse can clarify many of the important succession issues. Your children will breathe easier with a contract in place that controls the disposition of your property after your death. They will also be more likely to endear themselves to your second spouse, because they will know where they stand and not be suspicious of underhanded influence.

I also recommend that you compel your children to execute prenuptial agreements that include acknowledgments from your child's prospective spouse that the family business is now, and will continue to be, a family asset. Your kids may argue that their romance is above business contracts that contemplate divorce.

You should respond with the following thoughts. There are many dimensions to a marriage, including spiritual, emotional, physical and business. The business dimension of marriage is by no means the most important, nevertheless, this is an area that requires forethought, preparation and cooperation to avoid misconceptions that lead to hurt feelings. In the complex area of business, the only way to avoid misunderstanding is to reduce understanding to writing. This record is a prenuptial agreement. It is not realistic for you to assert that a prenuptial agreement is a requirement for marriage. As adults, children can marry as they please; however, it is reasonable for you to dictate that a prenuptial agreement is a requirement for being the recipient of stock. With any reasonable recognition of the benefits of stock ownership, this should provide adequate motivation to adopt a premarital agreement acknowledging family assets. If receiving stock is not a big deal to your child and his or her spouse, then you could be saving yourself some major headaches by holding on to it.

In conclusion let's revisit a few key concepts:
- Listening and coaching are the keys to communication.
- Communication with your children is essential to succession.
- To be heard, you must speak as a coach, not as a parent.
- Coaches optimistically look upon individuals with the goal of helping them be the best they can be, rather than judging who they are not.

- In most family businesses a stock transfer restriction is put in place prior to the marriage that limits stockholders to direct family members.

As the owner of a family business, you have the primary responsibility in succession planning. You have few greater responsibilities than promoting the unity of your family in business succession. Your first responsibility is to consider succession, realizing that selling is better than transferring to incompetent managers. Examine the potential benefits of succession, evaluate circumstances and consider feelings. As the family leader, you are the one who will determine if a plan is ever activated.

Your greatest challenge will be to identify and train your successor. Your final, most challenging responsibility is to get out of the way.

When you have passed your peak, and when training, teaching and lecturing have reached the saturation point, have the courage and wisdom to pass the baton to your successor and get out of the way. Then he can have the opportunity to learn by his own mistakes, use you as wise council and continue the family legacy.

Conclusion

*T*he miracle, or the power, that elevates the few is to be found in their industry, application, and perseverance under the promptings of a brave, determined spirit.

~ Mark Twain ~

Conclusion

We have reviewed the critical factors of family business succession. Specifically, we have discussed achieving success, strengthening the family unit, developing successor managers and the various aspects of financial planning. By reading this book, you have come to realize that family business succession is far more complicated than you ever dreamed. We have dissected the family business organism, identifying the body, heart and soul of the family business, and how it can continue to be strong and vibrant as it passes from one generation to the next. You have been informed, encouraged and, hopefully, inspired to seek your succession dream and to apply every resource at your disposal to that goal.

Hopefully, I have not over-complicated what can be a convoluted, uncomfortable subject. Discussions about death, retirement and control of your business are not particularly inviting. Dwelling on the minute details of one or more of the aspects of succession runs the risk that you'll be left confused and intimidated. On more than one occasion I have watched families argue endlessly about relatively minor issues, such as what attorney to use or if life insurance is a good investment. The potentially tragic result is that important progress is delayed and, in some cases, never achieved. And so, with this book, I have provided an introductory roadmap you can use to get started.

I have endeavored to help you better understand the issues by sharing experiences that you may have found unusual or even hard to believe. These are real case studies and it is my hope that you can learn from others that you are not alone in your concerns and that you can feel optimistic about the process. Please take encouragement from realizing that others have shared your goals and circumstances. They have stepped out to overcome the same challenges you are facing. Your situation is not unique and it is manageable.

Regardless of your familiarity with succession planning or the impact of this book on your thinking, the important question is, where do you go from here? What role are you going to play? I challenge you to become a doer, an initiator, a catalyst for action. Succession will never happen if you do not get started.

If you need help, contact a succession planning organization or ask your attorney or accountant to help get things started. Do not be reluctant to ask, because you are going to need help. Succession planning is a complicated subject that needs experience, technical expertise and organizational ability.

Additionally, while succession can be gratifying and satisfying, it is at the same time frustrating and disheartening. Staying on course and maintaining the planning momentum needs a guiding hand from someone who has traveled the path before.

Succession does not need superstars; succession needs steady, reliable team players.

If you ask for help or ideas, you may find that "experts" will jump out of the woodwork. Organize your planning team based upon the contribution that can be provided. Keep your team lean. Excess team members will only slow the process. Further, a control freak will frustrate other team members and ultimately undermine your succession planning effort.

If your advisors are unfamiliar with the critical factors of succession, give them a copy of this book. Discuss your goals, circumstances and concerns with the planning team and reaffirm the need to take action. Identify the next five action items that are necessary for progress. Never end a planning meeting without reviewing your action list and identifying the next five action items. Keeping a short action list will empower a realistic vision of what is needed to maintain planning momentum.

If succession planning looks too big, complicated, or involved, hold fast to the most important requirement for success: a positive attitude. It is not at all uncommon to want to throw your hands up in the air and just say, "It's not worth it! I'm out of here! Find me a buyer!"

If you feel yourself approaching a break in patience or conviction, step back, get some space, find time to think and reset your convictions.

Stop thinking in terms of the Hail Mary touchdown pass and start thinking in terms of first downs.

Remember, with affirmed goals and an action list, you can maintain your vision. When you start to get depressed about family attitudes, the vast amount of work that must be done or your slow progress, just focus on what is in front of you and do not worry about the big picture. Steady progress is more important than an overnight overhaul of your family's financial planning structure, attitudes and philosophies.

Keep in mind that, if you are in a succession hole with finances, relationships or management development, it took time to dig that hole and it is going to take some time to get out and refill it. There is no quick solution, but there is a reason for optimism as soon as you recognize "The Three Laws of the Hole."

- The first law is "You never hit bottom until you stop digging." With this in mind, focus your energies on terminating negative attitudes and actions that work against succession. Positive things will then start to happen.

- The second Law of the Hole can now come into play: "When you stop digging you can find the way out." Digging holes is literally the pits. Initiating positive attitudes and actions will ultimately bring about the positive changes required to get your business succession out of the hole.

- The third Law of the Hole is, "In order to get out of the hole, you must follow the light." Knowledge of circumstances, problems and opportunities will enlighten you and your efforts to achieve family business succession. Be patient. Be steady. Be smart. Be dedicated to the goal of succession. This is a dream worth dreaming, a goal worth seeking.

If you are the senior generation and have a reluctance to step forward into action, have faith that your problems can be resolved and your goals can be achieved. As you can trust in God, Yankee ingenuity and the rising sun, you can trust that there are compatible answers to your questions.

The disposition of your business is your responsibility. Unwillingness to face this responsibility will put your dream at risk, along with the welfare of your loved ones. Have faith that, if you address this responsibility, your fears can be satisfied and those sticky problems can be resolved. Miracles probably will not happen overnight. And you may well have uncomfortable times before peace of mind is achieved.

The harder you work, the luckier you will be. Stepping out of your comfort zone will put you in a position for growth. Compel your advisors to press forward with ideas and plans that address your fears and concerns. Let your children and every advisor know that planning may be uncomfortable, but not planning is unacceptable. Focus upon making progress and, eventually, this progress will lead you to the achievement of goals that have heretofore appeared impossible.

If you are a motivated successor, enthusiastically support your parents' efforts to develop a succession plan. Endeavor to share your motivation and insight with your parents, siblings and advisors to encourage them to continue in the succession process. Try to get involved as a member of the planning team. If your parents will not discuss the subject of succession planning with you, their attorney or accountant, don't give up. Relentlessly endeavor to motivate them. Do not lose your cool, but remain enthusiastic, persistent and optimistic. Be as diligent as possible without creating chaos. Be ready to seize every opportunity for progress.

As I mentioned earlier, "If you fail to plan, then you plan to fail." Certainly this theory applies to an undertaking within the scope of succession planning. Staying focused and on track is imperative. To help you stay on track with the succession process, consider the following acronym as a plan for your ongoing **SUCCESSION** program:

1. Set a goal of succession.

2. Understand the critical factors of succession: Business success, Success through Teamwork, Intra-family Relationships, Successor Management Development, Strategic Business Planning and Financial Planning.

3. Challenge the "status quo" to achieve improvement in each critical area.

4. Create an advisor team to provide planning leadership.

5. Establish succession planning as a business priority.

6. State the planning goals of both generations.

7. Seek family involvement in achieving stated goals.

8. Initiate a program for regular review of feelings, finances and the federal tax laws.

9. Operate based on the Family Golden Rule: "Do unto family members as you would have them do unto you, and give them the benefit of the doubt."

10. Nurture an interdependent family business environment.

It is tempting to think about selling your company, investing tons of money and living the simple life clipping coupons. But keep in mind that a sale usually creates more losers than winners. In most cases, the unique hyper-productive family business environment is destroyed. You also typically lose significant income-producing capital to income taxes. The return on the net-after-tax proceeds of a sale rarely equals the internal or even the external return that was being realized prior to the sale. The tax collector is the acknowledged big winner and the peace of clipping coupons is not what it is made out to be.

Don't believe that you would be free of worries regarding family harmony or business matters if you sold out. Wealth and worry are partners for life. It doesn't matter if your wealth is tied up in a business or in Treasury bills. If you worried over your business, you will worry over your money. If your children did not get along while in the business, they will not get along out of the business. If you were directly or indirectly supporting your children or in-laws through a job in the family business, you are going to continue to be involved in this sticky situation if you sell. And if you sell, your pockets will be full and your children may be out of a job and asking for help. The net result will be that you will continue to be involved in their lives.

With a plan that addresses the critical factors of business succession, you can have your cake (business) and eat it (spending money) too. It will undoubtedly require sacrifice, thought and effort. But what else is new? However, when parents, children and key employees closely examine the negative impact of a sellout, creativity typically receives a real shot in the arm.

I am amazed at the productive programs developed by motivated children or key personnel when they recognize that, if they don't get their act together, the business is going to the highest bidder.

I encourage you to hang in there. Reach for the brass ring of succession and expect success. Your efforts will be perpetuating a family legacy into which so much has been invested. You will be perpetuating an environment that exemplifies the values and principles of your family. You will be maintaining your personal independence and the philosophy of liberty by perpetuating an opportunity for your children to remain self-employed and achieve the just rewards for their talents, work ethics and attitude. Regardless of who you are and the part you are playing in the succession program, do your part to stretch for the baton, as if the completion of the relay depends solely upon you.

If you fall, get up. Success is not a reflection of the length of your stride, but the willingness to keep getting up and not accept defeat. Be a voice of optimism, not an echo of defeatism. Do not overlook that your attitude and your tenacity are vital links in the succession of your family's business. You are a leader and that you are setting an example for others. Succession of your family business is worth seeking. It has a multidimensional price in money, time, emotion, energy and patience; however, succession is worth the price.

Succession of the family business is a win/win/win/win affair. The parents win by maintaining and preserving a lifelong independent asset that can provide them incomparable security, benefits and flexibility. Parents also win the gratification of perpetuating their own legacy of achievement and perhaps that of their parents and grandparents. As a fifth generation client said, "I am passing this business to my son whether he wants it or not. I am not going to be the one that history records as the one who dropped the ball."

Children win by maintaining a career path, an economic opportunity, a respected position in the community and a forum for family fellowship. The employees win by maintaining their jobs and the supportive, considerate environment that family business provides. Their jobs are stable, as they will not be replaced by the reductions and changeover of staff created by a sellout. Whatever the Japanese can produce through engineering efficiencies, America can outdo through the creativity, tenacity and hyper-productivity of the family business. What General Motors cannot do, the American family business can.

America wins through perpetuation of its most active political action committees (the family business) that constantly strive for less government, more freedom and continuing opportunity. America wins through the perpetuation of the business foundation that creates more jobs, pays more taxes and is pound-for-pound more productive than any other institution in the world. What is good for the family business is good for America; as the family business prospers, so prospers America.

The peace of mind and gratification achieved by succession are worth every ounce of effort and every dollar of cost. Considering the achievement and investment of time, money and effort by everyone involved, you owe this goal your best effort. You owe yourself, your spouse and your children your very best effort at achieving succession.

Because you have made the effort to read this book, it is evident that succession is important to you. I challenge you to use the technology and experience shared here to seek succession. Take to heart, to mind and to action the critical factors of succession. I challenge you to use all of the intellectual, spiritual, monetary and human resources at your disposal to consider "Seeking Succession" of your family business. Your efforts will bring you the reward and gratification that you seek.

Surely, if you reflect on what Lou Bachrodt, Jr. said as recorded at the beginning of this book, you will have the peace of mind that you have given succession your best shot. In the midst of frustrations and challenges, remember that "Seeking Succession" is not about money. "Seeking Succession" is about family. "Seeking Succession" is about those of us who consider your family business a living entity reflecting the love, pride and dedication of your family.

Keep your business alive. Make sure your family business has every opportunity to live on and be a witness of God's favor to you and your stewardship to Him.

Go for it!